A Stranger and Afraid

Some other books by G. S. Fraser

The Modern Writer and his World
(Penguin Books)

Vision and Rhetoric
Lawrence Durrell
(Faber)

Alexander Pope
(Routledge)

Essays on Twentieth-century Poets
Poems of G. S. Fraser
(Leicester University Press)

A Short History of English Poetry
(Open Books)

G. S. FRASER

A Stranger and Afraid

the autobiography of an intellectual

I, a stranger and afraid
In a world I never made.
A. E. HOUSMAN

CARCANET NEW PRESS · MANCHESTER

First published in 1983
by the Carcanet New Press
208 Corn Exchange Building
Manchester M4 3BQ

090057

British Library Cataloguing in Publication Data

Fraser, G. S.
  A stranger and afraid.
  1. Fraser, G. S.—Biography   *2. Poets, English*
  —20th century
  I. Title
  821'·912   PR6011.R/

ISBN 0-85635-460-0

PR
6011
. R38
2476
1983

The poems in this book, from Poems of G. S. Fraser,
are reprinted by kind permission of
Leicester University Press.

The publisher acknowledges the financial
assistance of the Arts Council of Great Britain

Typesetting by Anneset, Weston-super-Mare
Printed in England by Short Run Press Ltd., Exeter

Contents

I dedicate this book, with humility,
to the memory of my father

The Point of Departure

1

A FEW months ago, I spent a week lecturing at a residential adult college in Wiltshire: Urchfont Manor, a pleasant red-brick William and Mary house, in green bosomy grounds. I talked there about some of the more important English writers of this century and what we can learn from them. With me, also lecturing, was the poet, John Heath-Stubbs. He talked particularly about the novel, and he claimed that in this country the novel, in the traditional sense, was finished. The great English novels had belonged to a period lasting from the mid-Georgian to the late-Victorian age. That had been a period of profound and startling change. Nevertheless, it had been a period in which, for the people in the middle station of life about and for whom the great English novels were written, there was still a stable social background. The typical hero of the classic English novel, of *Tom Jones*, for instance, *Pendennis*, or *David Copperfield*, is a young man who discovers the world, rebels against it, comes to terms with it, marries, and settles down. Our own world, John thought, will not stay put to be discovered nor will our young men have the chance of settling down.

The real subject, John Heath-Stubbs pointed out, of the great traditional English novels is not character as it displays itself in some crucial decision or violent act—that is the subject, rather, of drama—but character as it displays itself in a series of small, everyday decisions and acts, against a background of accepted and customary standards. The real subject is, in a word, the manners of society. But what are the manners of our own society? What customary standards can we fall back on, with what world can we come to terms? Perhaps, indeed, we learned certain traditional standards from our families, or at our schools and universities. The practical world around us is increasingly indifferent to these; and at any moment some public catastrophe, wrenching us up by the roots, may make nonsense of whatever moral structure we have built round our private lives. Society, the society in which he lives, is no longer a tangible medium for the

1

writer. He is thrown into himself or out into the acceptance of some systematic scheme for bringing order back into the world. So the only types of narrative that can be written to-day, Heath-Stubbs thought, would be those corresponding to the forms, older than the novel, of the intimate journal and the philosophic fable: narratives, like Mrs Woolf's, dealing with shifts of mood rather than with action or character; narratives, like Mr Rex Warner's, expounding social theories through allegory.

I thought these remarks very plausible; and the narrative on which I am about to embark, since it is the story of my own life, may often have the flavour of an intimate journal; and sometimes also (since it is the significance of such a life as mine, in such a world as ours, that concerns me) of the philosophical fable. Nevertheless, I intend, so far as I can, to make my story a narrative of the plain, old-fashioned sort. My subject, in fact, is manners; I have to describe a life without crucial or violent incidents, and a series of small, everyday decisions. For, though John Heath-Stubbs did not exaggerate the instability of our modern world, he did perhaps exaggerate that instability's immediate range. One feels it in London; but, on the other hand, John Heath-Stubbs and I did not feel it in Urchfont village, when we sat in a bar parlour, drinking cider, and surrounded by prints and photographs that suggested the moral persistence of the past: Fred Archer, the jockey; Captain Scott, the explorer; the round, choleric face of Buller, that impetuous, unlucky general of the Boer War; the sleepy yet compelling mask of Kitchener. In the provinces, there is still a living sense of tradition. And I am a provincial myself, brought up in a corner of Scotland where life still goes on, in its old roads, with a dour steadiness; and that background still remains with me as a measuring rod for what has happened since—the scatter of my life over Egypt, Eritrea, London, and South America. I do not feel quite sunk, yet, in the shifting sands. And is my case so uncommon? I think that there are, even to-day, some general experiences we have all shared, some general questions we have all asked ourselves. Our time, like other times, has its types and its patterns. It is with these, if one wants to carry on the plain old tradition of narrative, that one should deal.

I say narrative rather than fiction. I thought at first of making this book a novel. But all first novels are autobiographical more or less, and it seemed more honest, as well as more convenient, to make my narrative quite frankly that of my own life. Yet I choose myself as a peg to hang the story on not so much because I think I

2

am interesting as because I think I am, in a way, rather ordinary. I am taking myself as a reasonable random sample of the modern artist and intellectual; and I am trying to give a reasonably full answer to the question, how did I get to be that way. The lives of all of us are prolonged attempts to answer certain questions. What are we, and why are we here? What sort of a world are we living in? What should we do about it? Each one of us, till he dies, is always trying to mould his experience into some significant shape. I differ from the ordinary sensitive man of our time merely in so far as, since I earn my living by writing, this groping for the sense of it all is for me almost a whole-time job. And from some points of view, of course, this book will be too full of gropings. I offer it to the reader as a 'frank contemporary document' rather than as a finished work of art. It will be too near life to be free from confusion, though struggling, like every individual human life, against confusion. I shall be trying to find answers to large questions; and my answers will be inadequate, like all our answers, but the questions are curt.

I might make a more comely design if I were to invent some fable, that would describe nothing I have experienced, yet express everything I have come to believe. But my memories weigh too heavily upon me, and, in any case, invention is not my talent. Even as a poet, my gift is not to imagine but to perceive. I go through life in a rather vague mood, but occasionally, quite unexpectedly, when I am sitting among friends, listening to their talk, or wandering by myself in a muse about the streets, the scene about me seems at once to concentrate and to expand. It concentrates in the sense that I suddenly grasp it in its completeness; it expands in the sense that I am aware of all that it implies. Some significant detail, observed casually, will make clear to me a whole structure of events. It is my business, therefore, as a writer, to be faithful to the living detail; we exist, I sometimes feel, in a world so very strange, so full of momentous choices, that we should observe our surroundings—even, perhaps especially, on those occasions when little seems to be happening—with an almost religious care. At times, it seems to me to be an impertinence to invent anything.

And yet, no doubt, without intending to, I have invented a great deal. I am covering, in a very short space, thirty years of my life, relying mainly on my memory; and I know how memory simplifies and foreshortens. At least, I have tried to keep in charity with the boy I no longer am without growing sentimental about him; to grasp the direction of his struggle, without reading

3

more consistency and purpose into his life than was really there. I have tried, too, not to forget things that were painful, and not to remember pleasant things that did not quite happen.

2

It is as well to begin at the beginning. Our first few years, of which we remember little and that so vaguely (and what we remember is more like a dream than a reality), shape all the rest of our lives.

I was born in Glasgow, in 1915. My father, a captain in the Highland Light Infantry, was fighting in France. He had studied law at Glasgow University and, before that war, had held a post in the Town Clerk's Office in Glasgow. He was of Scottish Highland descent. His mother was a Sutherland from Caithness. On his father's side, our family, according to my aunts, could trace its descent from the famous and wicked Simon Fraser, Lord Lovat—old Simon the Fox—who had his head cut off on Tower Hill for his share in the '45 rebellion. He had sent his son out to fight, while protesting his own loyalty to the Hanoverian dynasty. He had played both sides against the middle for many years, and it is possible that he might still have suffered for his intricate double-dealing, prolonged over many years, even if the Stuarts had won. George Borrow, who had a churlish hatred of Scotsmen, says that this ability to see both sides of every question is a hereditary trait of the Frasers, a clan, he suggests, of trimmers. If it is, I have inherited it. But our connection with old Simon the Fox is probably a family legend. All I know for certain is that the earliest Fraser ancestor we can definitely trace was cast up north of the Moray Firth, when a ship, on which he was escaping to Holland after Culloden, was wrecked. He was sheltered by a farmer's daughter, who in the end married him. And my ancestors after that were crofters, fishermen, soldiers in the ranks of the Highland regiments. My paternal grandfather broke this tradition. He came to Leeds and later to Glasgow to seek his fortune; did very well in Glasgow as a wholesale clothier, was a prominent local figure, and a member of the Glasgow Town Council; then lost all his money, through some business disaster which has never been fully explained to me; and was killed, before he could re-establish his position, and while still a man in early middle age, by a fall from the open top of one of the Glasgow trams. I know little else about him, except that, though he was a self-taught man, he had a taste for letters, and used to recite the

4

poems of Edgar Allan Poe; and that, like many Highlanders, he was a heavy drinker. His children remembered him as a dominating figure.

They inherited, for their part, the vigour of his character. Two of his daughters, Anne and Helen, were suffragettes, and Anne once spent a fortnight in Holloway jail, went on hunger strike there, and was forcibly fed. Helen, during the Great War, toured the United States, lecturing on women's war work. In the 1920s she took up politics, and stood as a Liberal candidate at several by-elections, but always for hopeless seats. Of the sons, my father, George Sutherland Fraser, was the only one trained for a profession. The others had been going to take over my grandfather's business. After serving in the Great War, most of them emigrated. Like many Highland families, we are now scattered throughout the Dominions. Those who remain in Great Britain are in or near London. There is none of us now in Scotland.

My mother's family was a mixture of Welsh and English, though she herself had been born in Glasgow. Her father, Charles Francis Jones, who had begun life as a Liverpool supercargo, had become the secretary and accountant to a big Clydeside shipbuilding firm. He was a prosperous man, with a big house and garden in the pleasant residential district of Dalmuir. His wife had been a Miss Johnson, and there was supposed to be some family connection with the great Dr Johnson—a connection of which my mother was not particularly proud, since she thought of that great man chiefly in terms of snuffiness, dirtiness, and a habit of spitting out hot soup. There is certainly a hereditary melancholy in my mother's family, that might be explained by such a relationship; except that my maternal grandfather, to whom the relationship did not apply, suffered from the melancholy, too.

The Joneses were a slower and steadier family than the Frasers; they have not shown the same tendency to disperse and emigrate, they are not, like the Frasers, intellectually combative and passionately political. My mother's great interest, when she was a young woman, was in the theatre. She acted and sang in Glasgow amateur theatricals and had even, rather daringly for her class and her period, performed professionally two or three times in the Scottish music halls; she had a repertoire of humorous or sentimental songs, with a whimsical flavour, which she sang to her own accompaniment at the piano. She was lively, sociable, no great reader. My father, during their courtship, used to read

5

poetry aloud to her—Kipling, particularly, who was a great favourite of his—and this she found rather a bore, though she was too polite to say so. She and my father, after one of the long engagements which were usual in the days before the Great War, had married shortly after its outbreak; he was then about thirty, she in her late twenties, and they had known each other since their schooldays. I was the first child of their marriage.

<h2 style="text-align:center">3</h2>

While my father was away at the wars, my mother stayed with her family in Dalmuir, and it is with my grandfather's house there, Brooklands, that my earliest memories are connected. My very earliest memory is of a vision. I was christened in the dining-room at Brooklands, and every night and every morning, when I said my prayers, there appeared, against my shut eyelids, an exact visual replica of that room, with its rich browns changed to a swimming transparent white. Possibly the shock of the baptismal water on my head had imprinted that scene on my mind almost photographically. I thought it was a vision of heaven, and I thought that all people saw such a vision when they said their prayers; heaven was a double of the world one knew, but in a more exciting colour.

Brought up by women, I was a pensive little boy. I liked to sit and stare at the coloured shapes of things in a long brooding dream, from which all at once I would waken myself, with a sudden shake, like a dog wakening itself, and there would come over me, like a panic, the thought that there were all these things, coloured and shaped and in their places, but where and what was I? Then I would catch my face, the small, transparent, coloured ghost of myself, in the bay window (it was on the window-seat of the dining-room that I liked to sit and brood), the ghost of a handsome little boy, with large dark eyes and silky fair hair, a ghost all sunny and green with the garden that shone through it, and putting my hand upon the glass, near that reflection, I would be able to say aloud to myself, reassuringly, 'Here I am, George Fraser, sitting on the window-seat in grandpapa's house.'

The dining-room was a very brown room indeed. There was in it what I thought of as a brown smell, a smell of leather and plush and furniture polish and grandfather's cigars. There was also a brown silence, a brown gloom. My feet moved across the deep, dusty thickness of the carpet without making a noise; yet there seemed to be something tickly and muffling in the air which made me want to hold my breath, to cough, or to sneeze. The whiteness of the vision, the cool shock of the vision, at bedtime and in the morning, when I said my prayers, was pleasanter.

I had been accustomed to say my prayers only at bedtime. It was grandmama, when mother and I came back to Brooklands when I was about four, after we had been away some months on holiday somewhere, who taught me to say them in the morning, also. Grandmama I specially loved. She was very stout and sweet, gentle and old, and she had a broad face with a short hooked nose and hooded eyes, that seemed to me like the face of a wise old owl. She dressed, too, differently from other ladies, in long black silks. There was always a shawl round her shoulders, and she carried a long stick in her hand, on which she leaned heavily, as her skirts hissed over the ground. As a very little boy I used to creep under them and pretend that I was hiding in a dark tent. When I was staying at Brooklands, I usually slept in a little bed in her room, and in the mornings I would creep into bed beside her, and she would tell me stories, to which I would lend only half an ear, for I was fascinated by two or three large moles on her hands, and one on her cheek, which I used to rub at patiently with my fingers, trying to rub them away, till grandmama would catch my hands and hold them. 'You are a great leveller, George,' she would say to me then, in her deep, hoarse, chuckling voice, 'a leveller of all surfaces.' But often she was more serious and would tell me stories about Adam and Eve, and their beautiful garden, and about Moses and the Children of Israel, and how the Red Sea had opened for them, and about how Adam had talked to God in a garden and Moses in a burning bush; God was always ready, she said, to be talked to, and if in the mornings I would ask God to make me a good boy, God would listen. The first morning that I heard about this, I thought I would try it out, but, perhaps because I was not feeling well that day—I had a little sore spot on my tongue that made it painful to eat, at luncheon, even a chocolate shape moulded like a rabbit—I was especially fractious and difficult. I told grandmama sadly in the evening that her scheme did not work. 'George, George,' she said, 'you can't expect God to make you a good boy if you take no trouble to be a good boy yourself. The way that God will help you will be by helping you to take trouble. But you haven't been such a very bad boy, you know. Your poor sore tongue . . . Now, George, say your prayers and go to sleep.' I shut my eyes, said my prayers, felt again the cool shock and the whiteness of my vision, and was soon

7

calmly asleep. God's ways, like grandpapa's, who was a little grumpy and moody, and only to be approached with caution, might be mysterious; but grandmama was good and wise and could always put things right.

4

I clung to my vision. It was certainly better than the brown of the room: curled on the window-seat, however, I could look out on a lawn, and admire a holly tree, its leaves smooth and glossy like the wood of the table and sideboard, but of a more living colour. And this lawn sloped steeply down towards the garden wall, so that, looking out of the window, I could imagine the sensation of rolling over and over down it, which I was allowed to do sometimes, and it made me sick and giddy, but it was very pleasant. In my vision, I was never able to see out of this window, and I used to wonder if the holly tree, too, had become a sort of dead cream-colour in heaven or a shiny papery white; or whether heaven, for its outdoors, had even livelier greens. Yet the vision, being simply recurrently there, did not cause me much inquisitive anxiety; heaven was a permanent place, of which I had glimpses, and which could be explored in due time. The worldly scene, meanwhile, was worth exploring, too. Dark and sad as the dining-room was, it was a very important place, for it was the scene every year of the family Christmas dinner, the one late meal for which, as a little boy of four or five, I was allowed to sit up.

I attended at that age, as children do, more to things than to people. On the long mahogany table with both its flaps out there had been, that first Christmas that sticks in my memory, very many things to attend to: the polished surface of the table covered with little lace mats; crystal wine glasses, whose sharp facets I would like to have explored with my fingers—but my own glass was a dark red tumbler that made the fizzy lemonade, squeezed in sugary gushes from the syphon, the lemonade that caught in my nostrils so, seem of a new colour. I did not really like lemonade very much, but was pleased to get it, because I knew it was a treat; and the big red crackers, with their bang when they were pulled, great bowls of them, rather frightened me, but then they were a treat, too. There were large and small bowls also, made of china, glass, and silver, full of bonbons in twists of paper, chocolates in little pleated cups, tangerines with silver foil still clinging to them, darkly blooming blue grapes, and crystallised fruits, fascinating because of their glazed, glaucous colour, and because they were dry and fibrous, where I expected fruit to be a juicy pulp, and because the sugary surface, though soft and sticky, could be torn off here and there in little crisp splinters. I had few words for such impressions, though the impressions themselves were real and sharp; if I was often a silent and brooding little boy, it was because I spent hours trying, without words, to fix such impressions. When they seemed to be fixed, they would suddenly fade away. And so at night, for instance, I would dream sometimes of eating delicious things, whose names I could not remember in the morning, but whose flavours I thought I remembered, and yet in dreams food has no taste.

Yet I was beginning to attend just a little to people. I have some vague impression still of the family atmosphere of these early Christmas dinners. There were more people round the big table at Brooklands at Christmas than at any other time of the year, and their mere numbers, the mere noise they made, impressed itself on my memory. There was grandpapa's sister, my Great-Aunt Cecilia. She had the Jones melancholy, and I think her presence, in some subtle way, aggravated grandpapa's habitual slight grumpiness. She had a habit, at these annual festivals, of dabbing her eyes (which were rather sunken, with pouchy lids) and of saying, 'Ah! poor Agnes, poor Emily!'—referring to sisters or other relations who had 'passed beyond'—'For people of our age, Charlie, Christmas is rather a *sad* occasion!' Grandpapa, busy carving the turkey, would look up and growl at her in the tone and phrase of the English Midlands from which the family had originally come: 'Oh, give over, Sissy, do give over!' I noticed these little bickerings, but I can hardly have known anything about their roots in the famous 'Jones melancholy'—though grandmama, who used sometimes to talk to me in a rather confidential way, as if I were grown-up, once mentioned that to me. I had been playing near grandpapa's chair as he sat in the evening, a shawl round his shoulders, over his cigar and his book beside the parlour fire; he had suddenly barked something at me, a little tetchily. I had scampered off in alarm to grandmama. 'Your grandpapa, George,' she had said, with a certain pride in her voice, 'is a true Jones. He has *black moods*.'

Black moods: these must be even worse than a thing which I myself was liable to fall into, called a brown study. In Aunty Sissy, black moods took the form partly of this obsession, natural in an elderly maiden lady, with the passing of time and the disappearance of familiar faces; but partly also (like the rest of the

9

family, she was a devout Evangelical) of an increasing anxiety, as she grew older and more lonely, about the state of her soul; an old lady, boiling herself eggs in her bedroom, drinking tea, reading *Home Chat* and cutting out cheerful little poems from that weekly, she found herself wondering whether she had done something with her harmless and empty life that might make her deserving of eternal punishment. . . . With these insistent remarks of hers about our dear ones who were gone, she would stir up, like a poker thrusting through a grate at smouldering ashes, some answering gloomy fire in grandpapa's bosom. Thus, in a sense, he dreaded these Christmas reunions.

For in my grandfather himself the family spleen rarely expressed itself directly in words. His melancholia had become crystallised, rather, in a number of habits, the most important of which was (as I seem to remember my grandmother's phrase for it) 'your grandpapa's way of locking up all the doors at night'. Every night, before he went to bed, he made the rounds, shutting and latching all the windows, and carefully locking and bolting the back and front doors. Finally, he went to his own room, which lay in the most inaccessible part of the house, along a short corridor, the door at the entrance of which he also locked, finally locking his own room. What would happen if suddenly, in the middle of the night, a fire were to break out, and grandpapa, waking up, still bemused by sleep, had to fumble for the key of his door and the key of the corridor? *That*, apparently, was not what he was afraid of. 'I do not know about the rest of you,' he once said to one of his daughters, 'but at least *I* like to feel safe at nights.' He did not, however, usually go immediately to sleep; my mother, whose room, when she was a girl, lay directly under his, used to hear him, sometimes for an hour, in his flopping carpet slippers, pacing to and fro . . .

Yet it would be misleading to suggest that Christmas at Brooklands was mainly an occasion for a display of the darker side of the family temperament. The Jones family and my grandmother's family, the Johnsons, delighted in the pleasures of company and the table. The great trencherwoman of the family had, indeed, died before I was born: Great-Aunt Emily Johnson, of whom I was to learn in later years that she was a woman of saintly kindness and of such enormous girth that, when she came to Glasgow to visit my grandfather and grandmother, she had to be hoisted up to street level on the luggage lift at Buchanan Street station. Aunty Sissy, compared to her sister-in-law, Emily, was a little bit of a thing, but her general diet of boiled eggs, morsels of steamed fish, thin bread and butter, and countless cups of tea, had not abated her peckishness at Christmas; and her conversation, as the good things piled up on the plates, tended to lose its funereal note. 'I must say, Ada,' she would remark to my grandmother—there was little love lost between these two—'I must say this, at least, for you, that you are a comfortable provider.' And then she would turn to my grandfather and watch the carving knife move expertly in his hand. 'Well, I am partial to a *wing,* if you insist, Charlie . . . Well, just a little breast . . . Just a thin, papery slice or two of *ham* . . .' Then there would be silence for a little, broken in a few moments by an appreciative remark, invariable year after year, addressed by some female relative to my grandmother: 'What a deliciously *juicy* bird this is, my dear!' On one occasion I remember that I piped out, an infant pedant: 'Oranges, not birds, are juicy,' but the family talk flowed over me, and everybody agreed, yes, it was a deliciously juicy bird.

I remember this one pertinent remark of mine. I also remember how at the end of the dinner, when turkey, plum-pudding, mince pies and jellies had been disposed of, but we still had to begin on crackers, fruits, and sweets, grandpapa, after brushing his great moustache (it was white, but stained brown and yellow by his rich cigars) with his napkin, stood up, balanced a glass, and said, in a special deep and throaty voice, 'Absent friends!' Then we all got up and held our glasses in a stiff way and sipped and said, 'Absent friends!' This excited me as something grave and portentous, which I did not understand: a ritual. But while I sat brooding over the inner meaning of the ritual, I saw grandpapa's pink bald head with a red frilly paper crown on it; and I burst out laughing, and he laughed, too. Grandpapa could be very grumpy sometimes but then, as grandmama would say to me, 'My dear, your grandpapa can be very droll!'

What was drollest about grandpapa was his famous joke, which he repeated Christmas after Christmas. It was about Moses and Pharaoh. He told it in the broadest of English provincial accents, mingled, as I now realise, with some touches of the Jew of the music-hall stage. 'And there was Pharaoh sooming and sooming in the sea. And he said he would take the Children of Israel back into Egypt again, and said, "Saif me, saif me, Moses!" And Moses said nothing at all. And Pharaoh said he would give Moses all his treasures, and he said, "Saif me, saif me, Moses!" And Moses said nothing at all. And Pharaoh said he would make Moses the First Minister of Egypt, and he said, "Saif me, saif me, Moses!" And Moses looked at Pharaoh very long,

11

and he shook his head, and he said, "I haf seen you before, Pharaoh." And Pharaoh and the Egyptians were sooming and sooming in the Red Sea. But they could not soom for ever, and soon they were all drowned.'

Now I look at that story on a page (and I have got it more or less verbatim) it does seem to me to have a melancholy and grotesque humour; it is the sort of thing I find funny. But the real joke for grandfather's children was that while they found themselves laughing, they saw no point in the story at all. The joke, for them, was that there was no joke. Perhaps certain modes of sensibility skip a generation; or perhaps what we inherit through our parents are some of the characteristics of our grandparents. I could not say, any more than my mother could, what was the point of my grandfather's joke. But then I belong to the generation of the shaggy dog story. And I rarely remember funny stories, in any case; but I have remembered this one.

I am mixing together, as one does when thinking of childhood, the memories of several periods at Brooklands. Probably it took three or four successive Christmases to build up these impressions, and on top of that all sorts of stories that my mother told me. For behind Brooklands, there now looms up another memory; of Lloyd Street, a little row of semi-detached houses in a working-class district in Glasgow, where my father, home from the war and back at work in the Town Clerk's office, had managed to get some temporary accommodation. I was now about five; and had been sent to Brooklands by myself throughout the spring and early summer, because my mother was expecting a new baby. Dreaming my days away, I forgot about Lloyd Street altogether, and felt that all my life had been spent at Brooklands. But Lloyd Street held an unpleasant memory for me, and that was suddenly as unpleasantly revived.

I was becoming an excessively dreamy and spoilt child, backward for my age, and this annoyed my Uncle Stanley, the husband of my mother's sister, Aunty Dot, who paid us occasional visits at Brooklands. He seemed to me very big and fierce (he had the breezy, direct manners of a naval man and a habit of striding about a house and flinging open windows, as if he found it a little stuffy to be enclosed by walls). He thought I was becoming a little milksop and spoke to me sometimes in a peremptory tone that I was not used to. Once, running blindly about the garden, I knocked my knee against a cucumber frame, and started whimpering. Uncle Stanley, coming over with a clean handkerchief to wipe the blood and dirt off, did so efficiently, and then, since I did not stop whimpering, said quietly but angrily, 'Stop it, now. Stop it at once. You're not hurt badly at all. For goodness sake, be a man.' I stopped whimpering and then realised that, after all, I was not badly hurt. 'Good,' he said briskly. 'Now, run away and play.' Later I heard him talking to my mother's unmarried sister, Aunty Win, about how at my age I ought to be able to do up my own buttons and fasten my own laces, and how it was time I was sent to school. The word 'school' hit me like a blow; it revived something; in these pleasant months at Brooklands, I had almost forgotten the incident that had terrified me at Lloyd Street.

A strange man in a blue uniform had come to the door of our little house in Lloyd Street and had said in a voice so fierce and harsh, so terrible, that I had at once run away to hide in my mother's bedroom, 'Is there a boy called George Fraser here?' I had heard vague echoes of talk, my mother's voice quiet and determined, the other's brisk and high. I had heard the man say, 'He ought to be starting at school next year.' My mother said, 'We hope to have moved out of this district by then. Taking this house was a very temporary measure. Then we'll look about for a more suitable school.' 'You'd better,' the man had said in a very coarse, savage voice, 'not say anything against this district or this school.' In terror, I had stopped my ears with my hands, and heard no more. But there was something about the briskness of Uncle Stanley that reminded me vividly of the man in the uniform.

That was disturbing. But my most disturbing memory of that last visit to Brooklands was one that I could never quite fix. It turned out, though I did not know, that this was to be the last time I would see grandmama. I have an image of her sitting on a deck chair, in front of the house, on the lawn, the flat part of it, just before it began to slope, on the fine June morning when my father came to take me back to Lloyd Street. Something had upset me that morning, perhaps my father telling me that when I got home I would find a new baby sister. I remember Aunty Win asking me urgently to say good-bye to grandmama. I was sulky and said, 'In a minute, in a minute', and went to the place where the lawn began to slope, and rolled down, and climbed up again, and rolled down once more, and went on climbing and rolling, climbing and rolling, again and again, so that each time I got up I felt dizzier, and grandmama, sitting on the lawn with her grey shawl over her broad black silk shoulders, seemed each time more remote and sad. And I seem to remember Aunty Win's voice, high and

13

exasperated, and grandmama's voice, patient and sad, saying, 'No, no, Win, let the boy play.'

But did I say good-bye properly to grandmama in the end? If she kissed me, was I cold and distant to her? I cannot remember, but I can remember that months later at Lloyd Street I was playing with a strange toy, a toy safety razor made of india rubber, which father had given me because, watching him shaving in the mornings, I wanted to play at shaving myself; and father had just told me that I would not see grandmama again, not for a long, long time, because grandmama was in heaven; and I went up to the bathroom alone, and stood on the little stool there, in front of the mirror, and slowly pushed the toy safety razor up and down my cheeks, and saw that, though I was making no noise, great fat tears were running down the sides of my nose. I seemed to see grandmama again sitting on her deck chair and myself climbing and rolling, climbing and rolling, again and again, and not going over to talk to her; and I tried to remember what had happened after that, but I could not.

My mother and father found me there and I turned towards them from my little dais. I asked, as I had been used to ask about Brooklands, 'When can I go to heaven and see grandmama?' They talked to me in a gentle, serious way, and soon I was calm again. I could not go to heaven without leaving mother and father, and I must not do that. I must think of grandmama as utterly happy and as watching happily, perhaps, over us all. I put the little rubber razor down on a shelf . . . These are sentimental memories. Our characters are fixed, perhaps, not by such memories but by earlier happenings, quite beyond recall. Yet of all the very early memories, these seem the most morally important.

5

I have never been back to Brooklands; I suppose it is a roomy enough old house, with a reasonable garden, but in my mind, as I grew older, it assumed palatial proportions. Lloyd Street, 'our own wee house in Lloyd Street', tended to be put aside, when I rambled among my memories, as something not quite worthy of us.

The phrase 'our own wee house', if it was of my own invention, showed a mixture of possessiveness and of a tendency, which I must have begun to develop even at that age, to propitiate by deprecation. The housing problem after the Great War had been acute everywhere, and my father, coming home from Italy towards the end of 1919, had been glad to get hold of this little semi-detached house at the end of a row, in a new housing scheme. These little houses had at least a freshly unpacked air that did not belong to Brooklands, a smell of new paint and plaster about them. There was a strip of communal green behind them, with individual patches of garden farther back (all I remember growing in ours were blue cornflowers), while at the front of the houses there were narrow lawns. The walls of the houses were thin. We could hear at all times of the day the McCandlishes talking and arguing next door and if we left our back door open the smells of what they were cooking would float into our kitchen. One had little sense of privacy, then; but one did have a sense of difference.

I knew, for instance, that when I visited the McCandlishes to play with Bill or Daisy, I would find the whole family in the 'back room', or kitchen, Mrs McCandlish cooking something, Mr McCandlish with no collar or jacket, his shirt sleeves rolled up, sitting down for a meal at a kitchen table spread with old newspapers instead of a cloth; and Daisy or Bill playing on the floor with a battered rag doll or tattered picture book. Mrs McCandlish would not worry about their knees being dirty or their hair untidy, or about the noise they were making, and when they became fractious, which was reasonably often, she would quiet them with a 'jeely piece', a thick slice of bread smeared with jelly; or sometimes she would hand to Daisy a small tin full of sweet condensed milk. I called it 'lovely stuff'. I would sit patiently while Daisy, with a single spoon, first took a mouthful herself, and then thrust the spoon into her little brother Bill's mouth, and finally thrust it towards me. Then mother would call me, and I would go back next door to my own house, with a sticky face and dirty knees, to a meal for which I had spoiled my appetite.

Our own meal, at home, took place in the neat 'front room', or parlour; a cloth was laid, and father certainly did not take off his jacket or collar. There were two worlds, in fact, at Lloyd Street, and Bill's and Daisy's seemed to me in many ways the more comfortable and congenial; but my own world had a certain elegance and importance, that were recognised, for instance, when I went out shopping with mother. At the local grocer's there was always a good deal of bowing and scraping, of smiling and talking about the weather, and few transactions were completed

15

without a small tribute to the 'little gentleman'—a pennyworth of broken chocolate and toffee, neatly whisked up in a horn of paper, and known in the argot of the neighbourhood as a 'penny poke'. Yet even the chances of that sort of recognition were a little uncertain. They depended on my being with mother. Once, with a penny of my own in my pocket, I had rushed along excitedly to this shop, and, ignoring the crowd of people waiting to be served there, had reached up as high as I could and, banging the penny on the counter, had cried out, 'A penny poke, a penny poke, please.' The shopman somehow seemed not so affable as usual. 'All right, all right, wee man,' he had said to me, 'an' can you no bide your turn?' And then, in a confidential but carrying tone to the woman he was serving, 'I'm afraid thon's a spoiled wean.' And when I finally got my penny poke, I found it not so big as usual, with no broken chocolate in it, but only hard, uninviting bits of broken toffee.

That had been a rebuff to my sense of difference. And again, playing with Bill and Daisy, or with the Jamieson children, Dick and Muriel, who lived farther up the row from us, I found it hard to convey to them the peculiar splendours of Brooklands: the garden so very big, the sloping lawn down which I liked to roll, the rich, dark rooms: the mingled odour, too, that hung about these rooms, of pot pourri, of a lilac branch in a vase, of grandpapa's cigars. I would wax enthusiastic. 'Aye,' Dick would say, 'we've got a bit garden here, too,' and exasperatingly I would find it quite impossible to convey that Brooklands was a different sort of thing altogether from the little houses tight together like teeth in a mouth. Nor was it of much profit, with Dick and Muriel, to enumerate one's possessions. Whatever one said one had, a large parti-coloured woollen ball on an elastic string, or a wooden horse—I did possess a wooden horse, covered with brown hair, and sporting a real horse-hair tail, a horse which I loved so much that I used, in spite of its uncomfortable hardness, to take it to bed with me—Dick Jamieson would refer, and his little sister would bear him out, to an even more splendid example of the same sort of thing to be found in his father's shop. 'Oor faither's got a better yin nor that in his shop,' he would say. 'Hasn't he no, Murie?' And Muriel, nodding her plump head, would say in a wise and deep and cavernous tone, 'Aye!' This wonderful shop gave Dick and Muriel an obvious advantage over me. Bill and Daisy, too, with their free and easy kitchen life, seemed to have an advantage, too. But they were generous, they let me share it. Dick never offered to let me see his father's shop.

16

If I tended in later years, then, to put Lloyd Street aside, when I told myself stories about the past, it was because I had found myself at a general disadvantage there. Some memories, indeed, were almost entirely effaced. I know, for instance, because my mother has told me, that when I came back from that last visit to Brooklands, I had been brought up by my father to my mother's bedroom, to find mother lying back in bed, and a small, strange creature, hairless, with a crinkly red face, cuddled in the crook of her arm. I had kissed my mother formally, and then had gone downstairs to the neat front room, where, taking my box of bricks, I had squatted down on the carpet and started building myself a house. Father had followed me down and he stood silently watching me for a little. 'Well,' he said finally, 'well, George, what do you think of your new little sister?' 'I don't think much of her,' I said. I was probably very jealous of little Jean. Mother could not spare the time now, as in the old days, to coax me into eating when I was fractious at meals. It would have been ridiculous, now that I was soon to go to school, for my mother to tell me a complicated story about Giant Stomach, who lived in a cavern, to induce me to open my mouth (the road to the cavern), upon which she would pop a spoon into it, saying, 'Down the red lane!' I had been, as Uncle Stanley saw, too much petted and sheltered. I did not want, though I would be forced soon, to come out of my shelter; and what made my behaviour embarrassing to my parents was a kind of obstinate infantilism.

Jealousy, thus, has effaced some memories. Another memory has been effaced by terror. There was an old friend of my father's who lived in Dalmuir and who had a son called Andrew. As a treat, one Sunday afternoon (and partly as a compensation, because grandmama was dying, and I could not go to Brooklands as I wanted to), my father took me to see Andrew. Andrew's house was a little like Brooklands, and there was an afternoon tea of the sort I associated with Brooklands: cups and saucers of fine coloured and gilded china, for Andrew and myself hot sweet milk-and-water with just a drop of tea in it, and thin, thin slices of bread and butter; I enjoyed very thin bread and butter more than cakes and more than bread and jam. I vaguely remember the house, with its big garden, and more precisely the afternoon tea, and more precisely still Andrew, a fat little boy to whom I took an instant dislike.

What I have forgotten is the incident of the mechanical tiger. Andrew had very many toys, but the tiger was the most splendid of them. It stood in a crouching and threatening attitude, it had fur, streaky and stripy, like a real tiger, and green glistening glass eyes, and terrible teeth, and a red mouth, and it was about the size of a small dog. So, at least, it has since been described to me. It looked so very real that I was afraid to come near it. Andrew coaxed me to sit on the floor in front of it and watch it. 'Now,' said Andrew, 'I am going to show you something very strange.' He put his hand under the tiger's belly, and there was a clicking noise. Andrew then withdrew his hand with a smug smile. There was a hushed pause, and then another little click. The tiger sprang upon me with a growl, opening and shutting its jaws. My father, in the end, managed to stop me from shrieking, but I was taken home in a thoroughly shaken state. About a year and a half later, I met Andrew again, on a school playground in Glasgow. I had been at a real school for only a couple of days, after two terms at a kindergarten, and I was looking around the playground in a lost and lonely way. Andrew, an old inhabitant compared to myself, approached me in the friendliest fashion. 'I know you,' he said. 'You're George Fraser, aren't you?' I drew myself up stiffly to my small height and tried to look as haughty as possible. I put out a hand to thrust him away, and said, in a phrase from some fairy story that had been read to me, 'Be off with you, sir, be off with you!'

I discovered, then, jealousy and fear while we were at Lloyd Street; and I made certain other elemental discoveries that are worth recording, too—of illness, of pain, and (though I did not realise it) of sex. The illness had come about in an odd way, through my fondness for raw green peas. One of the things I had best liked doing at Brooklands was helping Aunty Win first to pick peas and then to shell them into a big earthenware bowl. There was a special faint fragrance that caught delicately at one's nostrils; and an equally delicate alternation, as one munched a few peas while shelling them, between the young, sweet, and soft peas, with their peculiarly vivid green colour, and the older, harder and slightly bitter ones, in which that colour had begun to fade. Two peas in a pod did not seem to me as like each other as they are in the proverb. I would nibble each pea thoughtfully as an individual experiment.

One day, playing together on a patch of wasteland with Bill and Daisy, we came to a tall straggly plant with a single large pod growing on it. I thought it looked like the pod of a green pea. I said raw green peas were nice to eat and that I would eat this pod. 'Youse winna eat this raw,' said Daisy, in a shocked tone, and so I felt in honour bound to eat it. It was not a pea pod. It was solid all

18

through and very bitter. That evening I had terrible gripings, mother gave me castor oil, and later, lying in bed feeling terribly sorry for myself, I heard the doctor say, 'Worms, oh, yes, undoubtedly worms!' He asked me if I had eaten anything strange, and I said I hadn't, and then, once he had gone away, wondered whether, not knowing about the green pod, he would be able to make me better. I spent several miserable days.

The discovery of pain came about a week later when I was still convalescing from the discovery of illness. I was playing by myself on the hard path of crushed cinders that lay between our back doors and the communal green. I had in my hand a piece of sharp wood, broken off a packing case, which I was using as a sword, but also biting and sucking it occasionally, as I sat on our doorstep and told myself stories. My thinking in these days took mainly the form of telling myself stories and then rushing off to perform the actions that I had imagined. 'And the horses came galloping, galloping, galloping along!' I would say, suddenly, out loud, in an excited voice; and then go galloping, galloping myself till I banged my head on a wall or my shins on an ash-bucket. Chewing my sword, I suddenly thought of myself rushing with my sword on a dragon, and, without taking the stick out of my mouth, I got up and rushed blindly forward; I tripped and came sprawling down; the jagged piece of wood, gripped in my right hand, was thrust deeply down my throat. I felt terrible, unbelievable pain and my mouth was full of a hot stickiness. I heard feet rushing from the house and was hoisted in strong arms.

Again, for a few days, I was back in bed, the sharp first pain in my throat having become something slow, patient, and awkward, that was called an ache. Unable to eat, I could only, in little sore deliberate gulps, take nourishing liquids. The tall, gloomy doctor, whom I was beginning to regard as a figure of ill omen, was hovering over my bed. 'Gets into scrapes, your little man,' I heard him saying. 'A little deeper, another half inch, another inch at most, and then . . .' And then what, I wondered; but the doctor did not complete his sentence, merely clacking his knuckles in a very sinister fashion.

It was several days before, still shaky, I was up and about again, and I was hardly up before I made (but without realising its implications) the third disturbing discovery. Daisy was fond of me, she was perhaps the only one of my little friends who was impressed by my stories about Brooklands. Perhaps I had been much on her mind while I was laid up. That, anyway, would help to explain the queer little incident . . . It was a fine sunny day, and a day of carpet beating. Some inexplicable instinct, like the migratory instinct in birds, had come over the housewives of Lloyd Street, and the green at the back looked very strange, laid out with carpets like a great shop, while all day long there had been a noise of thwacking, and the sunny air had been thick with household dust. Evening was falling, and some of the carpets were being taken in, but not yet the McCandlishes' or ours. Dick and Muriel, from the other end of the green, had been along to inspect our carpets. 'Oor faither's got a better yin nor that in his shop,' Dick had remarked. 'Hasn't he no, Murie?' And Muriel, nodding her plump head, had said in a wise and deep and cavernous tone, 'Aye!' But as evening fell and the stout, angry, energetic women ceased their thwackings and dragged their carpets indoors, Daisy and I found ourselves alone, contemplating only two or three carpets scattered on the greying grass, and sniffing a purer air, for the dust was settling.

I had been telling her about my terrible accident. 'Another inch, another half-inch,' I said, 'and then!' 'And then whut?' asked Daisy, in an irritated tone. She seemed preoccupied. 'George Fraser,' she said suddenly, 'let's get under thon carpet.' We lay on the grass together under the heavy carpet. The carpet had a harsh smell though underneath us the grass was fresh and a little damp. 'George,' said Daisy, 'I want to see youse.' 'But you do see me, Daisy. Here I am.' 'Ach, youse are slow, George. I want to see you like this.' And Daisy, who was wearing nothing but a short cotton frock and a little woollen vest underneath it suddenly pulled these up to her chest. It was dark under the carpet, and her little body seemed pale and shadowy, but it mildly stirred my curiosity. 'You're different,' I remarked. 'I'm not quite the same.' 'Then let me see youse, George.' I put her off. It was not easy, I explained, in my case. There were buttons and braces which I had not yet learned to do or undo properly by myself, it needed help from mother. 'Ach, George,' said Daisy in real exasperation, 'youse are affa *handless!*'

What would have happened next, I do not know; for suddenly my mother was calling for me in a very sharp voice—'and as for you, Daisy McCandlish,' she added, 'I think your mother wants to see *you*.' Mrs McCandlish, indeed, was standing by her back door, with arms folded, grim and formidable, she seized Daisy by the wrist, and soon from the McCandlish kitchen there came a noise of skelping and bawling. My mother took me indoors. 'George,' she asked, 'what was Daisy saying to you?' I could not think what Daisy had been saying to me, really. 'We were playing under the carpet,' I said. 'She is a silly girl, Daisy.' My mother looked at me thoughtfully for a moment or two, and then said she would say no more about it, but perhaps in future Daisy and I had better not play alone together.

In a few weeks, in any case, we moved to a new house, a flat in a big red sandstone block in Broomhill, much nearer to the centre of Glasgow, handier for schools and for my father's work. Such moves, when one is young, jumble memories. Yet Lloyd Street, like Brooklands, became part of the décor of my dreams. Where Brooklands, in dreams, always seemed to be surrounded by woods that stretched out indefinitely, Lloyd Street was small and neat by itself on a featureless plain. When I was awake, too, certain sensations would take me back to Lloyd Street, the smell of new paint, or of sausage meat frying with onions, which mother, in the Lloyd Street days, always used to cook for her lunch and mine; and tins of condensed milk, and jelly pieces, and kitchens, all these would take me back to Lloyd Street, and rude and ragged little boys in the streets near our new flat, who used to say to me, as a crushing and cryptic insult, 'Your mother doesn't buy your clothes!' Lloyd Street and Brooklands perhaps already symbolised for me, in a vague way, what Disraeli called the two nations. Brooklands represented the connection I would boast about, the nation I wanted to belong to, but Lloyd Street had a certain wistful homeliness, too. At Brooklands I had felt I belonged to the past, to the generations of a family, enclosed within its high walls. At Lloyd Street I had lived in the open and got to know my neighbours. And if sometimes in Broomhill, sleeping at night on my side, curled up under blankets that weighed too heavily on me, I dreamt that I was back at Brooklands again, creeping under grandmama's skirts to make a tent of them, sometimes also I would dream that I was back at Lloyd Street, under the carpet, with Daisy.

6

At Broomhill, I began for the first time to be aware of my father and mother as people. My earliest sharp and isolating awareness had been of people less close to me, of faces that held, for my innocent, enjoying eye, a greater element of the grotesque: faces like grandmama's or like Aunty Sissy's, or grandpapa's. Such faces, as it were, projected pegs for memory to hang a hat on. But

21

it would have been more difficult for me to say what mother and father were like.

Mother, at first, was mainly an atmosphere; warmth, comfort, coaxingness; an intimate female smell of scent (the scent had the delightful name, *heliotrope*), of face-powder, of a fur coat in which I liked to bury my face (the fur had a pleasant name that filled my mouth like a marshmallow, *musquash*). Father was the look of a pair of smartly creased flannel trousers, the smell of an old tweed jacket, and of a favourite pipe. I could not have said what either resembled, but father, of course, even now that the war was over, was a soldier. During the week, he always set out in the mornings, an erect figure, in a black jacket, a grey waistcoat, striped trousers with a knife-edge crease, and with a polished walking stick, rather unusually long, hanging over his stiffly crooked right arm, of which the elbow had been shattered at the Front; a copy of *The Times*, neatly folded, would be thrust by mother between the upper part of that arm and his body. In the evenings, I remember him sitting very erect in an armchair, the floor around him strewn with papers from his office. He wore a large pair of horn-rimmed spectacles, that tended to slip down his neat, sharp nose, and sometimes he looked over the top of these at me, raising his bushy eyebrows in a comical way; his mouth, under its little clipped moustache, was tiny, sensitive, and beautifully moulded, and when he was reproving or admonishing me, though his eyes could blaze, his mouth had an appealing petulance, as if asking how I *could* be so tiresome; the odd contradiction in that glance, between the fierce eyes and the delicate and plaintive mouth, filled me instantly with remorse.

At week-ends, the horn-rimmed spectacles were discarded, the dark suit was replaced by a greenish tweed jacket and flannels, or by mustard-brown plus fours, the polished walking-stick by a fierce and knobbly alpenstock. Father became a figure of purposeful gaiety, organising trips to the Botanic Gardens or to Bearsden or Milngavie, pleasant suburbs that one reached only after riding for what seemed miles past dreary tenements on the open tops of trams, or to Grannie Fraser at Langside, or even farther afield, to visit a friend who had an estate in the country (with tethered goats and a fishing pond) or another friend who had a houseboat on Loch Lomond. Yet, pursuing work or pleasure, father was regularity itself. Mother escaped definition. She was as strange and irregular, as unpredictable, in the changes of her costume, in the rhythms of her movements, in the sequence of her moods, as father, in all these things, was definite and neat.

Early in the morning, I might expect to see her with hair in curlers, in a salmon pink wrapper, clopping about the flat with loose slippers; half an hour would transform her into a neat, sensible lady in grey tweeds, a jumper, and a plain felt hat, ready for her morning's shopping; again, on evenings when she and father were going out to a party, I would (after a nervous period, father pacing up and down, looking at his watch, saying, 'Ada, we shall be late!') see suddenly the emergence of a novel being, white neck and shoulders and elaborate dark coiffure surging, like some great expensive blossom, from a black silk sheath; there would be a glitter, too, of rings and bracelets, a whiff of scent, and as mother bent down to kiss me good-bye, the very slightest of creaks, suggesting rigid corseting. In her girlhood, my mother had been proud of being able to lace her waist in to eighteen inches. 'Don't I look beautiful, Georgie?' she would say, and I would agree, and with a rustling and eager motion, father straight and slim behind her, she would be off on her way.

Mother made no single and simple impression. To my little friends in the neighbourhood she appeared chiefly as an endless source of free meals. The chief of these was a boy called Fraser Mackenzie, and he used to say, 'No, Mrs Fraser', and, 'Yes, Mrs Fraser', in a false, ingratiating way that made me hate him. I call Fraser Mackenzie the chief of my friends; it would be more true to say that he had attached himself to me in the spirit of a contemptuous and insolent parasite. My mother was aware of this, yet she felt that I should move about more, mix more with other little boys, and she felt that I was too dreamy and vague to look after myself properly; for the sake of invitations to tea, of bags of sweets, of evenings at the cinema, Fraser Mackenzie, she felt, who could look so admirably after himself, might also look after me. So he and I had become special friends.

He was cunning and avaricious. He had a sharp eye for traffic, a sense of direction, and so he could be trusted to conduct me and toddling little Jean to Sunday school; but near the entrance, he would stop, he would say thoughtfully, 'A wee girl like thon disna want collection money,' and extract the penny or twopence that Jean was clutching from her chubby little hand. The penny or twopence would be spent on sweets or a comic paper at 'a wee shop that keeps open on the Sabbath'; Fraser Mackenzie always knew the whereabouts of such shops. If it was a comic, Fraser Mackenzie would have the first read of it; if it was sweets, he would dole them out grudgingly, but reasonably fairly, though Jean would never get as many as he and I, and he was sometimes

23

rather reluctant to give her any at all—'Ah'm no sure,' he would say, 'that sweeties is affa gude fur wee girls.' He was a slightly built, red-haired boy, with pointed features, and light, glittering green eyes, who looked and smelled rather like a fox; and it was as a fox that I always thought of him.

The trouble was that I could always foresee his tricks long in advance. In a sense, he was a transparent character. He was skilled in all sorts of little games, with cards particularly, or with marbles, and he would inveigle me into playing for money; we would play for pennies, and Fraser Mackenzie would win twopence or threepence, and then I would suggest that we played for fun only; I could never grasp the rules of his games, for indeed he invented new rules when that suited him; but as soon as we were playing for fun only, he would tell me I was winning; and I would half wish I had gone on playing for pennies, but half feel, also, that if I had, I should have gone on losing; and sometimes I would be tempted to start playing for pennies again, and would lose once more.

I thought Fraser Mackenzie very wicked and false; I knew, also, that he did not like me particularly, but that he went around with me because he liked what he could get out of me. When we were playing with other children, I would be teased, and Fraser Mackenzie was treacherous, he did not protect me, but joined in with the teasers. It bewildered me that I knew all about this duplicity of his and yet could do nothing about it. There seemed to be a sort of fatality that made me his conscious and reluctant victim. He was company, at least, and knew all the other children in the block. He had a particular friend, also, Gavin, who was big and protective and kind; and I could not have Gavin's friendship without Fraser Mackenzie's. I felt also obscurely that where Fraser Mackenzie was quick and cunning, and Gavin was big and strong, I myself had neither of these sets of qualities. You had better be wary of attacking when you are not sure that you can defend yourself. It is from these intrigues of the playground, no doubt, that we learn our first lessons in politics.

It annoyed me that Fraser Mackenzie should share a name with me; it seemed to make a secret link, and I used sometimes to wonder whether he was aware, while he cheated me at games, that I was quite aware of being cheated; I felt sometimes that I knew what it was like to be such a person as he, and that I could be like that, too, if I wanted to; and yet I thought that perhaps Fraser Mackenzie was not really like that either, but really more like me, only that he played at being a fox . . .

24

I understood about playing at being things that one wasn't, for that game ran in the family. Mother, putting Jean and me to bed at nights, sometimes used to frighten us both by pulling her hair down over her face, rolling her large dark eyes at us, and saying in a low, fierce, harsh voice, 'I'm a Red Indian!' We would rush to hide behind a curtain or under a bed. Little Jean, in the mornings, would sometimes strut into breakfast, her small head almost hidden in one of my father's large hats, and dragging after her one of his walking-sticks. 'Who can this be, coming to pay us a visit?', mother would ask. 'Why, mother,' I would say, 'it's just Jean.' 'No, no,' Jean would say firmly. 'I am not Jean Fraser. I am Locky from Americane.' 'How do you do, Mr Locky,' mother would say. 'Won't you have some breakfast with us?'

Where I had been thin, fragile, and nervous, Jean was growing into a chubby and brave child. She had little fists, which she bunched up, and hit people with, to see what would happen; and she would even toddle up to big dogs in the middle of the pavement, and punch them gently in the ribs, but the dogs took it in good part, as everybody did. There was a famous occasion, too, when I had been pushing Jean in her go-cart, up towards Anniesland, and a big fat policeman had bent down to pat the bonny wee girl on her golden head; Jean had beamed up at him and when his big red face was near enough had caught his nose between her finger and thumb, and tweaked it. Jean would take after her father; she had his active, restless, exploring nature. One of my early memories is how, when we were on holiday in Arran, and using her pram to carry shopping in, she began persistently to rummage in a parcel of mince, scattering it in small handfuls on either side of her. There was a destructive streak. At Broomhill, she came into the front room once, to find me lying engrossed in the pictures in *Alice Through the Looking-Glass*; she lifted up the book from between my hands, tore out about a third of the pages, and then, chuckling to herself, pattered away. She never appeared to feel any remorse for these deeds; and indeed she was so sweet, and round, and nice a little girl that nobody was angry with her.

I had to push her out in her go-cart two or three times a week, and she felt that a go-cart ought to be self-propelling. 'Han' away, Georgie, han' away, Georgie,' she would cry, and would wriggle round in the seat, and slap at my hands; I would give the go-cart a little push so that it would run by itself for a few yards, and she would clap her hands in delight; then, when it stopped, I would get ready to push it again, and once again, more loudly, more shrilly, more excitedly, she would cry, 'Han' away, Georgie, han' away!' If Jean was so good, could Fraser Mackenzie be so bad? Surely he must be playing a game of pretending to be bad. I thought of the world as very full of disguises. My mother had a series of stories that she told to Jean and me, the Pussy Stories. The hero was called Mr Pussy and he was a cat. He used to disguise himself as all sorts of familiar things, a tram conductor, a new maid, an inspector of schools; always he would behave in a peremptory fashion, but he would be shown up in the end, after he had created as much confusion as possible, by his tail sticking out behind. He was only Mr Pussy after all. It would be convenient, I thought, if life were like stories—if Fraser Mackenzie had a great fox's brush!

But I was growing older. It was not easy to go on living in a world of let's pretend. My first year at school was rather successful on the whole. I was still the prey of parasites. There was a little boy who was always borrowing pennies from me, because he claimed to have lost his tramfare home; I could never refuse him, and he became madly exorbitant; once, I remember, I gave him an old and battered penny, and he said he did not like it, he wanted a new one; so I gave him the bright new penny that was all I had left—there was no chance of getting the old battered one back from him in exchange—and walked home by myself. Still, I learned to read and write very quickly, and at the end of that first year won a prize, a book called *Stories from Don Quixote*. I was pleased with that year, though there had been the summer sports, certainly, which I had not enjoyed; I stood vaguely on the starting line, missed the pistol, was ploughing half way up the course while all the others were at the finishing tape, and I dived in shame and confusion under the ropes. Yet I read everything I could get hold of, usually out aloud, down to the labels on sauce-bottles.

In my second year at school, I found myself falling back. My sums, somehow, would never come right. I smudged my writing with my fingers and made blots. Once I was asked to read out some stanzas from a mawkish and embarrassing poem, about the child Jesus changing little clay birds made by his companions into real and living birds, which flew away; the piece seemed to me sacred, like my prayers, which I always said in a whisper; and I could not read it aloud except in a whisper, blushing and making myself ridiculous. I fancied that the teacher had spotted how awkward I felt, and had therefore picked me to read, out of my turn. I hated the teacher during that year. She was always finding fault with me and wondering how I could have won a prize the year before. She held me up as an example to the other members of the class of how not to do it. The boys who were an example of how *to* do it were brought out to the floor, and we all had to look at them, and she said, 'These are the cream of the class.' I hated the cream of the class. I hated myself for being stupid and clumsy, for muddling up figures, and having smudgy fingers. In the playground I began to keep to myself, in odd corners, and to get pushed and jostled by the rougher boys.

Once, walking to school, I paused outside a book shop, some of them open and showing pictures. A man was standing very close to the window, staring at some particular book. I had a perverse impulse to see what was interesting him so much, and I thrust myself in front of him, pushing between his legs and the glass. He gripped me by the shoulder and thrust me out of his way. The incident remains even now vividly in my mind—a symbol of my own stupidity, of the world's ruthlessness. Children, like other young animals, either thrive or do not; at that moment, I was not thriving.

I was aware of my shortcomings. I had not learned how to tell the time. I went to bed usually about eight, but there was one fine summer evening when I asked my father if I might stay up for another half hour. He consented and then I heard my mother's voice, annoyed and plaintive, in the next room. It was the school holidays and she had Jean and me on her hands all day. 'But I promised,' I heard him say. 'But after all,' she said, 'he can't read the time.' There was more talk, in rather low, conspiratorial tones. In what seemed a very few minutes, my father came in, looking a little uneasy. 'Time's up, laddie,' he said, not looking me quite straight in the eyes. 'It doesn't feel like half an hour, father.' 'Time passes very quickly when you're enjoying yourself,' said my father, briskly. 'But look at the church clock out there, if you don't believe me . . . You do remember the lesson I gave you with my watch, don't you?' I looked out of the window but the angle of the hands told me nothing; there was nothing for it but a civil and bitter goodnight.

That night, and other nights, I could hear my father's voice and my mother's, through the thin walls of the flat, rising and falling, before I could get to sleep, and one night, waking from a disturbing dream, I became so obsessed with the rhythm of these voices, with these words that I could not quite hear, that I got out of bed and knocked on the drawing-room door. I opened it, and my parents, tall and strange and fierce-faced, looked down on me.

The light, after the dark hallway, dazzled me, and I rubbed sleepy eyes. 'What *is* it, Georgie?'—my mother's voice was strained. 'I heard you talking, talking, talking, and I couldn't go to sleep.' 'Go back to bed, Georgie, go back to bed *at once*.' I turned away from the light and their sternness; the voices went on again, but on a lower note, with more even, less acute rhythms, and then either they fell to silence, or I fell asleep.

There was another evening when my father came home from the office in a hurry to get on to some official reception. I was sitting hunched up on the floor of the hallway, murmuring over some story to myself. My father in shirt sleeves and evening dress trousers, looking desperately for a stud for his collar, knocked into me without seeing me. Instead of apologising, he gave me a little kick. 'Georgie,' he said furiously, 'can't you do anything but sit about and talk to yourself and mope?' I got up and went to the kitchen where mother was busy. 'Mother,' I said with a conscious quaver in my voice, 'father kicked me.' Mother immediately went to have it out with him. My father finally came into the kitchen, looking harried, though immaculate in his white tie and tails. 'No doubt,' he said, grittingly, 'I ought not to have kicked you, Georgie, but I think you must feel yourself that you ought not to have told your mother about it. You cannot really claim that I kicked you very hard. And there are some little episodes that we men ought to keep to ourselves. Goodnight.' The door gave a little bang as he left the house. Then my mother came in with a bright, forced smile. 'Father didn't mean anything, you know that, Georgie?' 'Yes, mother, I was silly.'

7

I am describing at excessive length the experiences of a rather tiresome little boy. But I believe that our childhoods shape our characters, shape even our vision of society and our practical attitudes to our fellow men. Modern psychologists think this is so, but they often talk as if the family were a self-enclosed thing, consisting only of father, mother, and child, and they talk as if children had no social problems in the strict sense, no problems about their relations with their equals. Yet in the streets and on the playgrounds there exists a society of children, with its own strange laws and customs, and it is his failure to adapt himself to that society which seems tragic to the lonely child. I was failing to adapt myself because I lived, to a quite unusual extent, in an inner world of images.

I would imagine what it would be like to have my own football, and to take the lead in games of football that boys used to play about the streets of Broomhill. But when I did get the football, I found that they were too quick and rough for me, that the ball was snatched away from my feet, and I was standing at a little distance, the spectator of a rough and tumble with my ball. I had a kind of false advantage over the boys in the block, in that my parents could afford to buy me a football, and theirs could not. They had a real advantage over me in that they knew what to do with it when they got it.

It was the same in all games. For a year I was a member of the Wolf Cubs, going to the meetings there with Fraser Mackenzie and Gavin. I remained a tenderfoot, while these two soon got their first and second stars. They would try to teach me a boy's usual knacks, to tie a knot, to catch a ball, to make the correct movements in some singing and miming game, and it was not that I failed to concentrate, but that my concentration was concerned with storing up images, not with adapting my body to a task. I was perpetually being forced into the position of the one who cannot quite do it, who does not quite belong to the group, who has to be helped along, who enviously watches. It was breeding a sense of insecurity that reflected itself in fractiousness and unpleasant dreams.

The artist is a person who cannot quite do it, who does not quite belong to the group, who has to be helped along, and who watches, perhaps enviously; I imagine that many artists have childhoods rather like mine (perhaps not only artists but failures, criminals, and neurotics, too). My father thought that my backwardness in games, my shyness, my cowardice about taking a lead were all due to the fact that, while he was away at the war, I had been brought up mainly by women and petted and spoiled. That must have happened to many children of my generation, and they got over it. A factor quite as important in unsettling me was the peculiar social relation, both at Lloyd Street and Broomhill, of my parents to their neighbours. In both places, we were birds of passage. In neither place did we belong to the same social class as most of our neighbours. But there is a strong sense in children, when they play together, of the tribe. The children I played with seemed to me to be a tribe with their own skills and secrets and, however tolerant they might be towards me, they also felt that I was not one of them. In a way I despised the cunning of

29

those, like Fraser Mackenzie or the boy who half wheedled, half bullied pennies out of me, who took advantage of me. It was half in a wish not to shame them that I let them take advantage. And for the boys I played with my clothes, my voice, my choice of words all made a difference (one of our neighbours at Lloyd Street had ironically dubbed me 'Gentleman George'). Brought up so largely in a family of English origins, and with a father of Highland ancestry, who spoke, like many Highlanders, precise and almost pedantic English, I was never able to master the coarse and lively dialect of the Glasgow streets. I was driven to imagining friends more like myself with whom I could play the sort of game (the acting out of a long elaborate story, with much conversation) that appealed to me; since such friends were only imaginary, the game remained imaginary, too.

I would lie awake at night, telling myself long stories, till mother or father came into my room, and told me to go to sleep. There would be Douglas Fairbanks in my mind, as Robin Hood; there was material there, towers, horses, arrows, terrible confrontations, to twist and turn into an endless story, and this got mixed up, too, with an image of the Crusades, of horsemen in armour riding off, in long glittering rows, to some incredible clash at a vague distance, and with the image of the Round Table, for my mother had bought me some little twopenny books in which Malory's stories were retold in simple language for children. The book that I had won as a prize, *Stories from Don Quixote,* also played its part in shaping these reveries; for I did not consider Don Quixote as a comic character, and thought his adventures as romantic and splendid as any others. I had wept bitterly over the incident where the Knight rescues a boy who is being beaten by a farmer, and, once the Knight has gone by, the farmer ties the boy up to a tree again, and thrashes him twice as soundly. My head was full of this wild stuff, and Hans Andersen's fairy tales, of which we possessed a fat edition, with illustrations by Heath Robinson and others, added a particular flavour, melancholy, northern, cold, of distance and despair to the brew. There were some of these stories, certainly, that I could never bear to read twice, like that piece of torturing sentiment about the little mermaid, but others, like that of the little girl who trod on a loaf of bread and sank down, down, down into the horrible bog, were dreadfully fascinating; the stories had homeliness, dreariness, a wild humour, horror; had refrains, too, like the wind sighing for the proud baron's three fair, dead daughters; there was an atmosphere about them, which I had not so far found in anything else—the atmosphere of poetry. I too could look at the moon from my bedroom window and listen to the wind howling in the chimney pots.

But if I fled from reality in my stories, reality came back to me in my dreams. These dreams were always of Glasgow. Sometimes, when my tramfare had been wheedled out of me, I had been forced to walk home from school; and, coming home from the Wolf Cubs, I would have been lost without Fraser Mackenzie and Gavin to see me on the right tram. Glasgow seemed to me an endless labyrinth, in which one grim street so much repeated the pattern of another, that without such guides one might be for ever lost. Sometimes, too, we went on even longer tram rides, to visit my father's family at Langside; as we came back in the evenings, riding on the top of the open tram, passing long rows of tenement windows showing a bilious light through clogged muslin curtains—a fine imperceptible layer of soot seemed sooner or later to cover almost everything in Glasgow, like a dark bloom—I would have a sense of terrible melancholy. In my dreams then, I was always wandering through the streets of Glasgow, and I was always lost; I would walk for miles, through streets that were familiar and yet not familiar, looking for my own home. Night after night, I wandered in that hopeless labyrinth, and the dream, I can see now, reflected a deep uprooted feeling, a sense of not being really at home anywhere, as well as the sprawl and the confused repetitions of the huge city. No door was ever really mine.

Such a dream, psychologists will say, is the expression of a wish to return to the womb; yet the womb itself is only the most poignant symbol of some fundamental security, some sense of belonging properly, which we have either lost or not yet gained; and children, or grown people, who are rooted and active in their proper worlds do not have such dreams. It might be truer to say that I had never properly emerged from the womb; I had spent too many years, years of premature brooding reflectiveness, protected by the walls of Brooklands, with all my wants attended to, and no effort called for on my own part. Too young, I had become my own spectator. I am not sure that I have ever really moved out of that enclosure. During the war, in Cairo, a friend of mine, the artist Eric de Nemes, told me that I lived inside a transparent crystal ball; and that all the efforts of the world, and all my own efforts, would never succeed in shattering it. The labyrinth that I trod in my dreams was an interior one, and perhaps a protective labyrinth; while I sought for a centre that

31

was not there, dangers and realities lay in an open space outside. Nevertheless, I would awake sweating in the morning.

8

I should say something, before I leave Glasgow, of the other side of my ancestry, my father's family. When we went over to see Granny Fraser in Langside, I had always a sense of journeying into the past. It was a district of older houses than our raw red sandstone block, with its brisk allotments near it, in Broomhill; of terrace houses of grey or brown stone, their surface enriched, as all surfaces in Glasgow are enriched in time, by a thick grimy patina. There was a bald park near Granny's house of scurfy grass and with sooty iron railings; sea-birds, come on heaven knows what errand so far inland, would skirl over the putting-greens. Yet there was an air, not unpleasing to me, of mellowness about this district, if only the mellowness of sadness and decay. And Granny's house itself was full of family history. In one big room, with a large black iron grate, used half as a kitchen, half as a room for meals, there was an old-fashioned box bed, let into a recess in the wall; I slept there once or twice when I stayed overnight, with the warm ashes of the fire still glowing. The floor-covering of this room was of linoleum, and Granny would be up at six o'clock in the morning to start scrubbing it. All her life, in Leeds first, then in Glasgow, at last in London, till she grew very old and her mind began to wander, she kept to the routines she had learned as a girl on a remote farm in Caithness.

In another room, with plush chairs, a heavy mahogany table, and dark fringed curtains of some thick and durable but uninviting material, there was a bookcase with a glass front, containing my dead grandfather's library, classics of the Victorian age, now locked safe from dust and children's fingers, and never looked at. There was a portrait of my grandfather in his young manhood, a florid, handsome, bearded man, and other portraits and photographs of men and women in the costumes of fifty years back; including, I remember, one of a youth of eighteen, with an open collar and a shock of hair, rather like the young Shelley. As a last touch, this period interior was lighted by gas, popping mantles on curly brackets. This seemed to me a dwelling more solid and serious, more planted, than our flat in Broomhill: with something about it that recalled the brown gloom of grandpapa Jones's dining room at Brooklands, and yet sadly and indefinably different. Human life had not permeated the

32

walls in the same way. This house at Langside was more homely, more Scottish than Brooklands, yet where Brooklands conveyed—delusively, indeed—the atmosphere of a way of life with deep roots, persistent, ready to thrust into the future, Granny Fraser's house had more of an atmosphere of inanimate stubbornness; the Frasers, unlike the Joneses, would always move with the general current of the times; the heavy furniture, the dark curtains, the books which nobody read, the grate which had to be raked out and polished every morning, were as irrelevant to the thoughts and wishes of my father's sisters, as they moved briskly about, arguing about politics, as a sprig of lilac, suddenly laid on that heavy table, would have been. My father's side of my family, unlike my mother's, lived much in their minds and little in their senses; the Frasers had a family gift (for which I myself was to be grateful later, in dreary barracks and draughty army offices) for abstracting themselves at will from their surroundings.

There were three children in that house, but of these only Norman, my cousin, the son of my father's brother who was overseas, made a vivid impression on me, mainly by dint of knocking me down and kneading me with his knees. He was of my own age and size, so it could hardly be called bullying; that Highland pugnaciousness, which Aunt Anne and Aunt Helen sublimated in endless argument, was with Norman still at the natural stage. My squeals would gradually break through into the Fraser consciousness; Aunt Anne or Aunt Helen would scold Norman, and Granny Fraser, who was sorry for the poor boy without his father or his mother near him, would say in her soft voice that she was sure the laddie meant no harm.

Granny Fraser was a Sutherland, from Caithness, that bleak, flat county, of farmers and fishermen, on the extreme north-east of the Scottish coast. She was a very thin, tiny old lady, who wore neat black clothes and sat very straight in her chair, and talked, quietly but very persistently, in a soft, musical voice. Though she had lived so long in Glasgow, her old face had over its natural pallor a brown tinge, as if weathered by the sea winds of her girlhood. And like the furniture in that living room at Langside, she had stubbornly resisted change. Her talk was all of Caithness, which she had left behind her more than thirty years before. And it was typical Highland talk, for on the loose thread of one long story there would be hung a string of parenthetical anecdotes; she had the Highland preoccupation with kinship, and when she introduced some new character into her endless saga, I would always be told that he was 'your third cousin, that would be,

George, on the Sutherland side', or 'married, George, on your great-aunt Elspeth, I mean on your grandfather's side, my dear husband's sister.' She had certain locutions that had remained from her girlhood, when Gaelic had been her first, English her second language, so that she would say 'married on' instead of 'married to', and 'fond for' instead of 'fond of'; and she always spoke English in a slow, ceremonious way, with a savouring of every word that was typically Highland. She had learned useful things on her travels, the Leeds housewives, for instance, had taught her how to bake good bread, but Caithness had shaped her for life, she had absorbed none of the attitudes of people bred in towns, and her character, a typical character of that bleak and remote but not infertile or unkindly coast, was a strange mixture of gentleness and inflexibility.

Her speech was gentle, yet she had her way in that household; and she was inflexibly severe with her frail body, always rigidly upright, and up every morning before dawn to be busy about household tasks that her daughters would gladly have taken off her hands. Disguised by the easy, affable manners that are typical of Glasgow and the Scottish West Coast, my father had something of her inflexible simplicity.

Granny Fraser outlived my father, dying only a year or so ago, in London, in Aunt Anne's house, still surrounded by much of her old furniture, and still impervious, in London as in Glasgow, to the great labyrinthine city round her. She had been wandering a little in mind for many years—often getting up in the middle of the night to pack her clothes and set off on long journeys to see her long-dead sisters in the Highlands, and her talk about Highland life tended latterly to be mixed up with details from the latest John Buchan novel she had been reading. Yet, for me, she stands as a solid symbol of something which she herself could never find the proper words to express. As long as she lived, we were a family, with that awareness of an ancestral landscape, a landscape that we had never seen. 'Your great-grandfather,' she would say, 'was the first man, George, to introduce a wheeled vehicle into Sutherland.' One does not know if this was true, but it meant something; she kept us aware of the primitive vigour of our stock. Now that she has gone, London will melt us to the flat style around us, and in another generation we shall have forgotten that we are of a single kin.

The Death of My Grandmother

There's little personal grief in a quiet old death:
Grief for a landscape dying in our heads,
Knowing how London melts us to her style.
What if she got those touches in her talk
(The half-impression of a scene that had
Flowed in her youthful blood and set as bone)
From phrases in some novel by John Buchan?
A memory is other than the words for it:
Persistence was her gift, not literature,
A character no town could penetrate,
Not Glasgow's sprawl, nor London's repetitions—
No more that landscape now: no more the old
Books in the glass case, and the box bed
I half remember as a boy in Glasgow:
Caithness enclosed within a house in Glasgow,
Glasgow enclosed in London: time in time,
The past within the past, parentheses.
In laying her to rest, it is as if
We folded up with her brown age a landscape,
A ribbed and flat and rocky map of duty
That is the northern edge of every island
Where pleasure flowers only in the swollen south:
Mourn character that could persist so long
Where softer personality dies young.

These lights and glimpses lost now: only bones,
Shapes of our heads, only the arguing voice,
In a foreign milieu the improvised fine manners.

Think of these rock-stacks in the stony Orkneys
That, toppling, stand improbably for years,
The sea persisting at them: and at last,
Boys' bricks, they crash on the untidy beach.
So with her piled and uncemented past:
Its tottering tower seemed out of the tide's reach.
Time merely fretted at the base. No more
Of all the colour of her years was hers
Than brown rock's is blue sea's. O travellers,
Who take the stain of Time, as I have done,
Expose your fluctuations to the sun:
Yet, for such stony virtue, spare your tears.

The Change of Scene

1

WHEN I was about eight years old, there was a vacancy in the Town Clerk's Office in Aberdeen for the post of Town Clerk Depute, and my father put in for it, and got it; his looks, bearing and record all told in his favour. For myself, the shift was peculiarly important in that it meant a move from a city which sprawled out darkly beyond me, to one whose shape was clear and glittering.

Glasgow in its grim way, is a romantic city, a perfect expression of historical forces beyond human control. To be romantic is, in fact, to surrender oneself, for the sake of an intenser feeling of being alive, to forces beyond one's control, to be classic is to protect one's traditional individuality against such forces. Glasgow has surrendered whatever traditional individuality it may once have had for the sake of size and scope. If one lets oneself feel it at all *as* a city, and does not busy oneself, as most Glasgow people do, with one's purely practical concerns, one feels it as a strange, dark, shapeless dream: a great, sad sprawl of bewildered human lives. The air of Glasgow is damp and mild and sooty, the speech of the people is a kind of affable sing-song, neither good Scots nor good English, their character a queer mixture of energy and shiftlessness, of the kindly and the aggressive, that comes from the melting down in the Scottish central industrial belt of many stocks and traditions; nowhere on this island are there more skilled and devoted artisans, nowhere are there drearier slums. Yet, if there is a kind of horror about Glasgow, there is a kind of cosiness, too. It is, unlike London, a neighbourly place. One's friends, there, will not be, as in London, those with whom one shares some common intellectual interest, but those whose family knew one's own family, those who once lived in the same street, or with whom one went to school. That very cosiness—such an excellent, such a humanising thing in itself, and the reason why my mother, for instance, still looks back on dear old smoky Glasgow with the warmest affection—would have been fatal to me. The cosiness would have cushioned all my

36

surface resentments; and, inside, the horror would have ground me away. Glasgow will some day produce a great romantic poet, but I was too sensitive and not tough enough for that role. I needed more outward strictness and more inner security, and these I found in Aberdeen. I was lucky to leave Glasgow while the city was still only a symbol to me; in a year or two, it would have become a reality, and would have drained my own reality away. I was no blossom to flourish on that iron branch.

Aberdeen is, in almost every way, the moral antithesis of Glasgow. Glasgow is provincial in the sense of having failed to become a capital; the great dowdy creature, gathering up her own trailing skirts, has little thought to spare for the rest of Scotland, and for the rest of Scotland also Glasgow is something strangely alien. Aberdeen is provincial in the sense of being the strong outpost of a local tradition, with deep roots in the past. The very look, the very physical atmosphere, of the two cities pointed for me, from the first, this contrast. The relaxing air of Glasgow, its smeared windows and stained stones, its parks with their bald and scruffy lawns, its clanging trams on their endless journeys, its oily and tumid river, all these would encourage in me a sad and hopeless dreaminess; while the brisk, cold air of Aberdeen, biting one's cheeks, the frosty glitter of its granite façades, the hard stone setts of the roads along which the great drayhorses clattered, striking out sparks on cold days, and puffing steam from their nostrils, all these woke me up, straightened my back, brisked me into an unaccustomed alertness. The air, after Glasgow's, seemed incredibly clear and pure, and one had a new sense of perspective, of streets stretching out to a dagger-point in long, cold distances.

There was a new sense, also, of having boundaries. There was the boundary facing the sea, a long curve of smooth beautiful shore between the mouth of the Don and the harbour. The mouth of the Don bounded the city to the north, the mouth of the Dee to the south. Moving in from the shore, one moved in a tram along Union Street, past the baronial turrets of the Town House, where father worked, and the other absurd turret of the Salvation Army headquarters, and the city cross, a little rotunda, with medallions of dead Stuart kings, and past the grimly solid granite façade of the New Market, and across Union Bridge, looking down on gardens and the railway, pigeons wheeling above them, and so on to Holborn Junction, past first of all the terraces of Albyn Place, clubs and schools and doctors and nursing homes, and then past Queen's Cross to Queen's Road, the solid houses of the more prosperous Aberdonians, of grey or pink granite, set well back in

37

their gardens. There would come a gap where one looked across the Grammar School playing grounds to a green distance where the city was expanding in new housing schemes towards and beyond the Bridge of Dee, and then one came to the great ring road, embracing the city in the directions of its new growth, Anderson Drive, and then on past houses less solid and imposing, till finally one reached the terminus at Woodend, or perhaps the tram would swing left towards the great park of Hazlehead. There was a golf course there, and beyond the golf-course, moorland, across which one could stride springily, striking at some point the road that pushed on past Woodend, and finding oneself then in proper country, dry-stone dykes, and green or brown fields, and paths crunchy with leaves and lined with silver birches, and quiet farmhouses.

There, then, was a city bounded by two rivers, by the sea, and by a fertile countryside, a city with organic shape. It would be hard for the most obstinate of romantics to feel lost in such a city; it appeals to the sense of human order, adapting itself to natural order, where Glasgow appeals to the sense of natural force, blind and overwhelming, proliferating, using and discarding men. Aberdeen gave me what I needed, if my apprehensions were ever to be of any use to me: a rigid framework.

2

It took us a while, of course, to settle in. We came up in the early summer, in the time of the school holidays, and for a few months we lived in boarding-houses, while we looked for a home of our own. The first boarding-house was a melancholy, old-fashioned place in Queen's Road. The landlady's deceased husband had been at some time in Africa, and the walls were hung with assegais, which I was always wanting to take down and play with, but father told me that the stabbing heads were poisoned. They were rusty certainly, and a kind of rust, or fur, or hoarseness of the past seemed to be spread everywhere. Old people sat about, in shawls and spectacles, and Jean and I had always to be getting out of their way or to be talking in whispers so as not to disturb them. It was a house cluttered with funereal ornaments—and jet beads, too, bobbed on the scrawny necks of the old ladies—and there were many things, besides the assegais, that we were told not to touch. One afternoon, the blinds in the neighbouring house were all down, because someone was dying, and Jean and I had to

38

sit like statues, books open on our knees, not moving or saying a word. The faint distant whiff of how life runs down, grows creaking and elderly, oppressed me a little. But I could not really imagine death.

We moved in a few weeks to a more cheerful place at Queen's Cross, where we could play croquet on the back lawn in the afternoons, and snakes and ladders with the kindly old landlady in the evening, and where Scottish high tea was a fine traditional meal, at which, every night, I made a grand tour of the fruitcake, the shortbread, and the sugary buns. Now I began to grow podgy. The boarders petted me and a handsome Australian girl used to take me for walks around the town, between my frequent and starchy meals, buying me quantities of chocolate. With her I got to know the Art Gallery, and His Majesty's Theatre, at which a statue of William Wallace points dramatically with a raised sword, and Duthie Park, where there was a pond, with ducks, which we used to take stale bread in paper bags to feed. Mrs Benton, our landlady, took me to town when she went shopping; we would go round the stalls in the New Market, and she would cheapen meat and vegetables, and then as a treat we would go into one of the big tea-shops in Union Street, and I had a meringue, or a sort of spongy and creamy confection, covered with chocolate, called a niggerhead. It would always be a difficult matter to know which to choose; Mrs Benton would sit watching me with a quiet, ironical smile while I pondered alternative pleasures.

These early months in Aberdeen went by, and I thrived on them. I could not quite carry my corn for I used to chatter too much at mealtimes, and to show off, and I once made a rude joke at the tea table about an old gentleman, a specially privileged boarder, who had rather a jaundiced and veiny look. My own ready giggle roused then only the faintest of echoes, and in my bedroom later my father rounded on me. 'People will laugh out of politeness,' he said, 'when you behave in this rude, vulgar way, but they don't think you are clever, they think you are badly brought up.'

His words pierced me; I realised, as I was to do often later, that the times at which one is most in sympathy with oneself—in fact, at the close of my first decade, and before the onset of puberty, I was relapsing, as children often do at this fairly placid period in their lives, into something like a middle-aged complacency—are those at which other people are likely to find one least sympathetic. My mother and my aunts have all the pleasantest

39

memories of me during that earlier period of my childhood in Glasgow of which I remember, myself, only the patches of loneliness, bewilderment, and misery. But when my mother, who had been in the south for some weeks seeing her father, came back to rejoin us at Mrs Benton's she thought I looked bloated. It was not necessary, she firmly explained to me, at tea-time, for me to sample everything on the table. Aunty Win, who came up to visit us for a little from the bungalow in Kilmarnock where she was now keeping house for Grandpa Jones, was similarly worried to see me spending so much of my time curled up by the fire, sunk in detective stories. They filled my head, she was sure, with unwholesome fantasies, and I was already a sufficiently violent child. At Kilmarnock had I not once shot my sister Jean in the leg with an arrow, and then hidden in the bottom of the garden in terror for hours? Her fears were confirmed when she tried to snatch a book by Agatha Christie from me and I made as if to throw it at her. She censored my reading severely after that incident. I felt her judgment of my character was hardly fair, for if I had shot Jean in the leg, had Jean herself not once, with unpredictable violence, hit me on the head with a stone hot-water bottle?

After a longer summer break than usual, what I needed was to get back to school. My mother took me one afternoon to the Grammar School: the oldest school in Aberdeen, its foundations dating back to the early Middle Ages. In the grounds, at the front, there was a statue of Lord Byron, who had spent a year or two there as a very small boy, before his mother moved to England and he to Harrow—an unhappy small boy, because of his deformed foot, which was being wrenched and tortured by doctors to make it straight: 'Dinna speak o' it!' he had cried, in rage and tears, to the old Scottish nurse who tried to console him. He was hardly a pattern of Aberdonian morality, but he was a famous man, so the school honoured him, and it was divided, in an imitation of the English public school system—or perhaps more exactly of the Scottish University system of different 'nations'—into four houses, one named after the poet. Houses, indeed, in a purely metaphorical sense; apart from a few boys whose loyal Aberdonian parents had sent them up from London, there were no boarders, and members of all four houses were scattered among every class, so that for common tasks classes could easily be divided into competing teams. I found myself in Byron House, for what that was worth; and later, when I began to scribble things, took that as an omen.

40

The Headmistress of the Lower School asked me several searching questions. 'Can you do long multiplication?' 'Can I do long multiplication?' I repeated thoughtfully. I was not quite sure. 'You must not say that, Fraser,' she said severely—it was the first time in my life, I think, that I had not been called 'George'—'you must not repeat my questions.' 'I must not repeat your questions,' I said, and blushed, and bit my lip. 'And you must call me Miss.' 'Miss.' I left her with the impression that I was unusually stupid and so was put into a class that was covering work I had already done in Glasgow, among younger and smaller boys. In a way, this was useful, for it gave me a year in which I could relax slightly and yet keep easily up with my classmates; and at the end of that year, I skipped a class, and so once more caught up with my contemporaries.

Taller and older than most of the boys in my class, I ought now, for the first time in my life, to have taken a lead. If there was a chance to do that, I failed to snatch it; perhaps there was not, for here I was a foreigner. The rhythm of speech in Aberdeen is much slower than in Glasgow, and when I read aloud in class, clearly and intelligently, I nevertheless rattled through my sentences at a pace that took the other boys, and even the teacher, aback. And in the playground the boys spoke a language that it took me a long time to understand. They had a rather obscene game, of rushing past one and tearing the front of one's trousers open, and they had what struck me as a rather obscene phrase for it, too—ripping one's spaver. But very many words were strange. Boys were loons, or more often loonies, and I was in a huff several times before it dawned on me that I was not being called a lunatic. Girls were queans, or queanies (the word was pronounced to rhyme with 'wine'). School, in the broadest mouths, of the boys from farms in Buchan, was skweel, and a fool was a feel, or a feelie. I could make little, in my first few weeks, of such sentences as, 'Thon loon's mair like a quean, he suldna be at the skweel, he's a feelie!'—and if I was the loon in question, as often I might be, I felt all the hot embarrassment that comes when, on some holiday abroad, one knows, by the looks, the tones, but can find no words to answer back, that one is being shamefully insulted in a foreign tongue.

It was a strange tongue, but not unmusical: a shrill language of pure Italian vowels. Perhaps at that period, in the late 1920s, the common use of the racy Buchan dialect as a language of the hearth was dying out among the middle classes in Aberdeen, for, never acquiring the dialect myself, I noticed that my classmates as they grew older gradually dropped it in favour of a slow, thoughtful, rather precise, rather pedantic English, the kind of speech which is called in Aberdeen Albyn Place English, Kelvinside in Glasgow, Morningside in Edinburgh. They would always retain, however, certain idioms belonging to their older speech—the use of 'fair' or 'fairly', for instance, where in colloquial southern English, one would say 'really'. 'I was fairly taken aback,' they said—or if they wished to be more formal, they used a more precise and less colloquial adverb than 'really': 'I was properly taken aback.' All this helped to give me a special, rather self-conscious interest in problems of idiom and diction, and though I try to write in a simple, unaffected way, some of my friends tell me that my English has, like the English spoken in Aberdeen, a queer flavour of old-fashioned pedantry, a slightly stilted eighteenth-century air. Scotsmen, in fact, learning their English from books, do tend to use in conversation a large sprinkling of words with a bookish flavour. This often makes their speech seem, to a southern Englander, stiff; its large spoken vocabulary, however, can give it an unusual precision.

Stirred up, perhaps, by the nipping northern air, my companions, during these breaks in the playground, seemed to me much rougher and fiercer than the boys I remembered in Glasgow. They would rush about in little gangs, playing a game which I had been taught to call tig, and which they called tic and tac. A person is touched and has to touch somebody else. But often it would be a matter not of touching but of pushing over; or of snatching a tie from under a pullover, or of seizing a cap and sending it whirling, sometimes into a scrum in the middle of the playground, sometimes over a wall and into the street. Belonging to none of the established gangs, I was fair game for all of them, and one day our mistress said rather acidly, 'I see that in the playground you are always baiting George Fraser. I can't see why he doesn't look after himself, for he is a bigger boy than most of you, but anyway in future stop it.' I felt rather ashamed of having this protection, and in any case its main effect was to make my classmates realise that they were baiting me, so that what had been done on an instinct was now done on a system. I would be pushed against a wall by little groups, and they would punch at my ribs, and I would thrust out my hands to keep them at a reasonable distance.

One day, however, I decided to assert myself. There was one stout, red-faced boy, the leader of a little gang that had selected me as a special victim. I waited, during the break, for him to start on his tricks, but somehow that day he left me alone. I went up to him. He gave me a little push, a perfunctory one, and said something mildly disparaging, like, 'Run away, if you know what's good for you.' In itself it was a rather mild provocation; but there was a history of potent provocations behind it. I caught him by his cheeks, rather plump and pendulous ones, and squeezed and twisted these. He began to scream, and tears started in his eyes, but I did not let him go at once. I expected him to hit me, but he went back to the classroom, blubbering. When I got back, I discovered that he had told the teacher and that I was in disgrace. I felt rather nasty inside myself, but I said coldly, 'I was only defending myself, and I think it's very cowardly and mean to tell on people. There are lots of things I could have told.' But the general attitude to 'telling on' people seemed to me a queer one, for there was no sense of dishonour about it—as there had been in my Glasgow school, with its more earnest attempts to imitate English public school codes—and the threat, 'I'll tell on you!' could generally protect a boy who was being bullyragged. 'Fwat would you tell on me for, it's nae but a game?' his tormentor would reply in a surly way, and leave him for the time being alone. Indeed, I am not certain that it was my own sense of honour that prevented me from telling on people. I had strong enough resentments. But I hated scenes and situations, especially when I was the centre of them. I had the wish, fortunately rare in schoolboys, to be unobtrusive, on the edge; this, indeed, was what made me so awkwardly conspicuous; for healthy boys are little aggressive, self-assertive animals. Those of them who are really happily unobtrusive on the edge are those who have been pushed there after a healthy struggle for the centre. It was not wishing to be at the centre that made me seem odd to my classmates.

In class, certainly, I got nearer to achieving my unworthy ambition. I was quiet, reasonably but not excessively good at my lessons, and not awkwardly conspicuous. I was only in disgrace twice; once for the ugly little episode I have just described; and a second time when, misjudging the moral atmosphere of the class as usual, I was again 'told on'. The class had been naughty in some way, and was being kept in. Teacher had gone out for a moment or two, and there was a general buzz of discontent, an atmosphere of incipient mutiny. I was becoming known as rather a dab at composition, and, in an unlucky moment, I decided to curry favour with my fellows. I whispered to my deskmate, 'I've made up a rhyme about teacher.' 'Let me hear it.' 'You promise not to tell on me?' 'I promise.' 'Faithfully?' 'Yes.' 'Teacher is a cheeky cat, let us give her tit for tat.' Teacher came back and of course my deskmate was out on the floor in an instant, bending over the desk, whispering in her ear. As in the case of the earlier incident, she was grimly forbearing. When I had time to think it over, she said, I would feel ashamed of being rude and vulgar, and that, she hoped, would be punishment enough for me. I sat crimsoning like a beetroot. I forget whether I plucked up enough courage to apologise as I was leaving.

Though I was hard-working and docile, I was always making such blunders, caused by an imperfect sense of the conventions of the little community to which I now belonged. We were once having a discussion about Santa Claus. I no longer believed in Santa Claus. I put up my hand. 'My father tells me,' I began to say. I paused. I was suddenly uneasily conscious of being older than most of my classmates. My words seemed somehow too formal for such a juvenile discussion. Switching my tone to an affected childish treble, composing my lips to a simper of sweetness, I began again, 'My daddy says . . .' In my choice of words, I was known already as the little precisian of the class, and this was too much. There were sniggers all around me. Our teacher looked at me from under veiled eyelids, tapping the desk slightly with a ruler, as she always did when she felt that one of her charges was putting on some sort of a performance. 'Oh, yes,' she said mockingly, 'oh, yes, George Fraser, your daddy says?' I blushed and was silent. I thought of my father as a very high card and was therefore reluctant to play him. Our music master once asked each of us what our fathers did. 'My father,' I said sullenly, when it came to my turn, 'works for the Town House.' 'Good gracious, George,' said our mistress, when the music lesson was over, 'you should have said that he was Town Clerk Depute. You might have meant that he was a Corporation dust-collector.' He might easily have been that, however, for the Grammar School was a democratic institution, filled mainly certainly with the children of middle-class parents, but also containing a good sprinkling of the children of what the Scots call the 'good poor'. The fees were moderate and many working-class parents thought it worth their while to save up and pay them. Father had taught me that it was vulgar to insist on one's comparative wealth and position, and I was carrying out his lesson too much to the letter; and there was a certain basic insincerity involved in my attitude; for I would not, surely, have been so conspicuously bashful if I had not had a quite exaggerated notion of what our comparative wealth and position was. By disclaiming any importance for my father so vehemently, I gave him, perhaps, more importance than he really had.

And yet, for all this, I did not feel so lost as I had in Glasgow. These winter afternoons, when the light would begin to fade in the classrooms, and the bare yellow bulbs would be switched on, giving, against the blue expanse of the windows, an effect of grim cosiness, I would feel myself cushioned by the classroom fug; and then braced by the cold, as I trudged eagerly home, through the frosty dark, up Carden Place, towards a warm, lighted room with a sea-coal fire, and Mrs Benton's high tea with its indigestible starchy scones and cakes and buns.

And I was not always fighting or being tormented, on half days I would have some companion to struggle home with me, by a round-about route, through the sports field at the back of the school; we would choose the longest ways, working through alleys and sidestreets, with a sense of exploration, now racing each other, now dawdling, now snatching at each other's ties and caps, as a game and not to torment each other. The world no longer seemed so strange and confusing, and just as the cold of these winter evenings made the warmth and light of indoors more delectable, so, in class sometimes, the brisk and business-like manner of our teacher seemed to accentuate the value of her kindness. I came into school one afternoon with a throbbing tooth and a swollen gum; I said nothing about it, it was the end of the school week, I was being taken on Saturday to the dentist, and so I was bearing my pain with patient misery. The misery, however, must have been obvious, for our teacher said that it was absurd I should be trying to work, and I soon found myself ensconced in the staff room, beside a cheerful fire, with a cup of tea, and a boy's adventure story. Again, I was not made to feel so utterly out of it as I had formerly felt in sports. I was obviously the slowest of us all at football, but I was put in goal, and that gave me long periods when I could stamp about, and keep myself warm, while the others busied themselves at the far end of the field, and when the ball came near me I often managed to stop it and send it back into play; or if I was stuck by myself in goal too long, while the game moved about at the other end of the field, the sportsmaster would kick me a spare ball for practice. Here, as in the general life of the school, I felt myself at least marginally belonging.

My father had meanwhile discovered an old-fashioned house with what seemed to a child's eye an incredibly huge garden. It lay in a road which, though just off the Queen's Road with its trams and smart villas, had still all the atmosphere of the countryside; round it on all sides stretched fields enclosed with the low walls of rough stone which in Scotland take the place of English hedgerows. There was an atmosphere of wilderness, too, a patch of wasteland, with trees, lay just across the road; and the big garden of the house, long neglected, was itself a wilderness.

A curved drive, badly needing gravel, rutted and potholed, ran sweeping up between two lawns, very much overgrown, starred with dandelions and daisies, and beyond these lawns, with their backing of rhododendron bushes, darkly glossy, the garden stretched off in two oblongs, more or less at right angles to each other; one, behind a high hedge, was full of strawberry beds, border plants, rhubarb, sweet peas, and potato plants, all run to seed, with a square lawn, that had been used both for tennis and for drying clothes, at the far end; the other contained a dark clump of trees, and behind that squares of raspberry canes and gooseberry bushes that had run wild, and behind these again, protected by a high palisade, a shallow and turbid pond, surrounded by thick bushes, and fed, from under a high stone wall and a stone coping, by a thin, trickling stream.

The house itself was square and plain, with a brown harled surface, that had peeled here and there to reveal undressed stone. The two front rooms on the ground floor had big bay windows. There were three living rooms downstairs, and four bedrooms upstairs, two of them large; and there was a small room—my father used it as a dressing-room—from which a small ladder reached up to a great, exciting attic covering the whole top of the house. Downstairs, there was a long corridor that ran past the bathroom and various storerooms to a very large kitchen, with a great hearth and an old-fashioned iron grate, and to a big scullery, with a damp stone floor, overrun, on the day of our first visit, with cockroaches, and a round copper boiler for washing clothes. A corridor ran between the kitchen and the scullery, with a door out of it into a cobbled yard; and on either side of the yard there were outhouses, with low roofs that looked good for climbing on, to store wood and coal in.

The house and garden were both in a neglected state, and in taking them over there would obviously be the disadvantages that come from acquiring anything solid and old-fashioned; there was no electricity, we would have to make do with gas for lighting; we would have to spend a lot on painting, papering, repairs. Nevertheless, the possibilities of the place excited my father as they excited me; my mother, who foresaw the work and expense involved in keeping the whole thing up to scratch, was more

46

hesitant. In the end, it was decided that we should rent this spacious domain (so it appeared to us, though Seafield Cottage in its time had been one of the minor appurtenances of some great estate). While the garden was being got in order, and the house spruced up, we moved out of Mrs Benton's, and into humbler lodgings more in the centre of town, to save money. For the third time in a few months, I found myself shifted, this time to rather cramped quarters in a square off Union Street, where I waited excitedly to take possession of this new and magnificent background to my private dramas.

Meditation of a Patriot

The posters show my country blonde and green,
Like some sweet siren, but the travellers know
How dull the shale sky is, the airs how keen,
And how our boorish manners freeze like snow.
Romantic Scotland was an emigrant,
Half-blooded, and escaped from sullen weather.
Here, we toss off a dram to drown a cough
And whisky has the trade-mark of the heather.
My heart yearns southwards as the shadows slant,
I wish I were an exile and I rave:
    With Byron and with Lermontov
    Romantic Scotland's in the grave.

In Glasgow, that damned sprawling evil town,
I interview a vulgar editor,
Who, brawny, self-made, looks me up and down
And seems to wonder what my sort is for.
Do I write verse? Ah, man, but that is bad . . .
And, too polite, I fawn upon this tough,
But when I leave him, O my heart is sad.
He sings alone who in this province sings.
I kick a lamp-post, and in drink I rave:
    With Byron and with Lermontov
    Romantic Scotland's in the grave.

In the far islands to the north and west
Mackenzie and MacDiarmid have their peace.
St Andrews soothes that critic at her breast
Whose polished verse ne'er gave his soul release.

I have no islands and no ancient stone,
Only the sugary granite glittering crisp
Pleases the eye, but turns affection off,
Hard rhetoric, that never learned to lisp.
This town has beauty, but I walk alone
And to the flat and sallow sands I rave:
    With Byron and with Lermontov
    Romantic Scotland's in the grave.

3

These few weeks in Bon-Accord Square, before we moved into Seafield Cottage, remain in my mind. It was spring and the days were getting longer, the fresh, dusty spring days of the north-east coast. I began to wander out in the evenings, and to make friends with the boys who played in the streets round the square, and soon I found myself a member of a gang. Its captain took a fancy to me, and even appointed me one of his lieutenants, and though the post was purely honorary it gave me a certain cachet. He was a boy who shared my own taste for fantasy, and in these fine spring evenings we would play the sort of game that I enjoyed, setting out with wooden swords on expeditions against imaginary enemies.

There was some building going on in the neighbourhood, and we used to get over walls and stand on top of piles of planks or play 'Who's the king of the castle?' on heaps of cement. And sometimes, if there was a window that had not been boarded, we would clamber into a house that was in the process of construction, and climb up to the second storey by builders' ladders, walking daringly along shaky planks, looking down at the great drop below us. One of us kept a watch for policemen; and even if none turned up, we would work ourselves into a pleasant panic, and flee, hurrying down sidestreets and through lanes, till we were out of breath, and we came to a halt, and our captain reconnoitred. He came back to say we had shaken 'them' off. Our explorations, our invasions drew all their savour from the perpetual lurking in wait of this imaginary 'they'.

Sometimes, in the square itself, we paused and watched little girls and smaller boys playing at a more peaceful fantasy, the game of 'housies'. With chalk, they would draw upon the pavement the ground plan of a house, the parlour, the kitchen, the lavatory, and they would put their little rag dolls or their little

48

teddy bears in one room or another, and stand, it seemed to us for hours, with their arms folded, nodding wisely, and talking of their household expenses, in imitation of their mothers. Our captain sometimes looked a little wistful as we loitered to watch these household games. And there was also hopscotch, which tempted some of the younger members of our party.

I discouraged these loiterings. I did not want to play at hopscotch, or with rubber balls, or with skipping ropes, or to pretend that I had a house of my own; my imagination was purely military, and I reminded the captain that there was another fortress to be invaded, or suggested that enemy scouts, spying on us, were lurking across the square. We should start off on our way again. The captain threw out a hint to me about what we were supposed to be doing, and I elaborated this into a long story. He listened in grave silence, and then, when we reached our objective, translated the story into a curt order to his men.

Our followers began to dwindle, tired out by the length of our expeditions, or wearied by our persistence in a single theme, that of reconnaissance, risk, invasion, glory. We would find them playing hopscotch or even hanging on the edge of a game of 'housies'. But the captain's honour and my imagination were engaged, and, night after night, with a diminishing troop at our heels, we would set off on our forays. They were all working-class children but they seemed to have no feeling, as the Glasgow children had, that I was somehow hostile and different; they were quieter and more self-contained and more biddable. The captain was taller than the others and even quieter, given to long brooding silences; but he had, when it was needed, the curt and grave manner of true command. I was happy with this gang, happier than I had been, or was to be again, with any group of boys of my own age; but after I went to Seafield Cottage I did not see them again.

My father must have been cheered by this new interest of mine in manly pleasures, for he bought me two pairs of boxing-gloves; and explained to me that when I was fighting I must not flail my arms round and round like a windmill but must hold up one to protect my face and jab with the other. We had some practice, my nose was tapped, and my blood seemed almost to fill a bucket. Father also promised me some singlesticks, with basket handles, so that I could practise fencing. I already possessed a bow and a quiver of arrows, for toys that involved an image of combat were the only ones that attracted me. My father, as a soldier who had been wounded in the war, was now beginning to fill a special

49

place in my imagination. When he and I went out for walks, I would ask him to talk to me about these days, and he was all too ready to do so. Soldiering, even before the Great War, had been his life's great hobby. As a schoolboy he had learned drill and spit and polish with the Boys' Brigade (he had always a certain contempt for that comparatively unmilitary organisation, the Boy Scouts), as a student at Glasgow University he had been a cadet in the OTC, and as a young law apprentice in the Town Clerk's office he had been first an NCO and then an officer in the Territorials. He must have inherited a Highland lust for battle, yet when the Great War came, it in a sense cheated him, for he was kept at home for some time training others, and when he did get to France his elbow was shattered by shrapnel the first time he led his company over the top; and he spent the latter part of the war in Italy, using his legal knowledge in the preparation of evidence for often pretty sordid Courts Martial.

Of the war in France, however, he gave me rather grim little glimpses—the mud, the duckboards, the barbed wire, the rats that used to scurry over his camp bed, at which he would take pot shots with his pistol. 'Was that fun?' I would say, trying to be hearty about it. 'Oh, great fun,' he replied, in the tone of polite contempt he used when I had said something silly. Then we would talk about Italy, and his expression would change, his fine nostrils and sensitive lips taut with a kind of wistfulness. Italy had made the sort of impression on my father that it does upon most sensitive northerners. He talked of the harsh wine and sunlight, the simple meals eaten in crudely painted restaurants opening on a crudely vivid sea; minestrone heaped up with grated parmesan cheese, pasta, ripe figs, and then, for digestion, a stroll past houses washed pink and yellow, under lovely balconies, past palm trees, every flat surface throwing a glaring light back onto the sea.

People were poor in Italy, but it was not, I gathered, like the poverty of Glasgow. 'It seems to matter less,' my father said. 'Where there is a lot of sun, people do not need to eat so much or to work so hard. Or no. Not exactly that. They are a very laborious people, the Italians. But they somehow don't seem to worry so much. They take things more easily than we do.' And what did the people look like? My father would hesitate. 'They grow thick and heavy, fat even,' he said, 'while they are still quite young. But the boys and girls are sometimes like angels in paintings . . .' I thought perhaps that an occasional war was worth having if it allowed one to visit such places.

My father's eyes would sparkle when he talked army shop. In

the depths of his heart, for all his success in his civilian profession, he would have liked to pass his whole life in the army. Indeed, in his later days, he would sometimes almost persuade himself that he had done so. 'I,' he would say, 'who have been a soldier, on and off, for thirty years . . .' He had the qualities of a good professional soldier, spruceness, alertness, a crisp authoritative speech. He liked the fatigue that comes from strenuous exercise in the open air, he preferred the company of men to that of women, and he was very fond both of listening to long stories and of telling them. Yet though the Great War had given him a sort of lift, that nothing else had ever quite come up to—not even the rapid popularity he was achieving among the unresponsive Aberdonians—it had also perhaps, in some profound way, unsettled him.

It had given him a façade. It had fixed a certain image of himself in his own mind and it was that image, now, which he imposed on other people. At the time I am speaking of, he was nearing forty, but he looked at least ten years younger. He had the jaunty carriage, the springy step, of a very young man, and his face, though extraordinarily quick and sensitive in its changes of expression, was composed generally into a comely mask. There were few lines on it except two short creases of pride and determination, stretching from the edges of his fine, habitually slightly dilated nostrils to the corners of his mouth; these, and two other short lines, the result of occasional shortsighted frowning concentration, between his bushy eyebrows. In his student days at Glasgow, he had been a famous dandy, sporting a monocle, and uttering witticisms modelled on the early Saki; he still wore unusual clothes, his morning suit with cravat and dove-grey waistcoat, or his dress kilt, with an air, and even setting off to work in his ordinary rig he carried his stick and gloves with a swagger.

But behind the façade all was not wholly well. He carried more intimate scars than those on his stiff, shattered elbow. Never resigning himself to the complacencies of middle age, seeing himself to the last, even when a long and dangerous illness had almost shattered his splendid constitution and given his gallant airs a pathetic overtone of frailty, as the young captain, he was never free, either, from the young captain's repressed doubts and fears. He paid, as we all do, the full price for his *beau role*. For that had been a war to tell on a man: a slow and stupid war, in which soldiers lined up opposite each other in nasty ditches and with endless barrages patiently plastered each other into the mud.

Whatever heroic song there had been had risen above a cacophonous accompaniment; trench foot, trench mouth, rats, floodings, smells, gas, and all the repressed hysteria of a landscape of fields, roads, cottages all hammered and pounded as in a great mortar, into stinking, infertile pulp. The hammering and pulping was also going on all the time inside the soldiers. At the centre of all my father's splendid memories, there was some core of pure pain; and at times he felt the same compulsion to close his mind upon that core that makes us, when we have a sensitive tooth, touch it every now and then with our tongue, though if we leave it alone it does not bother us much.

My father's temperament, like his constitution, was resilient; but, just as his shattered and reset elbow would, in spite of his constitution, begin to ache devilishly in cold weather, so his mind, in spite of his temperament, would, when anything serious occurred to discourage him, be flooded with desolating images. In such moments of pain or discouragement, he would seek for distraction in company, trying to recreate some old atmosphere of mess-room comradeship, and never quite succeeding; at once wistful and gay in company, he had the charm of the gregarious lonely man. Behind his gaiety there was often this cruel core that he could neither express nor assuage, and, becoming aware of this as I came to understand him better, I felt that I was growing up not only towards the threat of a future war, but under the shadow of a past one. But at the time of these early talks I was unaware of that shadow; my father's war, like my own evening forays with my gang, was a game of fantasy, and when I thought of my father as a soldier, I saw him as a figure wholly bathed in light.

4

To explore Seafield, the house and the garden, is now for me like wandering in a landscape with a few figures in the foreground in fixed attitudes. I find it hard to separate one year from another. I can still in memory follow myself about in my wanderings to the pond, to the strawberry beds, to the attic where I would rummage among my grandfather's books, or in my clambers over the roofs of outhouses, but I am never quite sure what age I am. And the other figures in my landscape give me little help. I did not, in these days, notice change much, in myself or others.

Grandpapa, who came to live with us, selling his Kilmarnock bungalow, after Aunty Win went to America, was failing a little more, year by year, but to me he seemed always the same. Kate, our maid, who came to us from the country when she was half way through her twenties, and who left us, about eight years later, in her early thirties, did not seem to alter in any way. With her straight bobbed hair under her cap, and her high cheekbones like polished apples, she resembled a great wooden Dutch doll.

And all my figures have that sort of fixity. My father appears to me planted on the gravel drive, in his tweeds and checked cap, clutching his alpenstock, ready to take Jean and me for our Sunday morning walk. When we come back, we shall be a little late—for father has always met a friend on the way and perhaps has had a drink with him at the Golf Clubhouse at Hazlehead or at the Four Mile Inn, well beyond Woodend—and mother, who has spent the morning roasting the Sunday joint, will be a little flushed and irritable. There will be a dangerous look about her back, as she bends over the table piling up our plates, and sometimes, with a quick, sly gesture, helping herself to some tidbit with her fingers; for she is not only exhausted, she is famished. At last, she sits down. Father, a little nervous, launches into a long anecdote, and she will interrupt him by asking if he wants gravy with his Yorkshire pudding, which, she is afraid, has again been spoiled, by waiting too long. The joint will be followed by a jelly with pears and cream and by biscuits and cheese and coffee, and mother, in a better mood now, will say, 'Well, George, are you not going to say anything about the lunch I have spent the whole morning preparing?' and father, making an old joke, will say, 'An excellent lunch, my dear. A wonderful bit of cheese,' and mother will say that this is just like father; once when he was a young man he was taken to some amateur theatricals, put on by friends of hers, and, asked what he thought of the performance, had replied seriously, 'A very well-dressed show.' And the dresses had come from the costumier's just as the cheese had come from the grocer's.

But mother's mood will have softened and in the afternoon she will play and sing for us in the drawing-room, while father, with *The Observer* spread on his lap, observes her solemnly and sleepily from over the tops of his horn-rimmed glasses. Father and I have little ear and no voice. As mother improvises at the piano, or sings some song of her youth that goes off in trills and roulades, we follow the performance gravely, aware that we are missing all the finer points; but in the end, for a treat, we shall have some simple song that we know and like, 'Shenandoah', 'Danny Boy', or 'The Bonny Earl o' Moray', and we shall be able to luxuriate in its

53

straightforward sadness. Then it will be Jean's turn to practise her singing, her beautiful, petulant mouth, which so resembles my father's mouth, rounded to a circle, her eyes tightly shut (it is a trick she has got from my mother, who also shuts her eyes when she sings), and a small, high voice of quavering purity piping out from her, sometimes rather off tune. Jean loves hymn tunes and at night, in the bedroom which we still share, our beds at opposite corners, she will infuriate me by singing hymns to herself for a long time, preventing me from going to sleep; in the end, I will be able to stand it no longer, and will shout, 'Shut up, Jean, shut up!' and Jean will say I am wicked, I might as well interrupt a person saying her prayers; so I fall silent again, and Jean, her tone rather flat because she has no music to accompany her, will quaver out another verse or two for honour's sake, and then we will say good-night to each other—'Friends, is it, Jinissy?' 'Yes, friends, Geo!'—and so fall asleep.

Or perhaps it is a Saturday, it is high summer, mother and father have gone out to some social gathering, and Jean and I are left alone in the house with Kate. Grandpapa is up in his bedroom, where Kate will bring him his meals. Kate tells us to go into the garden and pick strawberries. Some she will make into jam and some we will have heaped up in a bowl with cream for our supper. We crawl under the net, which is needed because last year the birds picked holes in all our biggest strawberries, but even the net cannot frighten them away, and we find a brown dead bird with its neck caught and twisted, its strange open eyes at once glassy and dull, its little sharp feet poking up in the air. Jean whimpers, she pats at the brown feathers, she says, 'Poor bird, poor bird!' and before we can pick any strawberries, we must take it away and bury it, in the patch of bare earth behind the rhododendron bushes. Jean digs with her toy spade, and I gather little stones, and press them with my fingers into the earth, making an oblong border for the grave. Then we return to the strawberries, and pick them, slowly and sleepily, for the net catches in our hair, and the sun beats down on our heads, and for every three or four strawberries that we put in the basket, we eat one or two. The garden has a smell that makes us sleepy, the smell of dry, hot, freshly dug earth, of brick and brown stone warmed by the sun, and the spicy smell, also, of the stocks that line the herbaceous border.

When we have filled, or almost filled, our basket we move drowsily to the smooth lawn with its curved edge opposite the house. It is lined with rhododendron bushes, with dark glossy leaves (I think of these leaves when I read in poems about crowns of laurel) and waxy, fleshy, trumpet-like blossoms. Bees move about these blossoms, as drowsily as ourselves. We lie on this lawn, our strawberry basket beside us, and read our story-books, and a fat blackbird, pecking on the lawn a few feet away from us, raises its head, stands still and regards us with a beady, suspicious eye. The sky above us is blue but for a few flecks of white cloud. It is late afternoon and we are enjoying the last of the sunshine. As the moments pass, a faint chill comes over us, and an almost imperceptible change comes over the sky. A grey and filmy cobweb, silky and fine, is beginning to cling to everything, and it is so fine that when the eye concentrates on its presence it crumbles away, but it is always present where the eye is not concentrating, and I can feel it on the sky, the lawn, the glossy dark leaves, I can see and feel it curling over my own hands, lying in front of me in the grass beside an open book, whose white pages are also turning grey. This is the descent, in high summer, of the northern dusk; as I look up now, it has quite erased the coloured distinctions of the sky, floating clouds and profound vacancies are one, a single rubbed grey. The lights go on in the front windows of the house, it is cold, and Kate is calling us, a voice from a grey figure at the front door, calling us in to supper. A wind is rising, and it shakes the trees, and on the lawn beside me one, two, three little leaves from a high beech tree hesitantly fall. It will soon be autumn.

Inside the house, because mother and father are still out, Jean and I have our supper in the kitchen with Kate. Though it is summer, there is a fire in the grate, and the curtains are pulled, and so the big room, with the shadows flickering on the distempered walls, the scrubbed linoleum floor and the unstained wood of the kitchen table, with its covering of white glossy American cloth, has a homely air, at once bare and cosy. We enjoy our suppers with Kate. After the plates and cups have been cleared away and washed, Jean and I sit down with Kate at the kitchen table to a game of cards with a greasy, dog-eared pack, and we play a game in which, when you get three cards of a kind, you put them face downwards on the table, and then you have to pick them up again, trying to remember where you put them, or to guess where other people put them, so as to make sequences. Kate is very good at this game, she knows the cards in her old pack by heart, whichever side up they may be, and Jean and I always lose, but we sometimes win at Sevens, or at Old Maid, or at Snap—but we play that game rarely, as it always leads to quarrels—or at Rummy.

When we are tired of playing cards, Kate tells us our fortunes, not looking dangerously far ahead, but saying that next Saturday we shall go for a picnic, or to the pictures, which often turns out to be true, or telling Jean what fun she will have when she goes back to school again in September. Jean has not taken to school life. She has run home in the mornings once or twice, escaping during the eleven o'clock break, and sometimes after breakfast she has hidden in the bushes in the garden, hoping not to be found till it is too late for her to go. She listens to these prophecies of Kate's with polite scepticism. Finally, it is time for us to go to bed, and Kate makes us large mugs of cocoa and spreads thick slices of bread with butter and jam, and I linger over the cocoa as long as I can, till Kate says, with mock fierceness, 'Drink it up, here's grandpapa!' which is a joke, for I am not afraid of him, but I gulp the cocoa back with a kind of spluttering, glancing furtively at the kitchen stairs down which, at any moment, grandpapa might come, while Jean chuckles to herself . . . Is it worth recording such days and nights in which nothing of importance can be said to have happened? I think so, for it is strange to recollect that there was once a time, long ago, and yet so real that even now as a scene it is not only almost visible but almost tangible—when we were young, when we were innocent, when behind the round, recurring year the sky fell like a safety curtain, shutting out fire.

And yet does one deceive oneself, as over so many things, also over this? Is a child's life ever free from grief, fear, and bewilderment? Seafield is still for me the scene of a recurring evil dream. The particular background of the dream is the pond, at the bottom of the lower garden, where I used to go and sit and think by myself. Shut off from the rest of the garden and from the neighbouring fields by its high wooden palisades on three sides, and from the road by its high stone wall on the fourth; dark and shadowy, also, because of the thick bushes and overhanging trees which surrounded it, this sheet of shallow, muddy, almost stagnant water was a place admirably suited to gloomy reveries.

It was periodically, also, the scene of little dramas. When friends came to play with us, the pond would be the great attraction, but after a time it was put out of bounds for our games, for sooner or later somebody would fall or be pushed in—it was only a foot or two deep in water, but one seemed to sink as deep again in mud—and go home with a dress or a suit spoiled, crying.

And one afternoon, while I was sitting alone by the edge of the water with a book, some boys had clambered over the wall from the road outside, carrying old jam jars to catch tiddlers in, and I told them that they had no right to be there, and they said that the previous tenants had always welcomed them, and that nobody had any right to private possession of a pond; we fought, I got the worst of it, but they went away, frightened lest they had hurt me badly; and after they had gone, as I brushed the dirt off my jacket, and sponged my bruises, I felt that I had been very mean and petty, I should have welcomed them and they would have become my friends, there would have been another gang like the one in Bon-Accord Square . . .

I liked, anyway, in spite of such incidents, to sit by myself at the edge of the pond, reading, but sometimes I would sit alone long after it was dark, watching the reflection in the water (a thin stream trickled very slowly into the pond and out of it again) of the dark night sky and the stars, and sometimes stirring up this reflection with a stick, watching the stars shatter, thinking of the immensity of space, held so easily in this pool and so easily troubled, but itself stretching in all directions, for ever, which one could not think of, or perhaps coming to a stop somewhere, which one could not think of either.

I was oppressed by the thought of space, and by the lonely and small stars, whose reflections I could disturb so easily, shining at their huge distances. I was aware of myself, suddenly, as lonely and small also, and also surrounded by distances, concentrating for myself on this dark liquid mirror the reflection of that outer almost-emptiness, and I worried about what there had been before stars, or pond, or myself, before anything, before God had made the world. I knew from my earliest childhood the God of Abraham, of Isaac, and of Jacob: the stern yet homely guide of these wanderers with their flocks and their tents. I knew his voice, which spoke within me, also, when I had done wrong and offended my parents. But I was discovering that more remote and less friendly God, who evades the mind and has nothing to say to the heart, the God of the philosophers.

I would talk about these bewilderments of mine sometimes with Kate, who, as a country bred child, always aware of the night sky, had been also troubled in her time by the mystery of what lies beyond. She confided in me a puzzle that had occurred to her in her girlhood and that had never been solved to her satisfaction. If God made the world, who made God? I would try to solve it for her, but I soon got lost, for if a God made God, another God made that God, and I saw myself involved in an infinite recession. Yet might there not really be infinite recessions? What happened when two mirrors faced each other? I would try to imagine what it would be like if one could be invisible, like the man in the story by Mr Wells I had just been reading, and could look down a long corridor of recession in a mirror placed exactly opposite another of the same size; neither reflecting anything but successive glittering panes of diminishing emptiness . . . And the same antinomies that harried me when I tried to think of space harried me no less when I tried to think of time. One measured time by succession or alteration, by the ticking of a watch, the movement of a second hand, or by these more intimate changes, that were like a change within oneself, when the dusk announced the end of a day, or the wind the end of a season, by a thousand tiny but perceptible alterations in the look and feel of sky, leaves, and grass.

And there had been a time when there was only God, when there was no succession or alteration, when nothing changed, for God, being the changeless, could measure no change in himself; one could not, in fact, call it a time, but there had been only God; and yet the world had been created, and time had begun, and was not that creation a change in God, or if the image of the world and all its changes had been with God for all eternity—for one could not think of a notion suddenly occurring to God!—was not any notion of God's by its very nature an eternal object of the mind, surely for God to be aware of a thing (of the stars, of the pond, of my self) was for that thing to *be* eternally, and if God was eternally aware of what had been, what was, and what would be, was time real? Had the past vanished, or was it still there, like a country that one could explore if one would, and did the future already exist, and if all this world of time and change and immensity was still and complete in God's mind, and utterly enclosed in his knowledge, could time, or change, or immensity be more than clues and figments? Was not all life like a dream from which one might suddenly awake?

These thoughts passed through my mind, as I stirred those sunken stars with my stick.

And yet the evil dream which still sometimes troubles me, and which has that pool for its background, has little obvious connection with such early metaphysical flounderings. I have returned, in this dream, after a long time, to that scene, and men are digging by the bushes or sometimes draining the water, and dredging the scum below it, and what they will unearth at last, swathed with waterweeds, or entangled in the white roots of some blanched tree, is a human skeleton—the victim of some act of violence, committed in a dream deeper than the dream I am dreaming; so that I know that I am guilty and yet grope, in a thick darkness, for the grounds of my guilt. Or sometimes I know that I am not guilty; and then the searchers accuse me and I discover, to my horror, that though I can move my lips and my tongue no sounds come, I cannot speak the simple sentence that would prove my innocence. Or sometimes the criminal is a figure lurking in the bushes, whose presence I am the first to detect, and I point him out to the searchers. He takes to his heels, and we all pursue him, myself leading the pursuit; he flags and fails, we are going to catch him, and then I, who have been leading the chase, am transformed into the quarry.

I spoke once about this dream, which was coming back in its various shapes to torment me in my early days in the army, to my friend, the poet Tom Scott. He told me that the dead body, drowned deep under the water or twisted in the roots of the tree, was my sensual nature. My intellectual nature, in its fierce and foolish pride, had tried to kill my animal life, but that life with all its needs still remained buried within me, hidden, accusing, suffering; tangled in roots or weeds, it was the part of my life that belonged to the earth, and the tree that reached up from it towards the sky, or the water that lay over it reflecting the sky, these were my will and emotions, reaching out towards a starry world of cold distances, a world of pure and empty intuitions, and despising the earth on which they fed or flowed; which was why the tree, representing my will, was blasted, and the pond, which represented my emotions, shallow and sluggish, fed only by a thin trickle of outer life. The palings and the walls which enclosed the scene were the reserves with which I attempted to protect my personality . . .

It sounded plausible; but that buried body also represented the child who had listened to the God of his heart, and who was left there, for ever, some evening, under the bushes, while a cold and proud young sophist walked up the path, seeking, in a kind of dry ecstasy, to make God out of the gulfs that opened in his mind. There is no salvation, as everyone tells us, in such speculations. And they reach no end.

5

Grandpapa and I were intimate friends. I was too young to go out often with mother and father, or to join them in the drawing-room when they had friends in; and grandfather was too old. So we often found ourselves by a cheerful fire in the back parlour, accompanied by the cat, T'mon Zen—a name which sounds Chinese, but which is a corruption of the phrase, 'Come on, then!'—and by the dog Stumpy, an affectionate short-haired fox terrier, and provided by Kate with hot milky drinks and encouraging remarks, while we played game after game of cribbage together.

I am not fond of cards, and I have forgotten the rules of that game now, but I remember the serious concentration with which we played, and grandpapa's triumphant phrases, 'One for his heels!' and 'Two for his nob!', and his jaunty way of slapping down his cards on the table. The dog Stumpy would take a peculiar interest in the game, thrusting his nose under my elbow; he did this also when I was sitting by the fire, reading a book or drinking tea, making me spill my cup over my knees; he wanted to be patted and wrestled with, he resented my concentration on anything that made me ignore him. I would push his cold nose away, grasping it rather cruelly in the palm of my hand, but in a minute or two it would be thrust under my elbow again.

The cat T'mon Zen was more aloof, but sometimes allowed me to make up to her; but if my father came into the room, who said that cats made the back of his neck bristle, she would slink out. Otherwise she had her place at the side of the fire, where even Stumpy dare not disturb her. If Stumpy would not bark at her, my father would. One night, when she was still nursing a new batch of kittens, he had come from the office to find her at the front door, under his feet—on her way out to the garden to meet a friend. 'Out of my way!' he shouted. 'Immoral beast!' (Indeed, like most middle-class Scotsmen of his generation, he was very fiercely a puritan. He used to get into terrific rages when cars parked, in the evenings, in the dark country roads near Seafield Cottage. 'Brothels', he would mutter under his breath, 'brothels on wheels!') So T'mon Zen avoided father; Stumpy, on the other hand, the healthy, humanised creature, would desert me if father came in.

Grandpapa, apart from a perfunctory, 'Good dog . . . down, sir, down, sir!' or a, 'Puss, pretty puss, *meelk, feesh*!' would, on such evenings, ignore both animals. With a shawl over his shoulder, glasses low on his nose, a long cigar, at which he took occasional puffs, smouldering away on the ashtray beside him, he brought a grave and ponderous attention to bear on the cards; throwing down his hand, however, and sitting back with an air of sudden vivacity, when he had won a round. Though we said little to each other, we enjoyed these evenings. Sometimes I visited him in his bedroom, in which he had his armchair, his writing desk, and his constantly tended fire, and in which, as the years went by, he tended to pass more and more of his time, only venturing downstairs for special occasions, like parties and dinners at Christmas and New Year; I carried his meals up for him on a tray and lingered, savouring the solid darkness of the furniture and the atmosphere of old cigar smoke, impregnating curtains and carpets, which for me made this a room with more 'body' to it than the other rooms in the house; it led me by the nose to memories of Brooklands. Grandpapa and I would talk in a desultory way, but there was a sense of real exchange.

I did not always feel that with my parents. In conversation with them, it was my role to receive rather than to give. Their talk was anecdotal, and one anecdote led to another. What they were talking about became, as they proceeded, more real to them than the immediate reactions of the listener. My father's talk, as I have said, was mainly about his military memories; my mother delved farther back, into memories of her childhood. There were the stories of the first school she had attended. An elderly maiden lady teacher had been a stickler for refinement. My mother would ask her for a drink of water and be chided gently. 'Young ladies do not ask for a *drink* of water, Ada, they ask for a little water *in a glass*.' Or my mother would describe how, on the way to school, she had seen a bull. 'Oh no, Ada.' 'But I *did* see a bull.' 'Oh no, my dear, *that* is not what you saw. You must never use that word. It is not a ladylike word.' 'What did I see then, Miss Watson?' 'Ada, my dear, you saw a *gentleman cow*.' To hear such stories was a pleasure but it did not give Jean and me much training in putting our own points of view. We were always at ease with our parents and were never snubbed by them. Nevertheless, it was—very properly—they who held the floor. Jean and I grew up to be tactful listeners, hesitant when we had to hold the floor ourselves. But grandpapa had none of this taste for anecdote. When he and I talked to each other, it would be difficult to say that we communicated any facts and ideas, but we felt that we were reaching across to each other, there was a sense of a secret understanding. Talking to me in his bedroom, my grandfather would forget, for a moment, the steady and rooted melancholy which was becoming the mood of his old age; but downstairs we often heard him pacing to and fro in his carpet slippers for a long time, like one encaged.

61

One might have expected my grandfather, who had lived so much among his daughters, to be more fond of Jean than of me, but the relations between these two, though often affectionate, were also often stormy. There was an occasion when Jean, a cherubic creature, with a smile that was pure sweetness, was found pushing at grandpapa's legs—she can hardly have reached up much beyond his knees—while the old gentleman, supporting himself with his stick, stood poised on the top of the stairs. As she pushed, she chuckled to herself, and even the mild slapping she got could not prevent her from continuing to chuckle. She, for her part, accused grandpapa of giving her sly, testy little kicks when she annoyed him by crawling about on the floor too near his feet. Yet she had accesses of sentiment about grandpapa, and offered to sing to him, or brought up to his bedroom bunches of flowers from the garden, plucked rather short in the stalk; and he offered her, on such occasions, one of the boiled sweets he carried, to reward a good child. Yet even as she grew bigger and more responsible, there remained in Jean a tendency to tease grandpapa and he, while he retained the energy to growl at anybody, would sometimes growl at her. He and I were on a different footing; I was a strange, quiet, studious boy and perhaps too much like an old man myself.

Before he grew too weak to go out, grandpapa used to take me to the cinema; always on a Saturday, and often on my weekly half-day, if it were raining and there were no sports. We would equip ourselves at the little old-fashioned shop at the top of the road with a large bag of boiled sweets and take the tram into town. Aberdeen at that time had more cinemas in proportion to its total population than any other town in Great Britain, and yet the cinema always seemed crowded; grandpapa and I sat in the warm dark, accustoming our eyes to the slight rain and flicker of the old silent films on the screen, sucking pear drops, and listening to the snatches of music, heavily nostalgic, or briskly military, or thudding with suspense, with which a bored female pianist accompanied the shifting images. We were aware at first of stuffiness, of discomfort, of other people crackling paper bags and crunching bonbons, but soon lost ourselves in a projected world of strong situations and violent activities, knowing that peace and quiet, tea and toast, awaited us at home.

The film was often a Western: the rustlers, the sheriffs, the kidnapped heroine always chased round and round the table in a log cabin by the bearded villain. Then, just when one had given up hope, the hero and his companions appeared on horseback, breasting a distant rise, kicking up clouds of dust, and emptying their revolvers, for no apparent reason, in all directions; they would gallop like anything, without seeming to get anywhere; one seemed to recognise the same rocks, the same clump of trees, from another angle; there would be a cut back to the log cabin, where the heroine was still haring round the table, and the bearded villain did not appear to be getting anywhere either; a cut back, again, to the dusty and static gallopers; a cut to the log cabin once more, and then just as I and the pianist were getting really worked up grandpapa would break the illusion by whispering to me in his hoarse, sardonic tones: 'Old scatterguts again!'

It was his generic term for galloping cowboys. Similarly, in thrillers, at the moment when the secret panel opens, and the hero has his back to it, I would hear grandpapa's carrying confidential rumble, 'Our old friend, the clutching hand!' He enjoyed the movies, for he was getting to a stage where he found reading or talking too much of an effort. His enjoyment consisted largely in the fulfilment of expectation. I found the plots confusing and intricate. Generally, when we got home, and Kate asked me what it had been all about, I contented myself with a single word of explanation, 'Cowboys!' or 'Murders!' or, occasionally, in a disappointed tone, 'Love!' Kate, also fond of the cinema, was not so completely averse to love as a theme, but she became embarrassed if it was treated in too sentimental a way. She admired the manly charm of Clark Gable, but was often irritated to find him in roles in which he behaved with what she regarded as an unnatural softness. 'How was Clark Gable, Kate?' mother would ask. 'Ach,' Kate would say, taking off her hat, 'ach, Mrs Fraser, I thought he was awfu' *soppy*!'

6

My own feelings about the cinema were confined to a slight sympathy with the general class of villains; I could understand their wanting to dress up, wear masks, carry pistols, and emerge ominously from trap doors. I could feel the attraction of sitting like a spider at the centre of a web, plotting. The heroes of the cinema seemed, on the other hand, a wooden race, who blundered stupidly into every trap set for them, and wasted far too much of my time gazing into the eyes of their dogs, their sweethearts, or their horses. As for the glamorous women of the screen, these simply did not exist for me. Later I fell in love in rapid succession with Greta Garbo, Jessie Matthews, and Judy Garland, but the cinema was not yet my passion or my vice . . .

My passion and my vice was the printed word. It had been so almost since I first learned to read; since those early days in Glasgow when I strained away from mother, who would be trying to tie my laces or comb my hair, to read even the label on a sauce-bottle. Only a passion and a vice could have made me cruel to my grandfather, whom I truly loved. Yet there were afternoons when, knowing he wanted my company, I insisted that I must go into the public library to change my books. He would set off for the cinema by himself, and a little later, when I felt sure he was safely on his way I set off, took the tram to Union Bridge, and walked briskly past Union Terrace Gardens towards the library, past the pigeons wheeling at the corner over the inexpressive statue of some monarch of the House of Saxe-Coburg-Gotha, and the trains that rumbled through the sunken gardens far below.

On these raw, exciting days of early autumn, particularly, all the tall façades had a grey glitter, the great drayhorses struck out sparks from the granite setts, and like dragons puffed vapour from their nostrils, and I myself, with the iron tabs on my heels, skimmed sparkily along and felt my breath against the dry cold air as a sort of warm dampness. I appreciated the rigour of this weather more now that I was away from grandfather; while I was with him, slowing down my steps to suit his pace, it was as if he carried about with him, hung as he was in scarves and a heavy black coat, something of the atmosphere of his bedroom where the windows were rarely opened and a fire burned even in summer. The old man would be sitting lonely in the cinema, muttering sadly to himself, 'Old scatterguts again!' and with nobody to offer his pear drops to, and yet the sense of guilty ingratitude I felt was soon swallowed up in a fiercer sense of freedom.

The smell of the public library was itself stuffy. It was, however, a dry and ticklish smell that comes from the brittle pages of old books and from the dust that gathers along the top of them. It was a pleasanter smell to me then—not now, for I feel that I have lost too much of my life poring over books, and that I can learn most, now, by listening to people—than the damp and warm smell of confined human bodies. It led me by the nose to everything that was old, and odd, and dumpy, and voluminous on these shelves—to the old sets of Dickens with their painful small print and the grotesque detail, blurred in cheap reproduction, of their engravings: to Mark Twain, whom I read right through, his live works and his dead ones: to the complete works of Edgar Allan Poe, including his virulent criticisms of forgotten poets whom I never had read and never would read: to the contorted, headachy sentences of Carlyle, and the damp evangelical world, which yet had a dreary fascination, of *Eric; or Little by Little*, and *St Winifred's; or the World of School*. To anything, in fact, with a proper smell of the past about it . . .

I was seeking in the past (in these damp, indigestible, plum-caky Victorian layers of it that were most readily accessible to me) for things I felt a lack of in the present. I am talking now of the late 1920s when I was in my early adolescence. I was already beginning to notice, for instance, pretty young women with a vague excitement. But the way they dressed put me off. It was, in the history of costume, a deplorable decade. Women wished their bodies, from the shoulders to somewhere about half way down the thighs, to appear flat oblongs; below these oblongs, their legs swung unexpectedly out, as on a hinge. Breasts, waists, and hips did not officially exist; but since the artificial flat line had, after all, to take account of natural projections, women's bodies, above that startling exposure of leg that seemed to have no connection with the rest of the organism, appeared unnaturally broad and thick. One looked up from the body to the head; the hair, in any case bobbed or shingled, was hidden under a savagely pulled down cloche hat, which also masked the forehead, drawing a straight horizontal line just above the eyes; thus the face, like the body, seemed a rectangle, but tigerishly set with teeth. Thus the young beauties of that cubist decade were, to my innocent eyes, a spectacle more alarming than attractive. I would turn for relief to my grandfather's books in the attic, in particular to the two big volumes of John Leech's *Pictures of Life and Character*. John Leech's young women had trim waists and pert bosoms and wore broad crinolines which swayed sometimes in the wind to let one glimpse a trim ankle. In the evenings, their low, clinging bodices revealed gracefully sloping shoulders. Their black hair, parted exactly in the middle and gathered in a low bun on the nape of the neck, was so smooth that it seemed almost lacquered to their heads. Their faces were perfect ovals. One did not feel that they had been drawn with a set square; their line was the curve, the line of beauty.

It was the same with other aspects of the Victorian age. My grandfather had also a set of papers of the 1870s—*Judy, Fun, Will o' the Wisp*, and other short-lived rivals of *Punch*. The jokes, in these old papers, meant little to me (except in so far as they

65

conveyed a sense that a joke in the English tradition is a serious matter, not something to be undertaken lightly); but the great cartoons, sometimes spreading over two pages, showing a terrific Gladstone unmasking a cowering and villainous Disraeli—or a gay and sprightly Disraeli exposing a hypocritical Gladstone—conveyed, very admirably, the heroic atmosphere of politics in the Victorian age. I could not find that atmosphere in current newspapers. When I turned to the cartoons in these, I found no heroic figures, but an insignificant toothy person, in a bowler hat, known variously as John Citizen and the Little Man. He seemed to feel nothing of the eager Victorian interest in public affairs; he looked confused and harried, and laboured under a perpetual grievance about paying taxes. No doubt he was an accurate enough representation of the average worried little man of the years between the wars; I did not find him an attractive or inspiring figure, and I turned to the past for something to look up to, as I sought in these old pictures, too, for images of a lost grace and charm.

Among all the writers and artists who made the Victorian age real to me, Dickens was for a long time my favourite. Words for me at this time were entirely instrumental; they either failed to convey anything, or dissolved completely into images, and Dickens seemed more packed with images than anybody else I had read. I fell into the habit of reading him in bed. Straining over the small print and spoiling my eyesight, it was not the page that I saw, but his figures acting and moving—figures he made real to me down to the last button on their fancy waistcoats, the last twitch of their eyelids or gesture of their hands. It is his notorious magic. His first love was the theatre; and he gets inside his characters and, acting each part with mad, exaggerated energy, inspires the reader to do so too. It was a magic, however, that I exploited too greedily. The time came when I began to notice the sentences on the page and how they were shaped, the part played in the whole effect by such devices as elaborate periphrasis and emphatic repetition, and when I would realise with a start that I was no longer staging and acting the whole thing for myself—I was merely trying to work out how a page of prose had once had a certain effect on my imagination; and as I thought about that problem, the page ceased to have precisely that effect. To come to oneself, after a bout of Dickens, was a disconcerting experience. A whole world, more crowded, bustling, packed with observed details than the real world, would go out like a popping light bulb: I was merely myself once more, holding a heavy book in my hands, my eyes tired. I would clap the book shut and go to sleep . . .

But after I had ceased to visualise, in this magical way, a scene, I could still hear voices when I read; when Dickens, for the time being, had exhausted me, I turned to Thackeray. His images were not sharp and definite like those of Dickens, but vague and dissolving; he observed no more of the outer scene than one commonly observes; but if his images melted away, they melted in the current of a continuing voice, which I imagined as speaking to me, inside my own head, as my own voice speaks about the past, and so creating another kind of illusion. I began to read now, not so much looking as listening; for if I had lost the magic of my private cinema, the gift of dissolving words into an experience that seemed to have nothing to do with words, still the words themselves remained, and were themselves magical. Words were themselves mysteries. As I did not know how Dickens could make me see, with a precise observation that was not habitual to me, things that had never been seen, so I did not know how he could make me remember, with such a sense of melancholy and of the best chances somehow going wrong, things that had never happened. What sort of things were words that they could make me see and hear and remember and laugh and cry—while all the time here I was alone in my bed, nothing in front of me except black signs? Yet these black signs had abstracted me from the living world. At school and at home, I spent my time staring into the distance, building up worlds of my own, hardly noticing what was going on around me.

One day I picked up a different kind of book altogether—a volume of selections from Bishop Berkeley, dating from my father's days at Glasgow University. Here there were no images and no emotions. It was a strange, dry world in which people discussed at enormous length a question that seemed to be absurd, and yet I could not think of an obvious answer to it— what happens to the room you have been in, when you leave it, and close the door, and there is nobody there? Yet this dry world attracted me, for just as my greed for print had led me to exhaust, too early, my gift for evoking images, it was beginning also to exhaust my gift for facile response to literary emotion. I could read Thackeray flatly now, as I had come to read Dickens, seeing what people meant by calling him 'sentimental'; all those addresses to the reader, those appeals to one's better self, or one's knowingness, they were a kind of trick. There seemed to be no tricks at all in Bishop Berkeley, and he was an author to be read, not at night, in bed, but alertly by daylight. I would lift my eyes from the table near my bedroom window, from his clear yet puzzling sentences, and look out at the trees swaying in the fading evening light—the trees which were perhaps only there, with that particular look, at twilight, of being more or less than real, because I saw them so, or because God did. Then I would leave the book open on the table (did it vanish as I left it?) and walk out to the garden, or to the roads, quiet and edged with fields, around the house. I would see the world with its green of leaf, its grey of stone, its brown of path and field, with a sky of some indescribable mild colour above it, my world held together just so by my seeing it so, moving and changing its aspects as I moved; would feel it real and important, and yet feel also that all I could say about it was, 'I got tired and went out for a walk', and I would wonder how words could ever convey even the flattest map of all the colours and contours of reality.

I felt the weight of the world, a lovely weight, but not one that words could cope with. Words could be many things for me, but in the end, after being images, and emotions, and thoughts, they seemed to become once more merely themselves on the page. Were the images, the emotions, the thoughts something that I contributed myself? Or did they come from some mysterious invisibility, from however it was that words held together, from the structure of language—they certainly did not come from the separate, flat, meaningless words themselves! Or might they, after all? I wondered if they might, and kept for a while a notebook in which I put down every word or phrase that struck me; for I feared that not only images and emotions but thoughts themselves might begin to go dead on me, and for a time I read only to wrench loot from sentences, like a man walking in the country in a blind muse but tearing, distractedly, leaves and blossoms from the branches above his head.

I felt the world was there to be coped with, and language was my means of coping. But I felt also that I was not coping properly. It was this feeling which gave so much importance, a little later, to my discovery of poetry. In poetry, image and emotion and thought came together again; and with all my greed I could not tear these away from the words. The reading of novels, particularly the long, shapeless novels of the Victorian age, is likely to encourage a lonely boy in his most dangerous vice, that of daydreaming; partly he reads the story, but partly he makes it up for himself. The reading of our lucid early philosophers, those writers like Berkeley and Hume, who still write in the ordinary language of cultivated men of their time, with some care for the graces of style, can do him no harm; but it may perhaps turn his mind into a sort of logic-chopping machine, with nothing but straw to feed it. In poetry, image and emotion and thought do not exist apart from the words on the page, these very words, in that very order. Neither in dreaming nor in argument can the mind build up for itself some substitute for the poem itself. Poetry, of all uses of language, alone refused to yield to my laziness and vanity, to my weariness and my disillusionment. Without poetry, I would have been left, in the end, dumb in a rich world I could only point at. But in poetry the world spoke to me, and I felt that I also might speak to the world. So it was that, lonely and fumbling, I decided I would have to be a poet if I wanted at all to cope . . .

7

I have written enough, now, about these early days at Seafield Cottage to convey the flavour of my boyhood in that period of outer peace and inner solitude when my tastes and ambitions took shape. I was not left so peaceful or so solitary for long. My Uncle Stanley died and my mother's sister, Aunty Dot, with her three children, Freddy, John, and Stanley, came to stay with us. There were readjustments and occasional quarrels, but it was good for me to have other boys as companions, and if I was a difficult cousin, not good at games, and indifferent to the mysteries of clockwork railways, they could forgive me because I told them long and fantastic stories, of which they themselves were often the heroes. Time passed, changing them much, and me little. I was an undeveloped, thin boy with a childish face when I went to university at St Andrews at sixteen and at St Andrews I remained shy, sunk in books, with few friends, mad about writing. It is a grey old town, facing the sea, lovely in spring, with the same bleakness in winter that braced me in Aberdeen. The coming war hung over my generation there. The contemporary who was most like me there was probably Nicholas Moore, who had been sent up to St Andrews because leaving school young like myself, he was not yet old enough to go to Cambridge. His first and only year at St Andrews was my last. I was editing the students' magazine and he would send me three or four poems, in green and purple ink, in a beautiful script, every week; he wrote verse every day to keep his hand in, but, unlike most poets who follow this admirable rule, was willing to publish nearly all of it. As mad about writing as myself, he was as shy. He was pale and stooped slightly, though he was sturdily built, and the expression of his eyes was hidden by his thick glasses, and the expression of his mouth seemed to me rather sardonic and cruel. We rarely talked to each other, for it was impossible to know what to say. I remember once at tea I passed him a plate of cakes, all of which were exactly similar, except that some were pink and two were yellow. He carefully turned the plate round to choose a yellow one. 'They all taste just the same,' I said. 'Yes,' said Nicholas, 'but I prefer this colour.' I had the impression that his mind was working hard all the time making these slight, impalpable discriminations. Communication between us was further made difficult by the gulf between my harsh north-eastern burr and his flat, slightly nasal Cambridge accent. But when he settled in Cambridge, and I started work as a journalist in Aberdeen, he started sending me admirable letters, and we became (as we had never been, when we had the opportunity for daily meetings with each other) fast friends.

I forget, now, whether it was Nicholas who held the other end of the banner when, with some of my contemporaries who were very political, I walked in that last year in a May Day procession in Dundee. I had no very settled political attitudes; I could be coaxed and badgered into thinking myself a revolutionary; the friends whose company I enjoyed, however, over a coffee or a glass of beer, were the elegant and the reactionary. I liked to sample most things and the only two movements in St Andrews from which I retreated, after the faintest of whiffs, were the Oxford Group and the Peace Pledge Union. I had, in fact, joined the OTC when I first went up in 1933, partly to please my father, partly because it seemed reasonably clear, even then, that a war was coming. I was a singularly inefficient cadet. The smell of cordite, the feel of khaki, the white stain made by brasso, the seagulls pouncing over the open-air lavatories, all these held for me an intimate mixture of fascination and horror; escape from these, each year, as our summer camp broke up, was exactly like a reprieve. When the real war started, there would be no such reprieve; the smells, and the shouting, and the sense of being a criminal half-wit because one could not march in time properly, these would go on indefinitely; I savoured that fact with a sour ironic relish.

Yet, if I could only have breasted these insuperable preliminary hurdles, there were things about these summer camps that I would have enjoyed. I had my first bout of hard

70

drinking at one of them, and found I had a good head. At an inland camp, I discovered the pleasure of swimming in river water—more delightful, in summer, than the sea. I liked the grass, and the hills, and the solitary country walks, when I could get away from camp. The drumhead services, with their sermons about the pious motives of great military leaders (including, if I remember rightly, Attila the Hun) appealed to my sense of irony. I looked on it all as an initiation rite. That seemed to be the view that others took, too. 'It will make a man of you, you know,' they would say. In one sense, that was not true; the role of the warrior brave, in paint and feathers, was never to be exactly mine. In another sense, it was too true. My mild and settled melancholy in these days was partly that of a boy who feels he has failed to pass the tests that would give him a right to be treated as a man.

The tests, I sometimes thought, ought to have been wider and more thorough, ought to have included sexual ones. As I listened, in the tents at night, to the bawdy, boastful talk of my companions, I felt that some experience like theirs might be the bridge for me into a world in which I was the same sort of creature as the others. As some coarse little friend described, for instance, the seduction of a servant maid, I would feel the pathos and charm of the pastoral background, which, so carelessly, he sketched in: an open field, sharp grass, and a clear night of summer. Adolescence is an obscene, poetic period; our sorrows then, and our joys, are more raw and particular than at any other time; I would listen to such stories with a green and sickly appetite, but all that remains to me now is their incidental poetry, how one young man, for instance, had talked one day for a long time to a young, fair girl, who leaned over the high stone wall of a big house, beside an apple tree, and, mocking his appeals to her, dropped apples on him . . .

I had an image, as such talk moved past me, of a foolish, happy, sunburnt world, that I could become heir to, if only I could harden my body and empty my mind of its burden of confusing thoughts. But I did not belong, really, even to the raw world around me. People came back to camp late from the neighbouring village, and would find me in my tent, pretending to be asleep. They would talk long in their heavy, slow, soft Scottish voices. They mentioned me rarely. Once one of them looked down to where I lay. He had been making a sort of catalogue of the characters in our platoon. 'And,' he said gently, 'and this poor colourless bastard.' I never came back to Aberdeen from camp, as I always half hoped I would, a different, a more formidable

71

person. I came back exhausted, needing to soak in a hot bath, and to be brought my breakfast in bed . . . And I came back also, in the end, from the real war, still needing consolation.

A Letter to Nicholas Moore

So few are lucky in the natural mode
And I was always an unlucky one,
With greed's shy gaze for the expensive treat
Of beauty, excellent in bone and blood,
Responsive to the same considering sun
That soured the grapes I never dared to eat.

Mine was the bitter gaze to pore upon
A profile or the modelling of an ear
Or the dry waxy pallor of two hands.
Mine was the pillow for the midnight tear
For all the deeds which could not be undone
And all the seeds wherewith I'd sown the sands.

Mine was the coward's humble insolence
That warms itself at an unheeding fire
And writes a poem to the kindly blaze,
Mine was the nibbling mouth without defence
Against the hook of any stray desire
That fractured the dead water of my days . . .

And thus, incompetent to speak of love,
I learned affection's humbler discipline,
And could be plain and easy with my friends
But yet stood still, where suns and planets move
Through love that turns their ellipses in,
For I had not their purposes and ends . . .

Or if I had, my density was such
That as another's star I could not move
Or I was tied to black and secret suns,
Lost memories, that held my heart too much,
A child's desire for universal love,
Or some blind, blank devotion like the nun's.

72

Or my own face in someone's flattering glass
That now my hateful mirror would not show,
Fixed to a pallor with a squinting eye,
Sir Death, expectant in the narrow pass,
A lame explorer nursing wastes of snow
That in his summer nightmares flower and die.

To My Friends

(on leaving St Andrews, summer of 1937)

We, born too late, in this unlucky age,
When charm and honesty had left the stage,
    Must watch heroic honour rant alone;
And yet we have controlled our politic rage
    And argued, sometimes, in an easy tone . . .
This little town from out the turbid tide
That lashes Britain, beating far and wide
    The ancient rocks with a still-threatening wave,
    We, whom the brass of war had not made brave,
By mask, by trick of manner or of wit,
    We saved! Or do they need to learn to save
Who safe, and ignorant, and sheltered sit?

So soon our trifling treaties have an end
These thoughts seem oak, though willow-like they bend . . .
    The real world waits us. 'Tis a rougher place,
Marshalled for marching. Here, they choose a friend
    Not for the careless talent, casual grace,
But bearing still in mind the crucial day
When pain and noise must batter out a way
    Here, in dead earnest, in no fit or start—
    O, batter where here? Here, we'll take our part
Not with the scribbler's paper, orator's breath,
    But solid arguments to touch the heart,
New logic; I mean, anger, hate, and death.

Such is our doom, we scholars. Honour comes
Always with marching feet and noise of drums,
    Music to drown the voice of common reason!
When life with hate, when time with anger hums
    Perhaps to think too coolly is a treason

To some new Caesar . . . Brutus was his friend
But thought too coolly and so made an end
    Of that great man of the democracy.
        Purse-proud patrician, empty reasoner he!
Traitor to justice and the common man!
        Cool reason paid the price at Philippi.
O scholars, back the winner while you can!

Shutting My Eyes

Shutting my eyes, I cannot see—
I can see no more
The tall walls, and the scud of the sea-spray
On the grey shale of the shore.

Shutting my ears, I cannot hear—
Or it lasts not long,
To drunken footsteps, the irreverent chorus
Of the drunken marching song.

Shutting my heart, I cannot feel—
But as a soft cloud
Shading the sun, the heart's branching ambition
By such dead foliage bowed.

Opening my eyes, I see too well
The daily task, the daily hell;
Opening my ears, I hear too loud
The sober nonsense of the crowd;
Opening my heart, I feel too weak
Towards the futile and the meek.

Open or shut, the eyes must see
What is, or can no longer be;
Open or shut, the ears must hear
A tale of folly or of fear:
Open or shut, the heart must know
How on the oak the ivies grow.

Shutting my eyes I long to see,
Shutting my ears I long to hear,
Some face that left no mask with me,
Some voice unechoed in my ear.

And when I come to shut my heart
I long to feel an old wound smart.

Shutting all these, I cannot shut,
No, not shut the mind
Still burning with the white weal of that beauty
That made ears deaf, eyes blind.

Waiting for the War

1

LEAVING St Andrews for the last time, I came back in the summer of 1937 to a disordered world. My mother was very ill, and would be away from home for months. We had given up Seafield Cottage, the pond, the garden, the attic, grandfather's books in their trunk, our childhood. Grandfather had been bedridden and wandering in his mind for three or four years now; and had passed quietly away during my last term at St Andrews. When I came home in the vacations, I would always, as soon as I got home, go upstairs to see him; he let me hold his hand, and asked after people vaguely, taking me sometimes perhaps for a brother, sometimes for a son. There was a kind of flicker of recognition between us, but no exact words to fit with it. He drifted to death placidly, free of the gloom that used to oppress him in the days when he and I would go to the cinema together.

All these were gaps. In the boarding-house in which father, Jean, and I were now staying, we felt uncomfortably large. Taking too long in the bathroom, scattering cigarette ash, shouting to each other over the bannisters, we got on our landlady's nerves. We felt we were being watched. One afternoon of early autumn I was in our sitting-room crouching over the electric fire. The landlady's sister came in and viciously switched it off. 'I am cold,' I said sullenly. 'Well,' she said, 'you should wear a coat,' and flounced out. I gripped a table and raged to myself: 'Insolent, insolent, insolent!' Jean tried to soothe me and my voice must have alarmed the poor woman (who did not really mean us any ill, but was just, like so many people who let rooms and provide meals, constitutionally incapable of leaving her lodgers to their own devices). I went out for half an hour to walk off my bad temper, and came back to find that the electric fire had been switched on again. Perversely, I switched it off. I never felt at ease again in that house. I was waiting, during these tedious and anxious weeks, to see if the local newspaper, *The Aberdeen Press and Journal*, would take me on and train me as a sub-editor or reporter. Meanwhile I spent much of my time in my bedroom, in a cloud of tobacco smoke, pounding out bad poems.

I was in low spirits. I had nothing very much to show for my four years at St Andrews; second-class honours; having won a prize for a play; having edited a magazine; having published, in remote literary magazines in London, which nobody read, a few pieces of verse and prose. Like every clever young man coming down from a university, I had a sudden flat sense of being, after all, nobody in particular. I was still shy, skimpy, insignificant, given to sudden tears and nervous blunders: an adolescent. Thinking of the dull sons of solid families in Aberdeen, the ones who had made a mess of farming in Kenya, and who now hung around clumsily at home, thrusting themselves, when a visitor came, just a little diffidently forward, I was afraid of sheer failure in whatever I might undertake; and it was in such a mood, an unpropitious one, that I started work on *The Press and Journal*. I would come into the night sub-editors' room about seven in the evening and stay on till after midnight, when the paper was put to bed. There was not very much for me to do. Teletype sheets from agencies came in on pale grey paper in blunt print; the chief sub-editor would tear off short news items, and I would scribble in headlines with a blue pencil and cut unnecessary matter; or I might put headings and sub-headings on some story sent up the chute by our own reporters, and break it into shorter paragraphs. Time hung heavily on me. There was a break about ten o'clock for coffee from a thermos and sandwiches from a paper bag, and sometimes I would sneak half an hour to flip through the piles of new books that had come in for review. It seemed to me that I had learned everything that I could be trusted with in the first evening . . .

I had a feeling of not getting anywhere and went round to the head of the local teachers' training college, to consult him about teaching as a profession. I spoke of the routine of sub-editing. 'I sit here,' he replied, 'and letters come in, and I answer them, and I answer them on the model of my replies to previous letters that have come in on the same sort of subject. Novelty hasn't much meaning except against a background of routine.' A schoolmaster's life, he said, if one had the gift and vocation for it—but had I?—was calm and secure, but in journalism there might be a more glamorous future, if that was what I was looking for; and I should remember that the mastering of any trade was a dishearteningly slow business. I felt the force and wisdom of what he said, yet wondered whether in the sub-editors' room I was really mastering anything, or merely (as in the drill-hall with the OTC at St Andrews) going through awkward imitative move-

77

ments without acquiring any initiative. I decided, however, to carry on.

Further family misfortunes helped, a little, to take me out of myself. While mother was still away from home convalescing, father fell ill: dangerously, we feared mortally. A severe pleurisy left him with an obstruction lodged in one lung, and he lay for almost a year between life and death, till one afternoon he had a fit of wrenching coughing that almost miraculously brought the obstruction up. He still lay sick for some weeks; thin and hectic, and with a hoarse, ghostly voice and with the merest ghost, too, of his old jauntiness. Visiting him in the nursing home, I felt the pain of my deep love for him, and of all his hopes centred on me, that I was bound to disappoint. The OTC at St Andrews had been partly a myth for his benefit and it was for his sake that I swam, and went riding on Sundays, and at St Andrews had played golf (going round the Jubilee, which is the old course, free to undergraduates, at an average of 130 strokes a round), and took long walks in the country and, sipping at my sherry, tried to appear a normal, brisk boy as I sat with him among his friends at the club. Yet at the back of his mind he knew perfectly well what a frail pretence all this was of mine. Illness brought out all the sharp, sensitive distinction of his face; the delicate nostrils, and the carved mouth, and the alert, hot, angry eyes that Jean, the beauty of the family, had inherited. I sat beside him for hours, telling him (what was not true) how well I was getting ahead on *The Press and Journal*. I was thinking that he would die.

If one acts a lie with enough courage and persistence, it sometimes begins to become true. I was making no headway as a sub-editor, so at *The Press and Journal* they decided to switch me, for a time, to the reporting staff. That might, they thought, cure me of my shyness. The News Editor, Mr Chalmers, one of the best friends I have ever had, was an irascible man with a golden heart; suffering from chronic nervous indigestion, that occupational disease of journalism, he was perpetually emptying small packets of bicarbonate into tumblers of water, and perpetually forgetting to drink them as he dashed away to answer a telephone, or to question a reporter who had just come in with a story. He barked at me as at everybody but I did not mind it. His very irritability reflected his almost boyish enthusiasm for his work; twenty years on a newspaper had not led him to take any detail of the daily routine for granted. Every minute counted. Every story might be some sort of a scoop. He sent me out to pick up half a dozen people on the streets, at random, and ask them all about their jobs. I wandered nervously round Aberdeen, drinking occasional cups of coffee, and popping into the reading room of the public library to soothe myself with ten pages about formal logic or the history of English metres; but finally my conscience cornered me, and I cornered my victims—dustmen, navvies, scavengers, porters, fair ground attendants—and found them surprisingly ready to talk. The experiment did not cure me of shyness. It is one thing to say, 'Excuse me, I represent a newspaper': another to get into easy conversation with a stranger. But I found that I had an eye and an ear, and could write easy, readable stuff, that was also accurate.

Quite soon, I formulated for myself two of the three important rules for the descriptive journalist. One is always to try, in as few words as possible, to give an exact visual impression of anything that is distinctive about a person or a scene. The second is always to try to convey the turn of speech of the person you are interviewing; a bald summary, in your own style, is not interesting. The third rule is to ask relevant questions, but I was still too ignorant about how the work of the world is done to guess, very often, what the relevant questions would be. But if I would usually start off my interviews on half a dozen wrong tacks, I at least soon learned to put in the random word that keeps people talking . . .

With every story of this sort that I secured, I was winning a bet against myself: I expected my nerve to fail or the stranger whom I approached to resent being accosted. Nobody did. People like to talk about themselves, and, in any case, with my eagerness and anxiety, I had probably a youthful charm for which I did not give myself credit. As I walked home, now, from the paper, late at night, I would still feel fatigued, but no longer futile. Mother was back home and we had rented a new little house right at the end of Queen's Road, near the big park of Hazlehead; as I walked slowly the whole length of the town, these cold nights, when the last tram had gone, carrying a walking-stick to stop myself from slipping on the frozen pavements, and looking around nervously for stray dogs, I had a sense of the dark, glittering, nipping space of the world, and of the excitement of moving in it. Yet the stray dogs would bark at me, as they will bark at any person who is not sure of himself, who is not at one with nature.

It was for the natural world, the world of greenness and growth, that I felt an occasional acute wistfulness—so other than my world of headaches, and paper, and books. Once as I was going home I got into conversation with a lad from the country. He worked on a farm, had been enjoying a day's holiday in town, and was trudging back home . . . miles and miles still to go, but he ate them with an easy pace. He talked to me in that slow, friendly way that always makes me (a townsman from my birth, but descended from crofters and fisherfolk) feel at home with rural characters; he told me about his work, up at five in the morning, gulping a plate of porridge, out in the fields all day, and at night a drink in the village or a dance in the village hall, and as he talked, I admired his handsome ruddy head. He walked off into the night at an easy, clumping pace, and I thought happily of that life close to the earth, with a usefulness that does not have to justify itself, where cleverness, money, social position are not obsessions, where a dance in a barn, a gill of whisky, a kiss behind a stone dyke, make up the simple sum of labour's consolations. In the country, the animal side of life is something natural; in the crowded and discreet towns it becomes something diseased.

Yet in the crowded and discreet town I was beginning to enjoy myself. I covered, for the paper, most of the regular weekly business club lunches, and in the evenings I attended public dinners, where I discovered that wine, liqueurs, and cigars did not prevent me from turning out a plausible three quarters of a column at midnight, with the aid of a menu with a list of speakers on it, and my very scrappy shorthand notes. My shorthand was quite rapid but not very legible, and I never knew whether I was using my shorthand to help out my verbal memory, or my verbal memory to interpret my shorthand.

Often the after-dinner stories were the ones that I could not use in my reports. There was the one, for instance, about the young lady of Riga; raped three times in succession after the first World War, as that Baltic capital was liberated, and unliberated, and liberated again by contending partisans, she had screamed very loud the first time, not quite so loud the second, and the third time she had still screamed a little for the honour of Riga. A fat naval officer told this story, his shoulders shaking with eighteenth-century glee. The year was 1938. I remember reflecting that perhaps, in a year or two, that sort of joke would be too true to be funny, even to him.

There were more sinister signs of the times. At the Junior Business Men's Club, I reported a talk by the local representative of the British Union. He was a tall man, very picturesque in his black shirt, and with only one arm. He had courage; I had seen him trying to make a speech, from a small car, in a working-class district, to a completely hostile audience, about the Spanish Civil War. They milled around the car. He stood erect, with a small megaphone, inflated cheeks, and a mouth turned down at the corners like the mask of tragedy. He made himself heard somehow, against a sort of murmuring groundswell, till he said something about 'the real interests of the common people of Spain'. The response was tremendous and overwhelming: a great roar from the crowd, 'Dinna you speak for the common fowk o' Spain!' and 'Lang live the common fowk o' Spain!' and 'Daith to bluidy Franco!' He stood for a minute or two, swayed backwards by the pressure of these cries, as if by the push of a strong wind; but putting his megaphone down, and not trying to make himself heard any more. And then the roar subsided, and he sat down again, a tall man bent awkwardly over the steering-wheel of his little car, looking crumpled, but not really frightened. I had watched this scene with the slightly guilty detachment of the professional spectator; whose sympathies may be swayed a little, as our sympathies are in the theatre, now this way, now that, but whose judgment of the play, in the end, is an independent and lonely one.

At the Junior Business Men's Club, this tall Fascist, meeting with no such overt opposition, could not produce such a dramatic effect. Indeed, the effect he produced was rather boring. He spoke with a monotonous, mechanical emphasis, a churning iteration, as if the words were being carried to his lips on a conveyor belt. It is a tone that can be noticed in the prose of some important writers of our time, often men of genuine gifts, who have had Fascist sympathies; I was to discover it, years later in Eritrea, in the writings of the Italian Futurist, Marinetti. It is a menacing tone; what Lionel Trilling calls the masked will in place of the modulated idea. There is an attempt to give continuous discourse the effect of news coming over, word by word, on a ticker tape, or even the effect of a set of fantastic, inaccurate, and sensational headlines. Perhaps an intellectual Fascist is a man who thinks in headlines, for whom all words and ideas have flat, hard, mechanical impact, and have lost light and shade. The pounding repetitions of this local orator had, at least, a disagreeable effect on me. The young business men suppressed their yawns, found no pertinent questions to ask, and murmured to me, after their guest had departed, 'Isn't it all rather nonsense?'

It was my first experience of a kind of person of whom I was to meet later (and on the extreme Left as well as the extreme Right) other samples; people who see the world in terms of plots, conspiracies, 'crooks', and for whom life is not interesting unless it resembles a cheap thriller. They are sometimes people of

81

romantic charm, of generous natures, and of real courage, but all their qualities are spoiled by being wholly at the service of a sort of frustrated aggressive fantasy; they reach peace in themselves, in the end, at the price of declaring war on the world. Fascism, at least as represented in the person of this one-armed orator, seemed to me then to have the sinister pathos of all kinds of voluntary self-deception. Life has drama, certainly, but not of the kind that the typical activist politician of our time imagines. The real drama lies in our struggle with a predicament that forces us to treat others, caught in exactly the same predicament, as enemies; in our struggle with impersonal destructive forces inside us and outside us. Knowledge and love are always seeking to outflank the nasty satisfactions offered by spite and resentment; and their long, loose line is broken by the enemy more often than not. For the hot little hates have punch.

But the politics of the 'man of action'—that is to say, of the man who is attracted, not appalled, by images of violence and cruelty—are on the side of the hot little hates. He is a man who has been hurt, and he wants to hurt others in return. A decent society consciously checks that wish to hurt; we keep aggression out of society by letting it work within and hurt ourselves—by being ready to remain divided against ourselves—or by turning it not on each other but on our common predicament. Fascism is an extreme case of the set of tendencies and counter-tendencies I am talking about. Self-deception is universal, and *all* political attitudes are in some degree sinister and pathetic. I have not met with cases of total sincerity. This tension between love and destruction is perhaps what life is about. If we forget this, we cannot achieve style, but only fragments and diatribe. It was of style more than politics that I thought as I watched that bony orator with pity.

Yet there are beams in our own eyes. One man does evil from voluntary self-deception, a coarse taste for melodrama, a misplaced desire to express his unlovely self; another can do as much harm from mere self-regarding indolence. I myself saw what Fascism was like, and I saw that Germany was forcing us towards a war, and that on our side it would be a just war, a war to destroy something evil and uncontained. But I knew also what a grim business that war would be for myself. My experience in the OTC in St Andrews had left me with no illusions that I had the makings of a soldier in me. I foresaw, once war had broken out, years of discomfort and possibly of shame ahead of me. And from German refugees, whom I had interviewed for *The Press and*

Journal, I had heard enough to feel sure that the coming war would be unusually barbarous. I knew about the tortures and also about the more ordinary humiliations: the Jews forced to clean out public lavatories with their bare hands—a bubbling over of evil like the sea. I did not think we could fight this without being in some way infected by it.

I had seen what the Great War had done to my father. It had done some positive things; it had given him confidence in himself as a leader; but there were scars, still, in his mind, images of pain and cruelty, and he would start talking, sometimes, in an uncomfortable way, about the rats in the trenches or about bayonet fighting, while mother would clench her hands, and try not to listen. Was it not that war that had strung his nerves and mind to this high pitch?—so that he was 'always on his toes', but never at his ease; needing always talk, and company, and especially reminiscences of that past? For war is one of these experiences, like an unhappy love affair, a shipwreck, a nervous breakdown, a quarrel with an old friend, that tie a man to the past; we date everything from it. So, for all these reasons, I felt a sense of guilty relief over Munich. At least another year, another year . . . My father did not. He knew Europe well enough, history well enough, to be certain that there was no dodging what was coming, and I remember him turning one evening at a concert and being uncharacteristically rude to a woman Town Councillor who had been saying, 'What we really need, of course, is *Moral* Rearmament.' He felt, perhaps, what I myself now feel looking back upon these years, the flabby unreality of our pacific dreams.

It was because I had a romantic feeling about the military life, as well as a fear and horror of it, that my own feelings about the coming war were so strangely mixed. In the summer of 1938, I went round Buchan, Mar, and Mearns on a mechanised route march with a territorial battalion of the Gordon Highlanders. We were away for a fortnight. I messed with the officers, and sent in daily descriptive reports to *The Press and Journal* which I afterwards put together as a recruiting pamphlet. At the end of my pamphlet, I remember that I suggested that the days of railway warfare were over and that the next war would be conditioned by the fact that troops could now be carried in large numbers, rapidly, anywhere, by road. As a military experiment, in fact, this mechanised route march had been illuminating, at least to a lay mind. The RAF had co-operated, coming low over our column, and dropping bags of soot in a near-by field; the soldiers repelled these imaginary bombs with imaginary concentrated rifle fire. That was on a road on Deeside, a lovely sunny day, far from anywhere. I revisualised that scene when I read, a couple of years later, about the role of the Luftwaffe in the fall of France . . . I enjoyed that fortnight. Colonel Buchanan-Smith, a man of exquisite politeness (whose sister, Janet Adam Smith, was later to become a good friend of mine in London), was kind to me, and suggested I should take a commission in his battalion. I made the excuse of my long hours at the newspaper, but really felt that I was shrinking from a responsibility I knew I was not up to. I admired then, as I admire now, the good soldier, but it is rather dangerous to admire an organisation intensely, and even romantically, on condition that you yourself remain outside it. But that fortnight became mixed up in my mind with pleasant, irrelevant things; young green birches, stippled against the sunlight; the purring of an old water mill; light flashing from lochans on a great tawny moor that itself seemed to ripple in the heat-haze; seagulls swooping, with a white incongruous grace, over the lavatory trenches, far inland, against a background of hilly dark pines; wine and good food and pleasant conversation at regimental dinners; and the feeling, which was consoling to me in my loneliness, of being made for a couple of weeks an honorary member of a rather good club.

A Letter to Anne Ridler

A bird flies and I gum it to a concept,
You trim your concept to the flying bird,
Your round words plopping open out in rings.
May your love's dreams be innocent and absurd
For dreaming of your verses while he slept
You mastered these oblique and tricky things . . .

But I was a reporter on a paper
And saw death ticked out in a telegram
On grey and shabby sheets with pallid print
So often, that it seemed an evening dram
Of solace for the murderer and the raper
Whose love has grown monstrous through stint.

I was a poet of this century
Pursued by poster-strident images
And headlines as spectacular as a dream
Full of cartoonists' dolls with paper visages;
I had no spare time over for reality,
I took things largely to be what they seem.

I had a headache from the endless drum,
The orator drumming on his private anger,
And the starved young in their accusing group
When I had written and could write no longer
Over my shoulder seemed to peer and stoop.
The adequate perspectives would not come.

It was not real, the news I got from London,
But made the immediate avenue unreal
And sapped my habits of their privilege:
Dreamy the granite in the evening sun
And like a vision, in their swoop and wheel,
The pigeons fluttering at Union Bridge.

The Communists were always playing darts,
The Spanish War survivor would not talk,
The Tory member only talked of peace.
In spring, the ash-buds blossomed in our hearts,
The tangle blossomed on the slimy rock,
The private impulse sought its vain release . . .

And in December on the ballroom floor
The girls in flowering dresses swayed and whirled,
And no girl leant on my protective arm.
From all the height of speculation hurled,
I stood and hesitated by the door;
I felt the pathos and I felt the charm . . .

Oh, I had hardly any will or shape,
Or any motive, but a sort of guilt
That half attracted them and half repelled;
My hand shook, and my glass of sherry spilt,
I wore a sort of silence like a cape.
The old historic constant pattern held.

And when at midnight in my lonely room
I tried to integrate it all in verse
The headlines seemed as distant as the girls.
If sex was useless, history was worse.
A terrible remoteness seemed my doom
Whether I wrote of bayonets or curls . . .

So the stiff stanzas and the prosy lines
Accumulated on my dusty shelf,
A family joke, like any secret vice:
Dud bombs, damp rockets, unexploded mines.
'This sort of writing isn't really nice.
Oh, George, my darling, can't you be yourself?'

You can; and I would praise your studied art,
Dry and stiff-fingered, but more accurate
Than all my brilliant angers and my blind,
Hot, hurt perceptions, energised with hate:
Would praise your calm perspectives of the mind
So coloured with the pathos of the heart.

For my slack words were awkwardly heroic,
Your noble mood assumes no airs at all:
A rock of anger in this world unstable,
Me other people's sufferings made a stoic,
But you, a hostess, at our hungry table,
Are kind; your atmosphere is germinal.

Loving the charity of women's love,
Too much a household pet, I see in you
The gentle nurture that now curbs my grief
As I grow tall, beyond that budding grove
Of all the beautiful beyond belief
Within whose shade my windflower passions blew,

Private to me, their shy and secret sun:
Who now with other private suns compete
And seek in man's inverted mode such love
As nerves the will to enter and complete
Its terrible initiation of
Man to these virtues that from pain are won.

And the sick novice whimpers for his home
Who shall be hurt and horribly alone
Before the historic vigil lets him sleep.
Yet for such hurt, such pity might atone
And such an Ithaca for those who roam
Far, that they may at last return and weep.

Why do the towers of Troy for ever burn?
Perhaps that old Jew told us, or perhaps
Since women suffer much in bearing us
We also must show courage in our turn,
Among these forks and dreaded thunder-claps,
Against an endless dialectic tearing us . . .

Or freedom, say, from family love and strife
And all the female mystery of a room
That half supports and half imprisons us
May tear a man from mother, sister, wife,
And every soft reminder of the womb.
Dead Freud in lost Vienna argued thus.

I hardly know! But Fritz, who's now interned,
(Sober and well-informed like all his race)
Told me this war might last, say, seven years;
But right would be triumphant then, the tide be turned,
Unless indeed (the night fell on his face)
Our hopes are just illusions like our fears.

Perhaps in London, say, in seven years,
We'll meet, and we will talk of poetry,
And of the piety of homely things,
A common past, the flowering library
In which the awkward spirit perseveres
Until a world of letters shines and sings . . .

Unless the vigilant years have numbed my face,
The long humiliation soured my heart,
The madman's silence boxed my veering mood:
Let time forgive me, if I fall apart,
And fall, as many souls have fallen from grace,
Through just and necessary servitude.

Or if we never meet, remember me
As one voice speaking calmly in the north
Among the muslin veils of northern light;
I bore the seed of poetry from my birth
To flower in rocky ground, sporadically,
Until I sleep in the unlaurelled night.

2

And my loneliness needed consoling. I remember, for instance, an odd incident that very fortnight. There was a dance at my sister's old school that I wanted to go to, so I left the troops for a day and took a bus back to Aberdeen. I was tanned with the summer weather of the countryside and for the dance I put on my father's evening-dress kilt, which suited me well enough. I felt that I had surmounted one hurdle, of getting on well in a rough male society, and that now I would surmount another, that of making an impression at a dance. But, alas, I made no impression. After the feeling of 'belonging' which had made me so happy to be with the Gordons, I felt miserably, all of a sudden, out of place.

There was a boy at the party whom I had known and disliked at the Grammar School, an undergraduate now at Aberdeen University, a dark-haired, thin boy, pallid and slightly blotched, with a loose, mobile, ugly mouth, but, unlike myself, a social success. I had remembered him, and he had remembered me, since an incident in the gymnasium at school when we were both small boys. Pale and sickly even as a child, he had been excused all but the mildest gymnastics, and he stood against the climbing rails by the wall, looking sulky, as the rest of us practised the high jump. I kept knocking down the bar, I held the others back, and at length the instructor said to me, 'You can watch!' I stood beside Willy. He whispered to me out of the side of his mouth, 'You're rotten, you're rotten.' 'Look,' I gritted back at him, 'I tried, at least. You didn't even try.' 'I can't try. But you *won't* try. You're rotten.' 'Shut up.' 'I won't shut up, you're rotten, you won't try.' 'Listen, I'll fight you outside.' 'I can't fight. You know I can't fight, you coward.' 'I'm not a coward.' 'Oh, yes, you are, because you *won't* try, but I'm not, because I *can't* try.' 'You're an ugly white slug,' I whispered. 'You're a pink coward,' he whispered back. It had rankled with both of us. We were not even in the same class; two classes were taking gym at the same time; and we were never in the same class after that, and had no acquaintances in common, but it seemed to be, on his side at least, hate at first sight and when we passed each other in the corridors, Willy, growing taller and tougher but no prettier, would make a grimace at me with his expressive mouth (at university, he was to become a notable amateur actor), while I felt myself growing hot, pink, and prickly and tried to stare at him as if he were not there.

Now, at this party, wearing my kilt, and seeing Willy, still pale, and sinister, and patently hostile, as I remembered him, in an ordinary dinner jacket (why had I not put on my dinner jacket, why had I made myself so stupidly conspicuous?) I found myself, in the hot, crowded room, flushing up pinkly again. Willy seized his advantage. We had not exchanged a word since that first encounter, years ago, but he addressed me like an old and intimate enemy. He looked me up and down with a pretence of awe. 'You know,' he said, 'you are the sort of person that frightens me.' The evening wore on, and I found myself without partners. My sister had many admirers. The other girls preferred boys nearer their own ages (after all, I thought, with a feeling that the best was behind me, I was now nearly twenty-three!). Willy was monopolising the girl, Oriana, whom I specially wanted to dance with. He seemed to be making himself extremely amusing. They were talking and laughing, and looking sometimes in my direction, as I stood, just as on that occasion in the gymnasium, and wistfully watched. Willy was probably saying to himself, 'He's rotten, he won't try.' This was a schoolgirls' party, there was nothing to drink but lemonade, and I needed a little false courage. I hung on the edge of groups, feeling like the frayed bit of the edge; asked three or four strange girls to dance, feeling that I was inflicting myself on them, and making the stiffest conversation. I felt my body unusually clumsy, stiff with my long marches with the Gordons on country moors; I was flat and exhausted. As the party drew towards its end, I found myself sitting alone in an alcove conservatory, full of potted plants, watching the dancers whirling around in the last old-fashioned waltz, the young bodies, the pert innocent faces, the sway of rustling skirts; and tears, born of some frustrated expectation, started into my eyes. Walking home with Jean, I wept, and we quarrelled violently. Why was I so terribly alone in this town, I asked, why could I make no friends, why were all her friends so young and silly? Young and silly, indeed, I thought bitterly to myself, but what a glamour they had, and how sometimes I wished that I were an undergraduate again, or something

89

ordinary and safe like a young doctor, a young lawyer; so that my social standing could be unequivocal; so that my evenings could be free, and so that, like everybody else, I could take girls out to coffee and the cinema, I could 'make dates . . .'

Parties, at this time, even such parties as that, at which I was so awkward and ill at ease, had become my secret passion. I was in love with the presence of young girls in a crowd. Individual young girls whom I knew, when I met them on the tram, on my way to the newspaper offices in the morning, did not excite me much, going to their university classes in their neat day clothes; but when I danced with them, stepping cautiously through a quickstep or yielding, with a good partner, to an old-fashioned waltz, their evening metamorphosis, the hair, the skin, the silk, the powder, the drawling soft voices, exercised a tremendous pull. I had really nothing to say to them, but even a quite pointless conversation that moved at the right pace, or any little joke, that would make them laugh a small artificial laugh, as we waltzed wildly around, would make me feel that the evening had come off. I felt that it was a serious moral duty to 'have a good time' and an unforgivable dereliction to sit in a corner glumly and appear the odd man out. Oriana, in particular, with her bright artificial vivacity (a vivacity that seemed to fit with streamers, coloured lights, and paper flowers, and that was perhaps no more an organic part of her personality than these are organic parts of a room transformed for a dance) could make an evening extraordinarily triumphant. To watch her smile and laugh was to say: 'I can attract, I can amuse', and the images of all these faces, these hands, these young bodies turning in the dance were as beautiful to me as flowers. Yet, except as artificial flowers, in a bowl of coloured light, I could not see these girls—I did not want to think of their personalities, their solid homes, the books they read, the lecture notes they learned by heart, their jealousies, spites, loyalties, and all the small sincerities of their natures—and so I would never make a true friend among them, still less win a lover. When I wanted a serious talk about anything, I turned to Jean, now herself at university and wrestling with Bishop Butler and Kant, or to my cousin Freddy, who talked for hours about the film as the great modern art-form. The solemn pleasure of the dance, the elaborate grave frivolity of the social evening, these, for me, were like a high ceremony, that must not be profaned by the slipshod usages of the world. It is strange, now, when a party is a gathering to which I go to drink and talk too much, to think of these evenings of early enchantment, composed of nothing but lemonade, conventional compliments, and the presence of a coloured cloud of plump and pretty girls.

And certainly our pleasures in these days, as they recall themselves to me now, had a touching pastoral innocence. Freddy and Jean and I would chatter about ideas, and while the summer lasted we would browse on the beach, picnic there, talk in a leisurely way about schemes for ensuring world peace—Federal Union was a favourite—or about the dances that would start again as soon as the days grew shorter, or about the prose style of Hemingway, or about the latest musical film with Ginger Rogers and Fred Astaire. The long golden beach stretched for its curved mile and the brisk sea beat upon it. In town, the glitter of granite, the flutter of pigeons, was like small change jingling in one's pockets. We went on bicycles to Stonehaven and spent all day lounging on the shingly beach. Where would we be, the same day of the same month, next summer? Or as the nights grew darker Freddy and I, each of us seeing the other home half a dozen times, would walk up and down Queen's Road, talking of a hundred things . . . When, and for how long, would the war interrupt our interminable conversation?

These were pockets of happiness. While I moved in them, I responded to other people like water, taking and losing their shape as I passed over. Left to myself, I would feel a guilt at being so adaptable and so uncommitted. I was trying to make provisional categories of human attitudes; my difficulty was that I could not see myself as a type or provide for my own reactions. My mind was full, as it were, of tangles of unsorted wool of different colours; left to myself, I would spend hours teasing them out, but would thrust them away at last—like unfinished poems and essays, also all in a huddle—to be taken out, perhaps later. And when the war came along, it was like a closing, almost for good, of that drawer. For the kinds of observation that I was beginning to make of this provincial middle-class society, clinging to many traditions that were out of fashion elsewhere, offered me delicate points of vantage; not so the rough democracy of the ranks. There was a very obvious symbolism, indeed, in the piles of uncompleted typescripts I left behind me in my bedroom chest of drawers. To begin; to go on pretty well; not to end prosperously . . . That had been repeatedly the rhythm of my juvenile ambitions, and these, too, for the time being, were shelved.

Social Pleasures

The Orchestra starts, slowly, I crush my stub,
I rise and I wait till the others
Have chosen their partners, and awkwardly
I smile, I say, 'May I?' she smiles faintly,
We move off stiffly, and . . .

Bunny perhaps, with her smooth dark hair, her pale
Heavily powdered skin, her little
Rabbit's smile, and the agreeable pressure
Of a fully-developed body. 'Well, George,
Been working hard lately?' 'Oh the usual,
The hours are long but the work is light.'
And, 'Really, you are dancing better lately.'
And a stiff bow at the end, 'Thank you, thank you.'

Bunny, the Gioconda of her province,
Inspiring durable and awkward affections:
With her little refined drawl, her pale smile,
Mystery behind a little malicious chatter
And maybe nothing at all behind mystery.
But then I have never seen her playing her game:
Heavy, and awkward, and dull, for her I am
Part of the burden, an old friend of the family.

Or perhaps Joy, with the charm
Of a creamy parchment skin on a neat skull;
The dark large pupils of unfocussed eyes,
And the honey voice, sticky in its sweetness.
Breaking with Joy, after the dance, I run
My hand down her pale warm arm;
Dancing, I am always thoroughly aware
Of the delicate contact of her small fingers.
I compliment her on her dress, ask her
About dances, parties, pictures. She sighs,
She didn't do so well in exams this term.

Or perhaps, Sheila, the thorough sportsman,
With her strong jaw and her boy's smile,
Abrupt, humorous. The music stops,
Then starts again. Falling in with her style,
'Anyway, I rather like holding you like this.'
She jeers back, 'How kind of you to say so!'

Or Rosemary, with her sunburn powder,
Her dark lipstick, her daintiness,
And her literary gossip. At Malvern
She bumped deliberately into Hugh Walpole,
Just to make him start and say 'Excuse me!'
She saw Bernard Shaw outside the theatre,
All alone, poring with simple vanity
Over his latest batch of photographs.
Or Italy, and the charm of Count Ciano,
Or Grenoble, and a mad Hungarian,
Who used to say for a joke that in Hungary
They ate young girls for breakfast, tea and dinner.
He was a cousin of the Archduke Otto,
And that was the week of the Soviet-German pact.
He absolutely hated Ribbentrop . . .

Those are the lucky who, like Fritz and Freddy,
Know what to say to girls, and know
Just what to feel about them. I hardly know
What exactly to say or what to feel.
The orchestra starts slowly, I crush my stub,
I rise, and I wait till the others
Have chosen their partners, and awkwardly
I smile, I say, 'May I?' She smiles faintly,
We move off stiffly.

I worry much about my quarter-turns.
I ask, 'Is this a waltz or a slow fox-trot?'
I see them looking down occasionally
To see what I am doing with my feet.
And, 'You can walk all over me,' says Sheila,
'I am as tough as a rhinoceros.'
'Shall we sit this one out?' says Bunny.

And later, trying to write lyric poems,
Expressing some intense and simple passion,
I muse upon these fragmentary contacts;
And remember a sentence of Louis MacNeice,
In *The Arts Today*, that in poetry
'One cannot force the empirical element.'
I remember a green net dress of Rosemary's
But find it makes a poor show in a poem.

Then, not for the first time certainly, I wish,
I glumly wish, at birth I had been given
A rasher, more impetuous temperament
And a less cautious, hesitating mind.

I meditate on Nicky and Lord Byron.
Stare at the typewriter and crush my stub.
The metre starts in my head, I type stiffly.

And it doesn't turn into a dance or a poem.

Christmas Letter Home

(To my sister in Aberdeen)

Drifting and innocent and sad like snow,
Now memories tease me, wherever I go,
And I think of the glitter of granite and distances
And against the blue air the lovely and bare trees,
And slippery pavements spangled with delight
Under the needles of a winter's night,
And I remember the dances, with scarf and cane,
Strolling home in the cold with the silly refrain
Of a tune of Cole Porter or Irving Berlin
Warming a naughty memory up like gin,
And Bunny and Sheila and Joyce and Rosemary
Chattering on sofas or preparing tea,
With their delicate voices and their small white hands
This is the sorrow everyone understands.
More than Rostov's artillery, more than the planes
Skirting the cyclonic islands, this remains,
The little, lovely taste of youth we had:
The guns and not our silliness were mad,
All the unloved and ugly seeking power
Were mad, and not our trivial evening hour
Of swirling taffetas and muslin girls,
Oh, not their hands, their profiles, or their curls,
Oh, not the evenings of coffee and sherry and snow,
Oh, not the music. Let us rise and go—
But then the months and oceans lie between,
And once again the dust of spring, the green
Bright beaks of buds upon the poplar trees,

And summer's strawberries, and autumn's ease,
And all the marble gestures of the dead,
Before my eyes caress again your head,
Your tiny strawberry mouth, your bell of hair,
Your blue eyes with their deep and shallow stare,
Before your hand upon my arm can still
The nerves that everything but home makes ill:
In this historic poster-world I move,
Noise, movement, emptiness, but never love.
Yet all this grief we had to have my dear,
And most who grieve have never known, I fear,
The lucky streak for which we die and live,
And to the luckless must the lucky give
All trust, all energy, whatever lies
Under the anger of democracies:
Whatever strikes the towering torturer down,
Whatever can outface the bully's frown,
Talk to the stammerer, spare a cigarette
For tramps at midnight . . . oh, defend it yet!
Some Christmas I shall meet you. Oh, and then
Though all the boys you used to like are men,
Though all my girls are married, though my verse
Has pretty steadily been growing worse,
We shall be happy: we shall smile and say,
'These years! It only seems like yesterday
I saw you sitting in that very chair.'
'You have not changed the way you do your hair.'
'These years were painful, then?' 'I hardly know.
Something lies gently over them, like snow,
A sort of numbing white forgetfulness . . .'

And so, good-night, this Christmas, and God bless!

Home Town Elegy

(For Aberdeen in Spring)

Glitter of mica at the windy corners,
Tar in the nostrils, under blue lamps budding
Like bubbles of glass the blue buds of a tree,
Night-shining shopfronts, or the sleek sun flooding

95

The broad abundant dying sprawl of the Dee:
For these and for their like my thoughts are mourners
That yet shall stand, though I come home no more,
Gas-works, white ballroom, and the red brick baths
And salmon nets along a mile of shore,
Or beyond the municipal golf-course, the moorland paths
And the country lying quiet and full of farms.
This is the shape of a land that outlasts a strategy
And is not to be taken with rhetoric or arms.
Or my own room, with a dozen books on the bed
(Too late, still musing what I mused, I lie
And read too lovingly what I have read),
Brantôme, Spinoza, Yeats, the bawdy and wise,
Continuing their interminable debate,
With no conclusion, they conclude too late,
When their wisdom has fallen like a grey pall on my eyes.
Syne we maun part, there sall be nane remeid—
Unless my country is my pride, indeed,
Or I can make my town that homely fame
That Byron has, from boys in Carden Place,
Struggling home with books to midday dinner,
For whom he is not the romantic sinner,
The careless writer, the tormented face,
The hectoring bully or the noble fool,
But, just like Gordon or like Keith, a name:
A tall, proud statue at the Grammar School.

Lean Street

Here, where the baby paddles in the gutter,
        Here in the slaty greyness and the gas,
Here where the women wear dark shawls and mutter
        A hasty word as other women pass,

Telling the secret, telling, clucking and tutting,
        Sighing, or saying that it served her right,
The bitch!—the words and weather both are cutting
        In Causewayend, on this November night.

At pavement's end and in the slaty weather
        I stare with glazing eyes at meagre stone,
Rain and the gas are sputtering together
        A dreary tune! O leave my heart alone,

O leave my heart alone, I tell my sorrows,
  For I will soothe you in a softer bed
And I will numb your grief with fat to-morrows
  Who break your milk teeth on this stony bread!

They do not hear. Thought stings me like an adder,
  A doorway's sagging plumb-line squints at me,
The fat sky gurgles like a swollen bladder
  With the foul rain that rains on poverty.

3

The war came, finally, when I was in the middle of one of these
pockets of happiness, when, in August of 1939, with my sister and
a party of her friends from Aberdeen University, I was spending a
fortnight in Paris. I liked Paris: the flavour of the whole great city
for me was like that of the sweet, cheap champagne, frothy and
tingling, like a sort of superior cider, round which I curled my
tongue every night before going across the road, into the grounds
of the Cité Universitaire, into the Franco-British House, and up
and up the stairs into my room on the very top floor, tired out with
enjoyment. The room pleased me, because it reminded me of my
old room at St Salvator's, the students' hostel at St Andrews. It
had the same desk and divan, the same broad windows opening
outwards, the same built-in cupboards; also, added luxuries, a
basin with a cold-water tap in a sort of recess, a light set in the
wall over my bed. I used to be very tired when I got up to my
room, about half-past one in the morning, but I rarely went
directly to bed. My rooms, on the inner side of the men's wing,
looked straight across at the women's, and I would switch out my
light and wait in the darkness, watching the women's rooms
in which the lights had not yet been put on and the curtains were
still drawn wide. Eventually, a light would flash, a figure would
move about in the room, arousing in me an agonising suspense,
until, finally, with a sudden suspicious look into the darkness, the
girl would draw her curtains. But sometimes one had better luck;
a naked girl, standing in the light, leaning out of the window with
the moon on her bosom, and then lying supine on her divan . . .
moved, I felt, by the same adolescent hunger, the same local rage,
that was moving me to such despicable spying.
  The adolescent hunger, the local rage: Paris seemed to me,
during that sultry fortnight, to be its home and its sanctuary . . .

In some street off the Rue de Rivoli, surrounded by red-backed copies of *Tropic of Capricorn*, I came upon the face, in a life-size photograph, of Henry Miller. Beside it was a page from *Time* in which (in phrases heavily underlined in red ink) some slick journalist stated that what Miller called 'the dithyrambic novel' folks back home would call 'plain old-fashioned pornography'. But I hardly looked at the book of the sales-talk; it was the terrible countenance, itself, that attracted me.

Why did that face shock me so? (The photograph, I must add, was probably not a good likeness, or else I projected into it all my own notions about Miller. For I have since been told by people, like Lawrence Durrell, who know Miller well, that he has a benevolent and austere aspect, like that of a Chinese sage.) Perhaps because of a naive vanity. I always thought in these days of writers I admired as conforming to my own physical type: the sweatshirt, the ruffled hair, the unlined face, boyish but for its tense look, and the lucid, short-sighted eyes, borrowing innocence from spectacles. I expected writers, in fact, to conform to the well-known type which one might call 'the permanent under-graduate'. Auden and Isherwood, from their photographs and their prose styles, seemed to conform to this type. Indeed, it still seems to me that this flippant, abrupt manner (varied by bouts of *very* serious debating-society rhetoric) is one of the safest masks for any creative thinker, these days . . .

But then Miller, as I should have known from his books, does not wear masks. I should have guessed that nobody could dive so deep down, and exist for so long under pressure, among marine monsters, and come up afterwards youthful, sweet, and smiling; I should have expected a battered, swollen, purple face, with the foam paddled over it, water runnelling down the sides of the nose, and the cheeks blown wide with wind. I should have expected this, but I did not; and I was frightened by the bald, ravaged, the terribly and at all points *vulnerable* face I saw.

The great writers of Paris, I suddenly remembered, *have all gone under*—have all sunk very deep, in that strange, that destructive but beautiful sea, that swims around our loins. I remembered a passage in the journal of the Goncourts in which Flaubert boasts how, as a young man, he used to go to the local brothel with his companions, and there pick out the ugliest girl, and demonstrate his prowess in front of his friends, still smoking his cigar and wearing his hat. 'I did this out of vanity,' I think the Goncourts recall him as saying, 'I took no pleasure in it.' And then there was Brantôme, with those astonishing court memoirs of his, the rich, stiff, brocaded Renaissance prose gilding and fantasticating his meagre and ignoble themes. The local rage! Paris is farther from the sea than any city in Great Britain, and in August its heat has a strange oppressive and yet stimulating dryness (I met an Algerian conscript at the baths, who said the greater heat of Algeria was more bearable, because less heavy); in that smouldering atmosphere, under a sky like the roof of an oven, in these streets with their dry, pungent, warm little wafts of chalky dust, of baking bread, of grinding coffee, of spilled petrol, of roses heaped in baskets and withering in the sun, and of scent drying away on women's temples and armpits, it seemed, somehow, extravagantly foolish to attempt to deny or sublimate that local rage . . .

Perhaps, I thought (I was still staring at Miller's photograph), perhaps it *was* foolish. But, after all, there were two sides to the question. How does a man feel when he goes under? Fine! But how does he look when he comes up? On taking in Miller's naked skull, his shapeless, battered, insatiate features, my first reaction was one of incredulity, I could not connect that face with my memory of his beautiful prose. I remembered how, when I had an operation to remove a squint in one eye, and for a fortnight my eyes were in bandages, a nurse with a beautiful, soft Inverness accent moved about the room; her voice charmed me with its sweetness and kindness; and then, when the bandages came off, I found that with the voice went a face not nearly so sweet and kind . . . a face that did not match. So Miller's face in his photograph did not seem to match his voice in my inner ear.

Nietzsche, no doubt, would have described these five minutes of meditation, in front of a bookshop off the Rue de Rivoli, as the meeting of two opposed types, the Dionysian and the Apollonian. In spite of all that local rage, I was, I suppose, even then Apollonian. I was interested in contemplating the finished work of art; in comparison to that, the impressions which the real world offered me seemed shabby, unrewarding, confused . . . and if I was always dreaming of special intimate atmospheres, of wits and beauties, of small talk that would turn itself as if by magic into a philosophical dialogue, that was because I had an instinctive need (if I were to grasp life at all) to make life itself an art, with its own recognisable style: the style of my own age, reflecting certain constant proportions, developing a local tradition, but offering, all the same, its own new emphasis and flavour. I would, as Nietzsche says, have had the vision my imagination conjured up eternal: 'In its light, man must be quiescent, apathetic, peaceful, healed, and on friendly terms with himself and all existence.' Man seems little likely, in our time, to be any of these things; new disasters, as I write, are nosing in on us like icebergs; but all that does not make the vision less true.

And yet the Apollonian, according to Nietzsche, though one can say all that for him, is by way of being a parasite. He is the spectator, the critic, or at most the creator whose work derives more from other art than from personal experience. The Dionysian, the creator as such, is a very different person; not interested in quiescence, apathy, peacefulness, or any of these semi-moral values (they are at least values of *well-being*) at all. He is not even interested, at least not to the same extent as the Dionysian, in the *beauty* of what he creates . . . that beauty is a sort of by-product, like lava (or even like Herculaneum) of a volcano. The Dionysian is chiefly interested in his own volcanic inner upheavals . . . Miller is a test-case for one's attitude in the matter. Is life worth living, in the way that he has lived it, that oppressive submarine existence, for the sake of the results? I think perhaps it is, and yet I feel that in saying this, a critic, like myself, would be at cross-purposes with a creator. Miller is interested in the strange sea in which he has lived, while what captivates me is the incongruous beauty of the fossil mermaids, the purple seaweed, the barnacle-encrusted figureheads which he has retained as souvenirs of his trip. And there is something else that puts creator and critic at cross-purposes. The creator thinks he is saying, 'This is the sort of world it is!' but from the critic's point of view he is saying merely, 'This is the sort of man I am, this is the sort of set in which I move!' The general situation around him is finally his own particular situation. The critic sees this. He tries, inevitably, to map out the objective limits of all these subjective universes; and since no universe likes being limited, the true creator just naturally hates the true critic.

My own feeling about the difficult problem I have been hinting at here is still fundamentally what it was in Paris in 1939. I think the anarchic energies of the vital factors ought to be respected . . . respected because they are not *fundamentally* anarchic, because the most untidy and perverse artist, if his gift and vocation are genuine, and if we neither thwart him too much nor help him too much, but leave him to find his own way home, will in the end produce a vision of order. It is in the light of such visions that the rest of us live, and without them our lives would be meaningless. And the art which embodies such visions is not produced by a reasoning attitude, but by peculiarly complicated patterns of

100

feeling that arise from the impact on us of some massive aspect of nature, our own nature, or the world's. On the other hand, in the bloody and dangerous times we are living in, I think it is the duty of creators, as well as critics, to develop a system of inner checks. I am not sure that such an artist as Miller has ever acquired, or is ever likely to acquire, such a system. In one sense, he is in the tradition of Whitman. Whitman accepted everything in American society and Miller rejects everything. Both, therefore, write with peculiar eloquence about death. For it is only, in the end, death that either accepts or rejects in this wholesale fashion; life is a discriminative process, and both Whitman and Miller, for all their praise of life, are too impatient to discriminate much.

Thus, they think they are praising life, but they are really praising a more fundamental process, the process that brought life into being and may destroy life, the process that crumbles away the profiles of mountains and builds new islands in the caves of the sea; they praise the flux of nature. We are caught in that flux, indeed. But the human image can assert itself significantly only in a certain artificial stillness, against the beat of these tremendous rhythms. And behind the beat of these tremendous rhythms, there may be something still more fundamental: Being or God. For when we say that everything changes, we still find, like Plato, that this, at least, does not apply to the notion of change itself; or if we say that nothing is eternal, that everything crumbles away, somebody may ask us, 'Is not the crumbling away *itself* eternal?' So we find that our thought is forced to transcend the idea of an endless natural flux and to rest in something in which the flux itself must be resting. We come back to the still, composed image in the end.

But, perhaps, after all, moralising to myself in this way, on a hot afternoon in Paris, I was wasting my time? 'In Paris and its neighbourhood,' says Saintsbury, with a delightful insular pompousness, 'morality has seldom been able to make anything like a home.' But art has been able to make a home, all right; and it was art I was after. As I went round the galleries, names that were only familiar counters in books—names that one knew because the best people mentioned them so often—began to acquire meaning for me. In the Luxembourg, for instance, I paused before a little picture, some clumsy elephant-grey pears, placed without recession on an astigmatic tablecloth of an equally uninviting green; and then peering a little more closely, to see who the artist was, 'Ah,' I said with a thrill of recognition— recognition not of a style, but of a name—'ah, a Braque!' And I

101

began to look for the composition, the precise and forcible design, which must, I thought, have made me pause in front of those dull pears on that tedious tablecloth . . . I was fascinated, too, to see a Rouault: a great head of Christ done (I ignorantly thought) as it might be by a clever child, with a very large box of crayons: deep, dark colours, broad lines like the leading that divides pieces of a stained glass window from each other, a peculiar rich splodginess, a naive exaggeration in the drawing and expression: I stared at it for a little, that huge, formless, clumsy, darkly glowing head, and then turned aside to look at some slick nude . . . I felt I was not up to the weight of all that awe and mystery.

The picture in the Luxembourg that I was most pleased to see (still checking up on my literary associations) was Seurat's 'Le Cirque', about which Roger Fry has a wonderful paragraph in *Transformations*. Seurat intended the pattern of upward curves in which this picture is built to suggest gaiety, and Fry says that this is the last emotion it actually suggests. I felt unsure about that— about the effect on my feelings of the clown, the lady on horseback, the rapt, simple-minded spectators, all fitted so exactly, so finally into the queer design. The picture is not melancholy, at least; unless there is an inevitable melancholy in any statement so exact and final. I felt detached, yet sympathetic . . . towards the intense, naive concentration of all the figures in the picture and perhaps of the artist himself, who had done it all, so surprisingly, in a sort of stipple, in little separate spots of colour, which extended beyond the picture to the flat wooden edges of the frame. If not exactly gay, the picture at least was wonderfully elegant, self-sufficient, consciously a little comic in its very extravagant poise: a dandy.

But, of course, the writer of whom I was most reminded in Paris (because I wished to be reminded of him) was Proust: in whose long melancholy masterpiece I had soaked myself, lying on my belly on the lawn at Seafield, through three successive summers. There was a very good French film on in Paris that August, *Régle du Jeu*, directed by Renoir; snobbish, corrupt, tender, subtly humorous, it seemed to me to have Proust's very note. Fundamentally, I fancy, it was a reactionary's film. Its modern feudal argument showed the maid bullying the mistress to come in out of the cold, the valet buttonholing the master, to ask him to stave off a jealous husband. The aristocratic hero collected the toys of the people: fair-ground mechanical organs, with coloured lights and dancing clockwork dolls, which he showed off, with a sweet, sly smile of conscious pride, to his friends. The tinkling, inane tunes from these formed a sort of background to the rather unreal melodrama of the plot. The hero had a mistress, which excused his charming wife (who, of course, really loved him, as he really loved her) for almost eloping with two different people on the same night. One of these suitors was shot, towards the end of the film, not of course by the hero, but by a simple character, a gamekeeper, jealous about his own wife. Very sportingly, the hero hushed this crime up, making it look like an accident. Such little tragedies were 'all in the rules of the game' . . . What was odd, however, was that this film, representing patricians as futile and childlike people, dangerous to others through their childishness, at the same time warmed my heart to them. It did not have the plainly satirical effect of my severely moral description of it. It made its appeal to a common weakness of all unsettled adolescents: the wish to get back and start again from an earlier and simpler stage, the pattern of regression.

And that, of course, is what Proust's great novel is about. Writing it, he found that it was possible, so to say, to have his life over again. And, in a sense, that pattern of regression is also that of the lives of all his characters. The huge, tepid, protected idleness of their lives allows them an unnatural development, like that of forced hothouse flowers. They are more themselves, more the selves of their most intimate and fragile fantasies, than people can ever be, exposed to colder airs and harsher pressures, in an actual world. They may reach the height of elegance like the Duchess of Guermantes or sound the depths of degradation like Charlus. They are full-blown, flower-show specimens in either case, where most of the personalities one meets in the real world are hardy dwarf perennials. For most people to-day, their own personalities and the personalities of their friends are a marginal concern. A life-history is something cut up in discrete chunks: school, an office, a war, a settling down again, a sudden realisation that one is nearing middle age and that nothing that one has lived through seems to belong specially to oneself, that it is all drab and typical. That is why the lives of the idle and the extravagant are so fascinating, why we find ourselves, sometimes, ready to condone frivolity, even corruption. Our own histories remain implicit in us, and there is something wonderful about any personal story, even the saddest, that has been fully told.

Proust's ghost accompanied me to the opera but he would never have climbed, as I did, to the cheapest and highest galleries. At the Opéra Comique, the really overpowering heat at the back of the gallery, and the fact that a pillar blocked my view of the stage, distracted my attention from the prolonged death-bed sentimentalities of poor Mimi. I waited patiently for the intervals, when I could drink a glass of orangeade, and smuggle back a lump of ice in my handkerchief, to mop my face with. At the Opera, for *Lohengrin*, I got a slightly more comfortable seat. There was a charming American girl behind me, who drawled, 'It does turrible things to my liver, but I sorta crave chocolate like a man craves licker.' Later she said thoughtfully, 'I guess Lohengrin turns out to be the swan in disguise . . .' But what really took up my attention, more than my neighbours or the stage, was my general surroundings: the brassy chandeliers, the marble staircases, the pillars, the opulently vulgar gilding, the red plush, all magnificently 1880. I tried to remember whether it was from a box at the Opera, or at the Comédie Française, that the Duchess of Guermantes had first smiled, or refrained from smiling, at the young Marcel.

Then there were the more usual tourists' amusements, the Casino de Paris and the Folies Bergères. I remember talking about these amusements with one of our party, an art student from Edinburgh, but for all his artistic vocation a typical Scottish puritan. The female body, he told me solemnly, was only beautiful at one remove—when put on canvas by the painter, when made safely unreal; so that it became purely a spectacle and ceased to be a temptation. I was not interested in such moral and aesthetic arguments; I found the spectacle of bounding pink girls admirably soothing to my floating libido (some is sublimated, some is concentrated, but some is always left to float). That was the local rage again, and one could not escape from that in Paris; but more general fevers (the omens of war, darkening every day after the Russo-German pact—the news of which I first read, in a glaring headline, over somebody's shoulder in the Metro, the words jerking before my eyes like the advertisements in the tunnel, the repeated *Dubo, Dubon, Dubonnet,* the Breton sailor with his long blond moustaches advertising Caporal cigarettes) drove us all home, a day before our fortnight was up. The deck of the steamer running between Dieppe and Newhaven was crowded, it was a sick journey, and hoarding impressions I felt as futile as a magpie. Paris had impressed me more than the Parisians. Against a background of spectacular avenues, the people in the street had struck me as hot, shabby, dusty, and insignificant. The women were dowdy as often as smart. The waiters had been amiable but grasping; so it had been, too, with the old women who showed us into church pews, or let us climb up monumental towers. Always that waiting hand, always the calculation of ten per cent!

I thought of all this, leaning on the rail, watching the choppy Channel.

'It doesn't matter,' I said, to one of our party, who stood beside me, and with whom I had been talking over these things, 'there is so much else there, they can rest on their oars!'

My friend looked up at a grey sky and shuddered. 'Oh, no,' he said, 'nobody at all, from now on, can rest on his oars.'

4

I volunteered in October, as a 'potential officer', with the thin hope of getting an Infantry Commission. It was not till December 1939 that I was called up, but I had left the *Press and Journal* a month or two earlier, so I enjoyed a last holiday. Once I was in the army, I started thinking of these two years of newspaper work in Aberdeen in a rather sentimental way; and they certainly had a great practical importance in my life, in that during them I learned the elements of a trade which was to stand me in good stead. But there was something unreal about them, all the same. I was performing in a cage, and thought of the cage as freedom. I thought of the war as coming to destroy my freedom, but it was coming, really, to teach me what freedom meant. There is an age at which young people, if they are to form their own characters, must cut clear for a time from their families. If they do not make the break at the right time—in their earliest twenties at the latest—two things happen. They are living at home and working somewhere in their home towns. The work they are doing, at that age, as beginners in some profession, will be comparatively unimportant in itself. The first thing that happens is that the family becomes the place where they shelter from their unimportance. The second thing is that it becomes at the same time the place that cramps them, that stops them from becoming themselves. It gives its love almost too easily, it makes too few demands, and yet it is not, and cannot be, sensitive to the growing-points in the mind. Because I had my family to fall back on, I never made any intimate friends among my fellow reporters in Aberdeen. My world fell into separate halves, 'life' and 'work'. And yet my family could not help with the most important part of my 'life'—the poems and articles I sweated over, to send to Nicholas Moore in faraway Cambridge; it was only, indeed, from

105

Nicholas's occasional letters that I got the kind of advice and encouragement I needed. I hid my serious writings jealously away; they had not the broad and popular touch, there was nothing in them that would ease my way to success, they were simply something that I needed to do. At a practical level, these early poems helped me to resolve emotional conflicts that would otherwise, probably, have been resolved by a nervous breakdown. But that could not be explained to the one circle of people with whom I was always lazy and serene. I came habitually to deprecate my poetry in conversation, to speak of it as an eccentric hobby of mine, like philosophy for Jean, or the cinema for Freddy. The fact that London magazines sometimes took my poems suggested, I would say indifferently, that I was at least fairly efficient at my hobby. But I tried to be dry and sensible in my manners, to avoid everything that would suggest the traditional romantic pose. I wanted nobody in that brisk and practical city to say to me, half with indulgence, half with contempt: 'Oh, George, you poet!'

The more I tried to be natural, the more I must have seemed all stiff pose. I remember one of the last dances I went to. I arrived late. It was in a private house. One girl, Caroline, fair and sturdy, with a strong jaw and a smile like a boy's, was standing by a sideboard as I entered, leaning on the polished wood with her sharp elbows, her square chin on her palms. She was a girl with whom I felt at ease, and once, I remembered, when I had tramped on her toes dancing with her she had said with quite genuine friendliness, 'It is all right, George, you can walk all over me, I am as strong as a rhinoceros.' We moved off now abruptly, alertly to the wakeful music; but (and how typical of me this was!) in the wrong direction, clockwise, just missing the other dancers, coming the other way round the room. 'Whirlwinds go clockwise,' said Caroline thoughtfully, and we found ourselves engaged in a long, solemnly nonsensical conversation about whirlwinds, Caroline mocking my owlishness, and I without the art of glancing off a subject at a tangent. Caroline, however, had that art. 'A new theory of whirlwinds,' she said. 'You must write an article about whirlwinds, George. To go with all the others. The international situation: humph, humph, humph! People's funny hobbies: chatter, chatter, chatter! The great traditions we are fighting for: bowf, wowf, wowf!' I giggled. 'And,' added Caroline, 'you are not in the least really interested, are you, it's not really you, I mean you personally, you are never the least, are you, the least bit involved?' She was rather breathless and, I suddenly saw, a little angry; I stopped giggling, for though this was what I felt privately about my exercises in popular journalism, I was taken aback to find the opinion so heartily shared. Caroline pressed home her advantage. She had a way of disguising a serious statement in an envelope of burlesque. 'But don't get me wrong, George, seriously, seriously, I think your articles are wonderful, I think our policemen are wonderful, I think, don't you, that life, all told, is just *the* most enormous fun!' I could not imitate the run of her patter. 'Enormous, enormous,' I echoed flatly. I found myself a little sulky. 'If the thing is worth doing at all,' I said defensively, 'I do it smoothly enough.' The music came to an end, and I bowed and moved away from her, storing up for consideration what seemed to be her judgment on me—that I was a refined person, with a vulgar talent. And yet as I turned from her, stiff and offended, I remembered how, when I went up to her, and put my right hand under her shoulder, and the fingers of our left hands touched, some consoling shock ran through my young badgered body, some pathos of mine seemed to penetrate her. She had been looking at a picture on the wall, pretending not to notice me approaching her. 'I'm sorry, I didn't notice you,' she had said. She had smiled with the rich smugness of her lie. 'The picture is much more beautiful,' I said gloomily. 'No, George,' she said, 'you are beautiful, too, but differently. More alive. You are alive and that is dead.' But as the image of Caroline, as the puzzle of what we had said to each other, of what we had meant by it, grew more precise in my mind, Caroline, the real unmanageable person, standing a few feet away from me, slowly faded away.

I chose another partner; and I seemed to be caught up in a soothing rather than a distressing dream, on the smooth linoleum, with the carpet up, the furniture back against the wall, the window lined for the black-out, in any pair of soft arms. Nothing seemed distressingly real, except perhaps Caroline; but as if, indeed, a whirlwind had carried her off, she remained for the rest of the evening out of my reach; but I danced a great deal with Oriana, whose tongue ran like clear water over a pebbly bed.

'What are you going to join, George?'

'The infantry.'

'Oh, why not Intelligence?'

'I don't know enough languages . . . I wish I knew German. Quotations, you know. From some little German book that hasn't been done into English yet. Saying man is a carnivorous animal and thought is a treason to his blood. That sort of thing. It would give my articles more weight.'

107

'Oh, but they are weighty. That one on Russia. How do you know so much about Russia?'

'I still owe the Left Book Club seventeen and sixpence . . . Oh, and I talk about these things often. With chaps in the office, you know.'

'I'm sure you don't get your ideas from chaps *in the office*.'

'What are my ideas, Oriana, anyway, what are yours?' The music had stopped now, and we were standing together in a corner. Oriana, like myself, was short-sighted, vain, and had literary ambitions; but she was a decorative creature to have near one, and she would put up, patiently, with my more portentous vein.

I tried to answer my own question. 'Fragments,' I said, 'from lectures at university, half understood. Things read in the papers. Attitudes we have taken over, without testing them, from our parents, as the proper thing. And all that history hands us, the dish we can't refuse.'

'Do you want to refuse it?'

'I find this life quite pleasant. The small room with the carpet up, the gramophone, the young people dancing, the older people looking on. It all seems harmless and steady, doesn't it? Respectability and charm. I wonder, though, but for this war that has come along to break it up, how long we should have gone on with it? Have you noticed how often older people have bad nerves—how good are our nerves, for that matter?—and how many of them drink rather a lot?'

'You mean that the Great War made older people nervous and taught them to drink?'

'It seems a sweet, self-enclosed life for us here. Dances, parties, the movies, picnics on the beach, flirtations. Knowing everybody, that is, half a dozen people, a dozen people, who see each other at regular intervals, who find that reassuring. It gives a frame for our private pictures. But what do the really ambitious, the really clever get out of it? Why are so many people excited and enlivened by the prospect of this new war?'

Oriana's attention was straying a little, towards more lively admirers on the other side of the room.

'Are you saying something awfully'—at the 'awfully' she put up her hand, and politely stifled a yawn—'deep, George?'

'War lends an interest, that's all I am saying. Has peace a public interest for us? Do people keep together, as they grow older, for friendship or reassurance? My old friend finds this life worth living, and therefore so should I. But I am not sure that I do really, often. What would the interest be, anyway? I am a man of substance, say, in this city. I hold on to the substance, I let the rest drift. And if I am not a man of substance, it is harder to see what my stake is . . .'

'People are nice, life is nice, George.'

'Wearisome, sometimes, I think. Listen. The music has started again. Let us dance.'

We moved off.

'What would the interest be, anyway, George, what would the interest be?'

'Listen to the music, the music, Oriana . . . I must try to keep time.'

5

I was called up in December. I was to be trained in Perth. And it was a dark and dreary afternoon when my train pulled out of the Aberdeen main line station; my last impressions were waving hands, the proximity of tears, the smell of salted herrings in wooden boxes. The train, screaming under a tunnel, was a birth trauma; and I felt, like the newborn infant, that I wanted to open my mouth and scream. There were too many people in the carriage—its windows painted blue for the blackout—for that. I sat back, feeling an uneasiness in my diaphragm, an unsteadiness in my hands. When I reached Perth, a pitchblack night had fallen, and I had the sense, trudging up the hill towards the barracks, of a world new, cold and quite ineffably sinister.

Breaking In

1

DECEMBER was a bad month to join the Army in. We would march three miles, out to the butts, through the heavy slush; and stand there, for half an hour, watching the mist fall more and more heavily, till it completely shrouded the targets, two hundred yards away. No shooting that afternoon. With blue fingers, we crowded round the lorry, half way up the hill, for our mugs of tea and cold mutton pies. And on other bleak afternoons, we were sent out on runs round town, in sandshoes and singlets, up on our toes; my ankles wobbled, my heart pounded, my cheeks were purple, and my companions cast me pitying sidelong glances. 'Break off, you can't stand it,' they said. I never broke off. I kept up with the others somehow, at a gasping hobble. 'You've got guts, anyway', someone said to console me. 'Yes,' someone else said, 'but all your guts are in the wrong place . . .' My courage, indeed, was in my conscious will; my body was a bad servant.

The hours I dreaded most, in the barracks at Perth, were those in the gymnasium. So singularly ill-coordinated were my movements that my feet would clap together, six inches off the floor, at the same time as my hands. The gym corporals would stop the general performance and make me do this again, alone, unable to believe their eyes. Drill on the square sometimes produced similar triumphs; I discovered one day that I was swinging my right arm forward at the same time as I moved forward my right leg. And there was always something wrong about my buttons, the way I had strapped my equipment on, or the angle of my cap. The instructor of our platoon, a fine old regular sergeant, became fascinated with me. His appearance, a striking one, reminded me of the traditional representations of the devil: a dead pale face, thick black eyebrows, curling upwards and outwards, a pointed, cleft chin, and crystal eyes, that retained, at the heart of the crystal, an icy reflection of the infernal fires. He had a soft Highland voice that made his gibes more scathing, and used to refer, for instance, to 'my friend, Private Fraser, who looks, this morning, rather like something deposited

110

on the square by the cat'. He taunted me once into taking part in an intercompany boxing match, and afterwards, as I leant over a bucket, bleeding profusely from the nose, he was grudgingly friendly. 'You have no sense at all of how to defend yourself, Private Fraser, but, man, you did stand up to your punishment.' He was a person of charm, originality, and character, but I was in no position to appreciate these qualities. His was the last face I saw, and the last voice I heard, when I finally left Perth to join the RASC in the south of England, and our relief at parting was mutual. 'Ah, Private Fraser,' he said, 'so we lose you at last?'

I did not spend very much time drilling on the square, or in ordinary infantry training, though the experience while it lasted had the quality of an eternity of humiliation rather than of time. I was soon edged off into a job in a Company office, and the Company moved, with the coming of spring, a mile or two out of Perth, to encamp in the grounds of Scone Park. Near water and trees and tall damp grass, I began to feel a passive animal happiness. I shared a tent with all the oddments of the Company, cook's assistants, messengers, orderlies—mostly old regulars with long crime sheets, liable to push off home at week-ends without leave; but I found them more congenial than the hearty stockbrokers and rubber planters from Malaya, with their smart commercial slang, their nervous cockiness, their manly obscenities, and their slightly spurious gentility. I listened patiently to the stories told to me by my newer companions, about detention barracks, about tramping the streets in search of work in their sour civilian days, about the relish, for a hungry man, of a hunk of bread and dripping and a mug of cocoa at a Salvation Army hostel; I sympathised with the man from the travelling circus, wistful for the fun-fair and the three-card trick and the caravans, and nursing an injured hand; I shaved with a razor blade the callouses on the red fingers of another soldier, whose eyes had a suspicious, affectionate look, and who at week-ends either overstayed his leave or came back to camp late, melancholy, and drunk. For another poor wretch I composed letters to his family in the slums of Glasgow, with whom he always quarrelled when he went to see them. And I lent half-a-crown here, a shilling there, which were always paid back promptly on payday, which was Friday, and usually asked for again on Saturday or Sunday . . .

In the end, I was separated from these picaresque companions. I slept near a telephone in the Company office, listening for air raids. There never were any, except one night when a stray

111

bomber dropped three incendiaries in a neighbouring potato field. In the tall grass, with the trees round us, the real war came near only occasionally: as when from the loudspeaker in the NAAFI tent, I heard Churchill thundering: 'As the will of God is in heaven, so let it be!'

My sense of peace at Scone Park was that of a convalescent. When I went to sleep at night, I was again back in the barracks at Perth, sweating and blundering through my training. A thin stream divided the two parts of the barracks; one morning (and often afterwards in sleep) I stood on the little bridge across that stream, and, looking down saw rusty kettles, an odd boot, and old tins covered with sodden paper out of which the water had soaked the colour and the print. A piece of cardboard came floating down under the bridge. Then, looking a little farther down the stream, I saw a terribly bored swan; it just sat there on the water, pecking fitfully at the strong triangle of muscle between its wings . . . That scene mingled in my dreams with a more consoling scene, when, on a day of suicidal melancholy, I stood on one of the bridges in Perth across the grey, monotonous Tay; just above a little island in midstream, covered in winter with withered rushes. I felt for a moment like hurling myself across the parapet. I left the bridge, strolled farther along the bank, and there were other swans, with their trite, assuaging grace, and a duck with a red bill and an emerald collar round its neck; and seeing life taking such a pleasant, harmless shape, I faltered in my resolution. Certainly, in these months, as a writer I had been like the first swan. It was not that things lacked interest, but that the interest (like that of all the junk rusted and rotted underneath the water) was of an unnourishing sort. I had the sense of being in the wrong stream; and I saw no way of reaching the river.

It was strange, for instance, to look up from my typewriter, to the three gibbets across the grass, where the squads were at bayonet drill. From each gibbet hung a sack stuffed with straw. In threes, brown figures advanced towards the sacks. They advanced at the 'On guard!', took a sudden leap, pointed, withdrew, on guard again, and passed: three paces past, they came to the high port, then turned about, and on guard again. The sacks bled straw. Some movements of bayonet drill were like ballet. One in particular seemed to me to have the beautiful kind of slow-motion inevitability about it of a cinema camera analysing the motions of an athlete. The bayonet is pointed at your heart: with your elbow, you thrust it aside, at the same time stepping forward, and bringing your own bayonet up over your

112

left shoulder your butt smashes in your enemy's face; as he stumbles, you bring your hands forward, and the edge of the blade slashes his skull; and then as he falls your hands continue their uninterrupted movement downwards and the point is at his belly. But if this movement is like ballet, the response to it is like pantomime. As the butt comes thrusting at your face, you drop your own rifle like a red-hot poker, grab your enemy's, and bring your clumpy army boot up to kick him in the crotch . . . War is not an art. It has no unity of tone.

2

And yet I was beginning to move out into the great river. I had fallen in with some other poets. An old friend of mine from St Andrews took me round to see Willie Soutar, one of the great figures of the Scottish revival of letters in this century; a poet rather too prolific, and when he wrote in standard English rather lacking a sense of idiom: but, at his best, lyrical and pathetic in his own Scots tongue—a purer lyrical poet, it seemed to me, in the narrower sense, than his master, Hugh MacDiarmid, whose impatient mind and irascible temper rarely permitted him merely to make a song. Soutar wrote too much poetry partly because there was so little else for him to do. He had been bed-ridden for many years. He lay supported on pillows in a long room, with a large window facing him, the walls at the sides of his bed lined from floor to ceiling with books; there was a large mirror at a sloping angle over his head, in which he could watch his friends' faces as he talked to them. He had long black hair, and a pallid face, in which the sweetness of his thought battled with and conquered pain. His voice was very soft and gentle and when he spoke to me (instinctively in English, not in the Lallans he used with my friends), it had a pleasantly old-fashioned turn of phrase. 'I like your notices,' he would say, meaning my reviews in some obscure, small magazine, which almost certainly nobody else in Scotland had read. In that long room, where we all instinctively lowered our voices a little, it was strange what a grasp he kept of the proportions of the outer world. It was natural, of course, that he should read a great deal; but what struck me was the shrewdness of his opinions, and the fact that the young friends with whom I visited him—Iain Christie, who had been business manager of the St Andrews' student magazine, *College Echoes*, in the year when I was editor, and the young St Andrews poet, Tom

113

Scott—turned readily to him for practical advice. Iain, indeed, had almost too small a sense of the sick-room. He would be slow and quiet when he first sat down in Soutar's room, but, being naturally an eager and bustling person, he would soon be pouring out his views with a hoarse and stammering conviction, and I remember once, when we were discussing Scottish poets, he blurted out (being one of those who took the side of Edwin Muir against Christopher Grieve in a great debate on the Scottish tradition that had been going on for about twenty years), 'Oh, MacDiarmid's daft!' MacDiarmid was Soutar's great master and model. A brick had been dropped. But Willie Soutar, who was used to Iain's ebullience, forced a smile, and went on talking in his humorous, soothing voice of something else. I wish I could recall more of his talk, which was marked by a homely sense of character and scene; one glimpsed through his words the Scottish landscape out of which (and, less certainly, out of his books) he had made his poems; and one thought of how long ago it was since, with the eyes of the body, he had glimpsed that landscape himself. He remained in my mind as a symbol of courage.

With Tom Scott, whom I met through Iain Christie on the occasion of my first visit to Willie Soutar, I formed a close friendship. He was the first writer of verse I had met who corresponded to the traditional romantic conception of what a poet should be. And traditionally romantic things were always happening to him; if he strolled along the banks of the Tay by himself, three naked young women would scramble out of the water and dash past him to their clothes hidden in the bushes; or he might come on a drowning man, going down for the last time; and if he picked up a girl at a dance, she would prove to be a gypsy, and would tell him all the folklore of her people. To see him turning a street corner in Perth—his hands thrust out in front of him, waist high, as if groping through an invisible thicket—was to recognise a visionary. He had the air of making an entrance (he would be singing to himself, in his vibrant tenor voice, some old Scots song) and the plain old houses immediately began to resemble the backcloth of a stage. Indeed, it was Tom's ambition to be an opera singer, and, neither handsome nor ugly, but very striking-looking, he habitually made the most dramatic use of his physical characteristics. He was tall and lean, and his body would sway forward from the heels, but be jerked back again by the countertilt of his flaming bushy head; his high nose, with nostrils like a horse's, seemed always to be snuffing the wind; his tight thin mouth curled readily in irony; and his voice, even when he was making the most ordinary statements, had a harsh tremor. Yet there was something kind, homely, and shrewd in his nature, that came from his working-class background—a stonemason by trade, he had given up his job a month or two before being called up, so that he could concentrate on his poetry. I turned to him in these summer months in Perth for excitement; he had the good sense to see that excitement was not what I needed, and would settle down with me, over endless cups of tea, to gossip, or to an examination of my poems (poems not romantic or lyrical enough for his own taste). We would 'tear fowks to bits'—examine the weaknesses of our common friends in Perth—and tear each other's poems to bits, too; though poems and friends, in the long run, somehow came together; I would trudge back to Scone Camp, late at night, feeling calm and soothed.

If Tom was a godsend to me, I often wonder whether I was a godsend to him. He felt guilty about trying to be a poet, since it meant uprooting himself from his background and becoming that contemptible middle-class thing, an individualist. My own tradition, after all, was the middle-class one and to break away, to make a name for myself, seemed to me moral duties; I failed to grasp the wrench that such an attitude implied for Tom, and—since it was the English poetic tradition, not the Scots one, that he was in love with—I encouraged him to transplant himself to London, not doubting at all that he would take root there. Yet when I came back in 1945 from my service in the Middle East, I found him, settled certainly in London, but not thriving there. I had meanwhile made a small reputation for myself, gathered a group of friends round me, published a volume of poems; Tom seemed just as I had left him, four years before. He was too intrinsically Scottish, too proud and intractable, to accommodate himself to the casual and off-hand gregariousness of London literary life, at the bohemian level. He liked personal relationships to be intense and sincere, talk to be an unburdening and a commitment. He was harried, too, by a strict social conscience. He had been trying to get a volume of his poems published, with no success; I looked through the selection he had made and found out that he had omitted what I considered his three or four best lyrics. 'Oh, these!' he said dourly. 'I thought these were morally defeatist!' I remembered how his singing of Burns and the ballads had been the first thing that had made me understand the Lowland Scots tradition; how, in the atmosphere of Perth in 1940, he had been a symbolic figure for all scruffy, uprooted intellectuals in khaki like myself; and how (as he told me) on being transferred to an English unit, in Manchester, he had felt his significance shrinking . . . he was no longer the poet of his unit, a voice for his fellow soldiers, but merely a rawboned Scot, out of place. My own case was so completely different; it was only after I left Scotland that I began to find my feet. Tom, perhaps, should have stayed in Scotland, once he got out of the army; even, perhaps, taken up his old trade again; in encouraging him to try his fortunes in London, had I sent him after a mirage? I should have encouraged his sense of local piety . . . Or should I? Perhaps in saying this, I am thinking too much of mere outward success. Yet I think even a very good poet needs a little of this, at some time; or he will turn in on himself.

My arguments with Tom grew specially lively over things I found time to write in that summer of 1940. I wrote a long preface for Henry Treece's and J. F. Hendry's anthology, *The White Horseman,* a preface that became one of the main platforms for the movement which was first called the Apocalypse and later, when it absorbed a wider stream of tendencies, the New Apocalypse. It was a confused movement, springing from a confused reaction; but it was not the product of a *clique.* About half a dozen young poets had, at the same time, and quite independently of each other, come to the same cross-roads; I myself, for instance, had not met Hendry and Treece in these days, and I have not met them even now. We were scattered all over Great Britain, and were soon to be scattered over several continents. We were people of different temperaments, contrasting principles, but what we had in common was a feeling that the prevailing tone of English poetry in the 1930s no longer rang true. The most important English poets of the 1930s (with the two exceptions, themselves precursors of our own reaction, of George Barker and Dylan Thomas) had been brought up as members of the English ruling class; their background was that of the public schools and major universities, their moral strength was in touching the uneasy consciences of young men of their own class, rather than that, say, of the industrial workers, who, in any case, would tend to take the Socialist position for granted, and would not be interested in the bad conscience of the ruling class, unless that resulted in some obvious practical benefit.

Thus, though the poets of the 1930s were sincerely concerned with 'social awareness', there were important elements in the feeling of the country with which they were out of touch. There could not, for instance, be a more striking contrast than that between the atmosphere of spies, feuds, conspiracies, the boy's

116

adventure story, in many of the earlier poems of Auden, Spender, and Day Lewis, and the progress towards power in this century— flat-footed, perhaps, but sure-footed, too—of the British Labour movement. There could not be a greater contrast, either, than that between the stretched, heroic tone of the poetry that was written in the 1930s about the Spanish Civil War and the glum, dour patience that was needed by a young soldier who was to serve throughout the war against Hitler; I expressed the feeling that many of my contemporaries had when I spoke, in a poem I wrote in the summer of 1940, of accepting a 'just and necessary servitude': of accepting humiliation, boredom, and unending petty frustrations. It was impossible, after Dunkirk, to feel that our national tradition was as rotten as the poets of the 1930s (looking at slums, unemployment, the ruthless war against culture conducted by the popular press, and the vacillations of our foreign policy) had made out. Somehow, unexpectedly, we had pulled ourselves together; even from the point of view of 'social awareness', a certain reaction against the Auden manner was called for.

Tom Scott I took as representative of all that was most alert and sensitive in Scottish working-class feelings, and after a decade in which 'poetry had been taken off its pedestal', he wanted to set it back there again; when I quoted Eliot's remark to him about poetry having to be at least as well written as prose, he yawned, and said he liked poetry to be 'poetic'. So I wrote my manifesto, full of rash generalisations, and even rasher bets on budding talents. It has pursued me down the years—John Waller, boggling at the word 'Apocalyptic', once described me as an 'Apocryphal poet', but it did not, I think, arrest my development. I was not to be taken in by my own plausibilities. I went on writing the poems I would have written anyway; so did Tom Scott, who also contributed to *The White Horseman*, and so did Nicholas Moore. The New Apocalypse was like a cross-roads through which we passed before setting out in our separate directions; but Treece and Hendry, I sometimes thought, as I read their later work, had remained there, desperately marking time and thwarting their natural growth. They remained too conscious of their position as leaders of a group, even when the best of their followers had deserted them.

The experience (and the banter to which I was later subjected on account of my preface, by poets in Cairo) made me, in the end, suspicious about the usefulness of groups, movements, and manifestoes to British letters. The French thrive on these, but it seems to me that in our country the good poet always advances on his individual front. When a good poet in our language is able to define what he is doing, he has finished doing it; he must go on to something else. Whatever can be reduced to formula is fake. I know this is so in my own case; I feel, not see, whether my writing comes off or not; I grope with a sort of blind tact, I slap my sentences for a hollow ring . . . I write too much, since I write for a living, and I have written some things that *are* hollow; but now and again I know (without being able to explain at all how) that a poem or a page of prose is just as it should be.

Tom, though he contributed poems to *The White Horseman* and discussed my preface with me, did not approve of the New Apocalypse or of my having a hand in it; yet without him, I would probably never have wanted to have a hand. He made me accept for a time a romantic attitude that was not natural to me but which I needed, at that time, as a contrast to the life around me. Yet that was not the main thing I got from him, or his friendship would not have been so important to me. He knew that ordinary life needs to be dramatised a little, if it is to be tolerable, but he was an enemy of my tendency to turn away altogether from ordinary life. Once, late at night, I went with him to a church canteen. We had been walking along the Tay, and swimming in it, we were hungry, and I felt fatigued. I sat on a crowded bench, listening with distaste to the loud, unmodulated voices, to the obscene epithets mechanically repeated before every noun—slightly bowdlerised in a church canteen, so that everything was 'ruddy' or 'blooming' or 'ropy'—and watched a voracious bandboy cramming the last of a cheese sandwich down his throat with a forefinger. A gramophone was playing some stupid tune. 'Tom,' I said, 'I wish I didn't have to live among these people, to watch them. They are disgusting.' 'It is you who are disgusting, George,' said Tom, grimly. I pulled myself together. Of course, he was right . . .

Tom was right to be afraid of breaking his roots. After he was posted to Manchester, melancholy and silence descended on him, he ceased to answer my letters, he was posted to West Africa and finally invalided out, and I lost touch with him wholly till, in 1946, I found him selling books—a seasonal rush job—behind the counter of a big department store in Kensington. Perth, and also my own writing, seemed to lose interest once he went. But in a few weeks, I myself was posted south to train as an RASC clerk. The days were monotonous and my new companions, with one or two exceptions, not congenial. The skies at night, at Weybridge and Woking, were a lovely pattern of crisscrossing searchlights, falling incendiaries, bursting flares; I looked at it with indifference, as if the sky were a screen on which there had been projected the jaggedness of my own nerves. I slept soundly, unlike many of my fellows, while the anti-aircraft guns thudded through the night. That mood of strange detachment remained with me till, at the end of the year, I left England. I was in London on the night of the greatest incendiary raid. Everything had been quiet, dark, and then suddenly bridges, buildings, statues glared out in savage white profile. I could have loitered and watched it as a spectacle, but I had come in to town that Sunday without a pass, and had to get back to Woking before the last roll-call. I was with a friend. Incendiaries had landed on the roof of our main station, but we got a bus that was picking up soldiers and caught the train farther out. When we reached Woking, we were told that an unexploded bomb was blocking the main road to the barracks. A private car with a soldier in it had stopped at a cross-roads. I opened the back door and we got in. 'Can you take us back with you to the barracks?' I said. We made it with five minutes to spare. Looking back, I realise that I was more worried at the probability of being put on a charge than at the possibility of being killed.

That mood of apathy did not last. We went overseas at the end of the year and in the spring of 1941 I was a clerk in GHQ in Cairo. The new scene around me was fascinating and I started to make friends once more; I disliked my work but in a month or two, by a stroke of luck, I was posted to *Parade*, the Middle East Army magazine. Like a Fury I began to write for it, and from then on my army fortunes started to look up.

s.s. *City of Benares*
(*Drowned refugee children, 1940*)

The bell that tolls my syllables can tell
An underwater tale, clang how there fell
Suddenly out of a surface shouting world
Into dumb calm doomed children, and there curled
(Currents' sick fingers whispering at their hair)
Round them a coiling clutch, was our despair.
Sea's soft sad pressure, like the sprawl of love,
Darkly spreadeagled, so they could not move,
The wide wet mouth was heavy, they would choke,

Till in that cold confusion pity spoke:
'This is a nightmare and one is asleep.
This is a dream, my brave one, do not weep,
Often may drown in dreams and not be dead:
Such weight is mother leaning on your bed.'

But having thought of this to cheat my pain,
That woe and wonder harrows me again,
Fat clouds seem bulked like whales, while through the green
Grave tons of twilight, in a submarine
Solidity of air like sea I move,
Pressure of horror how our hate hurts love.
Deeper than grief can plummet, mercy lies,
But not so deep as trust in children's eyes,
Justice is high in heaven, but more high
Blood of the innocent shall smear the sky—
Or think that red the flame of seraph wings,
See stained-glass heaven, where each darling sings
In God's dark luminous world of green and gold
As lovely as death's waters, but less cold:
Think what you will, but like the crisping leaf
In whipped October, crack your thoughts to grief.
In the drenched valley, whimpering and cold,
The small ghosts flicker, whisper, unconsoled.

3

When I think of Cairo, now, I think of something sick and dying;
an old beggar, propped up against a wall, too palsied to raise a
hand or supplicate alms; but in a passive way he can still enjoy the
sun . . . But who can possess a city? Who can possess it, as he
possesses his own body, so that a vague consciousness of its
proportions is always in his mind? When Harry Boyle, who had
been one of Lord Cromer's chief assistants, came back to Cairo in
1921—a figure in shocking, loose untidy clothes, with a drooping
moustache, plodding painfully, as I used to plod, through the
afternoon heat—he paused near the Bulac Bridge, and looked
around him helplessly. 'Your Excellency should know this street,'
said a policeman. 'You lived in it for twenty years.'

There would have been new buildings, shops, and blocks of
flats; but that would not be all of it; every street in Cairo has the
character of Cairo, but hardly any street has the character of

120

itself. Everything, every note that at first seems distinctive, is repeated again and again. The tenement which is crumbling away at one side, like a rotted tooth; the native restaurant, open to the night, from which there comes a soft clapping of palms on tables and a monotonous chanting; the maze of narrow streets that leads to a cul-de-sac, where a taxi has gone to die; the sudden green and red glitter of lights, glimpsed through a curtain, from a cabaret; the sudden patch of green wasteland, the glimpse of the river, the white glitter of buildings on the other side, the curved masts of the feluccas, pulled down at the top as if by invisible strings; these things, and not things only, but people and incidents, are repeated; the baldish purple-looking ox that has collapsed in the gutter and is having its throat cut; the street accident with twenty shouting spectators in white galabyehs; the woman in black, sitting on the pavement, nursing her baby at a dusty breast; the legless beggar propelling himself forward, on a little wooden trolley, with frightful strength, with his hands. Unknown districts of Cairo, as I used to pass them on the crowded, clattering trams, would terrify me; so much suffering, unexplored, inarticulate life. I used to go out to visit a friend in Shubra, rather far from the centre of the city. I knew where to get off the tram because beside the stop there was a great heap of pots beside a patch of wasteland; but if somebody had moved the pots, I would have been completely lost. Even as it was, when I had dismounted from the tram, I had to make my choice between three almost exactly similar sidestreets, each with a large tree beside its narrow entrance. No, I did not possess Cairo; Cairo possessed me.

Yet people can find their way about London south of the Thames or about the slums of Glasgow. And Cairo probably seemed to me a more confusing city than it really is because I saw it through a haze of heat and odours—the smells of spice, of cooking fat, of overripe fruit, of sun-dried sweat, of hot baked earth, of urine, of garlic, and, again and again, too sweet, of jasmin; a complex that, in the beginning of the hot weather, seemed to melt down to the general consistency of smouldering rubber . . . a smell of the outskirts of hell. Ceasing, soon, consciously to notice all this, I would sometimes, in the Garden City near the Embassy, pass a lawn of thin, patchy grass that had just been watered through a sprinkler; and I would realise, for a moment, how parched and acid my nostrils were. The smell of the Nile itself, of course, was different; by its banks, at night, there was a damp, vegetative coolness, that seemed to have, in a vague,

121

evocative way, something almost sexual about it. And it was voluptuousness, in a cool, large room, to bend over and sniff, in a glass bowl on a table, at a crisp red rose. But in such a room there would be European women; and their skins would have dried a little, in that cruel climate, and one would be aware of their powder, and their scent. Beauty, whether of body or character, lay, in that city, under a constant siege. In my memory, that hot, baked smell prevails; that, and the grittiness—the dust gathering thickly on the glossy leaves of the evergreens, and the warm winds stinging eyes and nostrils with fine sand—and the breathlessness, the inner exhaustion. Under the glaring day, one seemed to see the human image sagging and wilting a little, and expected sallow fingers and faces to run and stretch, as if they were made of wax.

In fact, against the background of Cairo, about so many of my friends, as I remember them, there was a garishness—a flourish and ostentation of every eccentric quality, that had often a deadness about it, exactly like that of posed waxwork figures. That inner exhaustion from which we all suffered affected that side of each of us that can be called the actor—the side of critical self-awareness—rather than the other side, that can be called the character. We were all too much 'in character', predictable in our responses; and these tended to be violent and shallow. Cairo was a place of quarrels and the making up of quarrels, of rows at parties, of little rival gangs, not a matter of these quiet and steady dislikes, and settled loyalties, that are a normal part of the British character. Partly this was due to the climate, partly to the intimacy of a small community, where everybody knew everybody else's weaknesses and where a passion for gossip, shared by us all, sooner or later brought to one's ears every unkind remark that had been made about one. Between rows, one might meet one's enemies over a drink, and seem to be getting on well; a gathering, on the other hand, consisting of one's friends of the moment, would often break up (when heavy drinking had broken down too many reticences) in bickering; so there was a constant shifting of alliances, and every friendship had its background of resentments and reconciliations. These tendencies were general, but they were accentuated in the circle in which I chiefly moved, one of journalists, writers, artists, each anxious to be admired and liked. Inner anxiety or boredom led to extravagant behaviour which aroused malicious comment; malicious comment led to quarrels which made a man shift from one group to another, leaving him, for a short time, in a state of isolation; isolation, in its turn, conduced to anxiety and boredom, and the wheel had come full circle.

I did not immediately sense this atmosphere; it belonged rather to my second period in Cairo, towards the end of the war. During my first period I was being driven hard by my Scottish social conscience. When my daily work was over I was to be found mostly at soldiers' clubs, helping to edit an unofficial magazine (very dull it was, too), taking part in debates, or giving talks, across a great gulf, about modern poetry. A soldier would get up and ask me why modern poets did not write something simple and moving, like 'Underneath the Arches'. A fat, pink officer (with a rather sheeplike baa and moustaches like the Golden Fleece) would read out long passages of Rupert Brooke, as an example of how to do it, and short passages of Mr Eliot, as an example of how not to. Communist soldiers would make, very briskly, the point that the poems I was reading reflected the culture of our present society, and that the masses did not want to acquire that culture, since it merely reflected the balance of pressures that held them down. They would create their own new culture, springing from a social order not based on the oppression of one class by another. I would shrug my shoulders at that, and say, 'You are fools if you think you can break quite clean away from the past.' But the past, they would say, was surely just what had landed us in our present fix—years of insecurity and mass unemployment, followed by a great war. The argument would continue amiably enough, afterwards, over cups of coffee, but I had a feeling of offering them something that they did not want. I should take a stand, my friends hinted, for some positive or passionate set of beliefs: Communism or Roman Catholicism, it hardly mattered which . . . what could be more tepid and negative than my old-fashioned liberal attitude of mind?

I escaped sometimes from these tasks of popular education, into more exciting company. There were in Cairo at that time a number of young poets, in civilian jobs, whose work I knew and admired. Lawrence Durrell, who had escaped to Egypt from Greece in a small open boat, was working at the Publicity Section of the Embassy. He was then not generally known, but I had come across a few pieces of his in Nicholas Moore's *Seven*, and they had excited me. In a threadbare time the nap of his prose was almost indecently thick; here, I said to myself, is a sumptuous writer, and that impression was confirmed by his early poems and by his novel, *The Black Book*, published in Paris and owing something to Henry Miller. Yet temperamentally Durrell was obviously a very different man; there was less spontaneous rhetoric in *The Black Book* than in, say, *Tropic of Cancer,* and much more conscious contrivance. I lingered especially over one or two meditative passages in a magnificently ornate style. Everything that Durrell wrote had a strong natural vitality that did not so much pour itself forth as work itself into a consciously elaborate texture of style. There was the same mixture of gross health and masterful artifice in some pages of *The Black Book* that one admires, for instance, in the painting of Rubens; and though Durrell was by no means unaffected by the melancholy of our time, that did not express itself in him, as it does in so many of us, as sag and hesitation. I fancy that my own sag and hesitation were wearisome to him when we first met; and, though he liked some of my poems, he hated my journalism, especially when I tried to introduce his work and that of such friends of his as Bernard Spencer and Terence Tiller to the wide army audience for which I was writing. He found my anxiousness to bridge cultural gaps dreary, and my 'personal touches' exasperating. 'The trouble with you, George,' he once wrote to me, 'is your vulgar sub-editor's interest in whether the poet picks his nose or not.' He once tore up something I had written about him, with the remark, 'Little poetasters making publicity for themselves out of their acquaintance with *great poets!*' I felt drawn to him, and also that I was a nuisance to him; this kept our relationship on a certain level of awkwardness, though when we did meet he was kind. He was a small, burly man, with a round comedian's face, and a light voice that fluted away in unexpected malicious phrases; monopolising every conversation, without appearing to do so, he could make an evening magically entertaining. He, for his part, can hardly have found me entertaining; he got angry with the gaps in my experience that made me behave in a juvenile way. On the whole, he showed as much patience with me as I deserved. He occasionally rapped my knuckles, even in print; but he exuded a kind of well-being that made me forget, when I met him, my resentments. It is not very common to meet a person of rare gifts who is in harmony with himself.

Another Cairo intellectual of that period, Reggie Smith, a great, brawny, black-browed man, who was extremely generous to me, used to call Durrell 'the magician': not that, being a combative rationalist himself, he really approved of Durrell's magic. For Reggie there had not really been a poet worth talking about since Auden and MacNeice, and he felt that poetry had gone off the rails since it had ceased to concern itself primarily with the social situation and the political struggle. He used to twit me mercilessly about *The White Horseman,* but he once rather weakened the effect of these energetic and sensible criticisms of his, by producing for my inspection a poem of his own, beginning, incredibly, 'H. copped it at Sidi Rezegh . . .' In the first place, why 'H.'? It is like these Victorian short stories that begin, 'In the great city of L—, in the year 18—.' If the man's name was Harry, call him Harry; if you do not want to use his name, call him 'he'. And why 'copped it'? That is a very archaic piece of slang; people do not use it, except perhaps in novels of the 1914-18 war, where the characters keep 'a stiff upper lip'. H. *got his* at Sidi Rezegh, if you like, but I think most soldiers would merely say he was killed. Yet though this little poem started off so confidently on the wrong foot (and I always thought of Reggie as a naturally sensitive man with blunt fingers), there was an effective image at the end, comparing the poet holding back his tears to a man trying to keep the bubble balanced in a spirit-level.

Reggie's kindness to me was all the more admirable in that, if he was no enthusiast for Durrell's poems, he was even less so for mine. He thought I had a minor, imitative talent and in an article in *Horizon* his wife, the novelist Olivia Manning, described me as writing 'pleasant Georgian verses'. I had a greater need, in these days, of kindness than of praise, and I felt at ease with Reggie; I liked his boxer's burliness, his pleasant, asymmetrical face, the eyes that saw so much behind their thick glasses, and his habit of singing folk songs to himself. Reggie's perpetual heartiness might give one, at a first meeting, an impression that he was a *faux bonhomme,* but one soon realised that he had strong principles, both about politics and about literature. They often led him to say severe things; but these were said to one's face, they were not personal in their intent and did not have an estranging effect. With his wife I was not so much at ease, nor was she so patient with me. She, too, had a fascinating appearance; slim and tubular, with a face at once oval and birdlike, whose pattern she completed with a turban, so that an artist of the school of Wyndham Lewis might have drawn her as a swathed, beaked egg balanced on a cylinder. Indeed, at a very early stage of our acquaintance I put myself in the wrong with Olivia. She had written a striking novel about the days of the Black and Tans in Ireland, and she showed me a book of manuscript poems, including several Irish revolutionary ones, which she had copied out when she was a schoolgirl. 'I suppose,' I said unthinkingly, 'towards the end of the last war?' Olivia, who in fact at this time was in her early thirties, was offended at a conjecture that added ten years or more to her age. Drinking late one night with Reggie in his flat, I tried to placate her, as she hovered ominously around, by quoting Byron,

> She walks in beauty like the night
> Of cloudy climes and starry skies
> And all that's best of dark and bright
> Meet in her aspect and her eyes,

but without, I fancy, very much effect.

I met Reggie and Olivia through the poet John Waller, then a lieutenant in an RASC water provision unit, some miles out of Cairo – 'waiting', as he put it, 'to lead my water tanks into action'. John was a link between the world of the civilian intellectuals in Cairo, in which I always felt an intruder, and my own shabby and harassed barrack-room existence. He would come into Cairo now and then in a truck, have dinner with me, and then late at night, with two or three bottles of beer under our arms, we would burst in on Bryn Davies and Reggie and Olivia, who, all having quiet, early-to-bed habits, were disconcerted to see us. John, in these days, at a first glance looked pink, hot, vague, slightly crumpled; with pebbly blue eyes and fluffy fair hair. Then one noticed that he had an unusually handsome face, marred by certain lines of indecision—as if he found it hard to decide whether he was enjoying himself or not—and by the faintly fretful and abstracted look that goes with the serious pursuit of pleasure; there is a similar expression in some of the portraits of Rochester. John, though not always fretful, did seem always a little abstracted; he was ready to talk, but when other people were talking, his eyes wandered and he stifled a yawn. He hated conversation on general topics but loved the sort of gossip in which people display not only their victims but themselves comically in character. When one was alone with him, he often seemed tired and flat, but when we were joined over a bar or a restaurant table by one or two new faces (any new faces, it did not matter particularly whose) he sparkled like an actor when the house fills up. He was most himself when he had the chance to throw himself into an artificial, public personality; he was happier with acquaintances than friends. It was not easy for him to be quietly intimate; as he told his long, elaborate, and often bawdy stories—interspersed with coarse sniggers—I watched his long, graceful hands with gnawed nails,

126

moving around nervously, touching things, expressing thoughts and feelings he did not put into words.

John, like many poets, was shy about his deeper thoughts and feelings. He had a fear of being excessively articulate, of flattening things out by abstract argument, and if his manner appeared defensively artificial, in theory he believed in being natural. 'I never use any word in a poem that I would not use across a bar', but, across a bar, he did not play the part of the poet. His great need was for sympathetic understanding; yet he laid himself open almost deliberately to being misunderstood. There were for him two worlds, a practical and a real one. The real one was that of friendship and poetry. About the practical world, he was cynically realistic: one got what one wanted by making the right contacts and pulling the right strings. About the real world he was sensitive, and it was in that world that he was always getting hurt. He would go out of his way to do things for people whose writing he admired; but often he would find that instead of increasing the circle of his friends, he had added to his reputation as a clever and unscrupulous wirepuller. To add to the complication, John, who had a strong sense of the comic aspects of the role he was playing in Cairo, enjoyed this reputation. He often invented, in conversation, an ulterior motive for his actions where none existed. Young writers in the ranks, like myself, or Erik de Mauny or Iain Fletcher, and older poets passing through Cairo without much money in their pockets, knew how capable John was of acts of kindness; but when we said so, we were usually told that he was 'exploiting' us, though it would have been hard for his critics to say of what this 'exploitation' consisted. It seemed to consist largely of taking us to parties, standing us drinks and meals, and putting us in the way of making pocket money by occasional journalism. These local feuds sometimes made John sulky and bitter; but they never affected his admiration for, or his readiness to praise in public, the work of writers who snubbed him.

A Bought Embrace

Holding the naked body I had bought
Half gingerly, my chin upon her shoulder,
And gently shuddering in her arms, I thought:
'We choose the easier way as we grow older.

127

'Ten minutes till the cinema begins,
And time to still the hollow vessel's grief,
Buy off the dream of sorrow; all my sins
Shock easily upon this cushioned reef,

'And all desires seem captious and remote:
On a calm swell, without the grief of wishing,
I bob in sunlight with my little boat,
And hardly notice where my thoughts are fishing . . .

'What could they dredge from all that sea, but love?
Those I desired and laid my hands upon:
Those me desiring whom they could not move:
And those desired, but not by me touched, gone.

'What matters, whom I wrote my sonnets to,
Whose letters hurt me, who disturbed my dreams?
I do not think I find them here in you.
I find myself, which matters more, it seems.

'I do not think my shillings buy your love.
What should she care about her customer,
Who knows, whatever he is thinking of,
He is not thinking specially of her?

'And yet I think you do not wish me ill,
So unexacting in your arms I lie,
So gently leave the voyage to your will,
Till the craft capsize and the steersman die . . .

'Why think, indeed? The body knows the story:
A single shudder brings the boat to wreck.
Purged of all ecstasies, I feel no more . . . I
Lightly with dry lips brush your placid neck.'

Three Characters in a Bar

(Cairo, 1944)

One who wishes to be my friend,
One who at sight hates my face,
Drinking late at the same bar.

128

Lurching colonial character
Technicoloured and wired for sound:
'Why don't you hurry out of this place?'

Charming gentle bohemian
Last, last of the Jacobites
Lighting my countless cigarettes:

'Pleasant to meet indeed, old man!
No one to talk to all these nights
About the prompters behind the sets.'

And there over behind the bar
A mirror showing my own face
That shows no love, that shows no hate

That cannot get out of its own place
And must hear me talking at night:
I drink to you, long-sufferer!

Three Profiles from Cairo

X

I thought chiefly of a
cat which approaches one,
rubs up against one's ankles,
then stalks away aloofly—
purr meaning spite and pleasure!
This elegant form curling
in its chair, and lapping up
its drink in a tidy fashion.

Some people's hairs bristle:
others (myself) like cats.

Y

As a child hides itself in a corner
(this face had a ruined beauty)
this face would hide behind the long
gesturing hands, or a new story,
or cold beer in a glass.

A face requiring lights and mirrors,
the painter, the photographer,
all the projections of Narcissus,
requiring evening and the wineglass:
dead face of the afternoons.

Thrust forward by an irrelevant
moving-on-its-own-path
river of war—and with the tide,
and near the shore: floating,
but with a sulky look as if to say,
'I choose, I *choose* to drift!'

I am reminded of a
lost child in the streets of Glasgow
whose hopes of home slowly founder
in that enormous labyrinth,
turning as the evening falls
to lighted windows in a sweetshop:
how bright the gaslight glitters,
how lucid are the colours,
how far the quiet bedroom
with all its blue pictures,
how far the green meadows,
how far the love!

Z

You, sir, whom everybody hates
because of your reptilian coldness
and the cold-cream unction
of your inedible voice,

whom we are tempted, too, to envy
since with a careful pumice
you smooth your dreary poems,
you, accomplished sir,

whom other poets fear
because your judgements are
cold, academical,
perception winged by spite,

130

talking in the serene evening
of food and drink in England,
I found you not unpleasant:
and thought with some amusement
of all those poems in which
lust points its knife against you . . .
and what a placid fellow
such a cruel poet is!

And had the sudden fancy:
this is no cold serpent,
coiling its cruel loves,
rather a kindly Indian
fluting his careful measure
(all its foul fangs extracted)
to his tame snake.

4

The real gap, which one would never bridge in Cairo, was that
between battledress and civilian clothes—for certainly my best
friends were those who shared with me the strain, the shabbiness,
the sourly ironical sense of isolation, of the intellectual in the
ranks. Two of the most interesting of these, in those first months,
were Bill Campion and Bill McKechnie; Campion I had met in
Cairo and McKechnie I had known as long ago as St Andrews.
They seemed to me temperamentally akin to each other but, like
so many of my friends about whom I have felt this, they disliked
each other.

'One can have too much blancmange and Meyerbeer,'
Campion would say to me, summing up McKechnie. McKechnie
never attempted that sort of thing. He dealt not in epigrams but in
gentle, involved, Jamesian sentences, heavily flavoured with the
correct RAF slang. One could almost hear the inverted commas.
He would indicate that Campion 'lacked coherence' or
was a 'bind'. In Campion's flow of metaphor and illusion
(Campion carried the style of *The Waste Land*, the 'cultural rock-
jumping style', into conversation) McKechnie would ignore the
surface brilliance and probe darkly for a central chaos. To
McKechnie, indeed, a Roman Catholic convert, all liberal,
relative points of view were distressing. Campion would pore
over the Islamic philosophers and visit El Axhar (the Islamic
university to which the faithful come from every country in Asia)
again and again; McKechnie would quote Sir John Mandeville—

131

'they worschippe a divell they call Mahound'. Heretics had carried to McKechnie's nostrils, in the early days of his conversation, he told me, a 'faint effluvium of decay'.

McKechnie seemed always to be the victim of a faint nausea, either spiritual or social. If he was devout, he was also fastidious; and he sometimes found it hard to put up with the loquacity of simple cradle Catholics from Glasgow or Liverpool. His sensibility to the feelings of others nevertheless caused him to seek and achieve popularity by making constant nervous but pungent little jokes. He was a mixture of the possible saint, the conscious snob, and the talented comedian, and few people gave me more stimulation or comfort. Bill Campion's personality had a cruder and sharper impact, and in a way he was a poet; in an abrupt, disconnected, allusive way, like the earlier Ezra Pound, whom he professed never to have read. McKechnie, of course, preferred music to poetry. What was all Shakespeare to one little chord of, I think it was, Tchaikovsky? 'What is a poet anyway? One of the lower animals, George, with sensitive antennae.'

If McKechnie represented the prose of life at its most subtle and sensitive (at its most wearisome and arid too, Campion would grunt, but is it not a condition of *form* in prose that it should sometimes be wearisome and arid?) Campion brought the winds and clangors of the Spain he loved alive about one's ears. McKechnie, with a sensibility—of which he made too much—to all aspects of human beauty ('But don't you feel the need,' he would ask me tragically, 'for contact with young human flesh? My hair is falling out, George, and my loins are withering away') was quite indifferent to what he ate or drank, and would choose the vilest and most draughty restaurant as an adequate background for his conversation. Campion, in fluent French and surprisingly adequate Arabic, could conjure up in unlikely places something worth eating and drinking. There was a little place where, at a moment when our funds had reached rock-bottom, we got a glass of wine for a piastre and a half and enough *meze* thrown in free— little bits of meat and salted peanuts and beans and beetroot and Arab bread and cheese—to stave off our hunger; and there we declaimed our poems at each other, and declaimed Villon, with rasping resonance,

> Et honnête Jehane, la bonne Lorraine,
> Qu' Anglois brulèrent a Rouen?
> Où sont-elles, vierge souveraine?
> Mais où sont les neiges d'antan?

and felt that with our poverty, what we fancied to be our learning, and the background of Cairo, our lives were Villonesque enough. While we were declaiming, to our surprise, Copts and Greeks started patting us on the back and shaking us warmly by the hand. 'Poetry,' said Campion, 'is an art which this country holds in public honour!'

Campion did, certainly, like to dramatise things. At the beginning of his service career he had almost got into the Intelligence (but he could never learn to ride a motor bicycle) and he had never got over this. He would see himself, in certain moods, as a Secret Agent. He used to go with me to visit a charming Hungarian artist, Eric de Nemes, and we would sit drinking tea while Eric mechanically and in utter boredom completed drawings of flowers or dresses to illustrate advertisements. His gift was for fantastic drawings in the Surrealist tradition but in Cairo, at that time, there was not a market for these. I once asked him why he did not do political cartoons. 'I would be afraid,' he said seriously, 'of giving Nahas Pasha the wrong sort of squint.' Eric had an excellent library, including English children's books such as *Alice in Wonderland* and the poems of Edward Lear, that have become French Surrealist classics. While he drew, I used to read out to him such things as 'The Dong with the Luminous Nose', but Campion, nursing his bony, khaki-clad shins, would mutter under his breath, 'Nemes? Hungarian? Ho, hum, ha!' There is a Hungarian irredentist motto that goes something like 'nemes, nemes, nemes' and means *never, never, never*—never, never, never will Hungary surrender her just territorial claims. Could, Campion wondered, Nemes be a plotting Hungarian nationalist? Eric, I would reply, was too busy with his painting, reading, and with scraping a living for himself to be any such thing—to dissipate such suspicions one had only to listen to his sensible, humorous talk, or to look at the flash of the gold tooth in his friendly grin. Besides the official machinery in Cairo for checking up on doubtful characters was extensive and peculiar enough already, without old Campion playing amateur sleuth. Campion did not really believe there was anything wrong with Nemes. He was indulging a sort of daydream in which his languages, his grasp of European history, his insight into character, got him a better job than his present one of fetching coffee (or whisky) for the Colonel and introducing a new degree of disorder into the office files.

Over all our talk and companionship hung a certain atmosphere of comic ineffectiveness—the fuss, the self-importance of the base area where everyone, from general to private, hopes that his task is necessary, but knows it is not heroic. It was refreshing, from time to time, to meet a man of action.

I looked up from my desk in *Parade*'s offices one day to find a very tall, gawky, bony young lieutenant in battledress looking down at me. I could place him at once as a Highlander, by something fierce and gentle in his whole bearing. His voice confirmed my guess, soft and lilting, with long vowels and snaky sibilants. 'Would you by any chance be Mis-s-ter George Fras-s-er?' I looked up at a strange face, with a short nose, a broad forehead and high cheekbones, fierce dark shortsighted eyes enlarged by strong glasses, and a wide, loose, sensitive adolescent mouth under an absurd small moustache. The wrists and the huge hands thrust out of a battledress jacket a little too tight and too short. The tall figure held itself with a military rigour but swayed a little on its feet, in a way that seemed to match the voice's lilting of its formal syllables. One large hand dived into a haversack to produce a little pamphlet, which it thrust on the desk before me. 'These are some verses of yours. And I am very pleased to meet you.'

The pamphlet was *The Fatal Landscape,* which Nicholas Moore had told me Tambimuttu, the editor of *Poetry (London)* was getting out: a dozen uneven poems. The young man was Hamish Henderson—or Seamus McHendrick, as he would call himself indifferently, giving his name a Gaelic form—a Cambridge friend of Nicholas Moore's. With Keith Douglas, whom I was also to meet later in Cairo, Hamish proved to be one of the two best battle poets of the war. His *Elegies for the Dead in Cyrenaica,* which I was to see during the years that followed in various stages of composition, won the Somerset Maugham Award for 1948. But in 1941 Hamish was still fresh out from home and still on the edge of battle. Though I thought of him, from the first, as a fighter, I was merely recognising a type. He had not yet seen any action. He took me out for a drink and began to tell me all about himself.

Hamish was a Highlander by vocation. Highland by ancestry, he had been brought up largely in England, going to school at Dulwich. I have been told that he acquired his Highland accent, during his schooldays, quite suddenly; going off to spend the summer holidays with relations in Scotland and coming back in the autumn with that lilt. Certainly, he had a fine ear, and it was his mastery of German that got him into Intelligence. He started off in the Pioneers because, as a Scottish Nationalist and a Marxist, he at first had little sympathy with the 'imperialistic war'. Yet temperamentally he was obviously a born soldier; and ideally fitted for Intelligence in that he had a spontaneous sympathy with the Germans and their romantic attitude to history—just as obviously, he was out of sympathy with the English, with their tepid self-control, mild dislikes, liberal hesitations, and their passion for compromise. Where Hamish loved or hated, he liked to be thorough.

It was typical of one sort of contrast between the English and the Scottish temperaments that, when we sat down over our drinks, Hamish at once began to discuss philosophy. I had written an article for *Parade* criticising in a superficial way German historicism, particularly in its Hegelian form, in which the real is equated with the rational, or what has happened in history with what ought to have happened. Hamish held the same philosophy, but as developed by Marx; and I tried to criticise that, too. Everything, for the historical philosopher, is to be considered as an instrument of change, nothing for what it is in itself; there are tides in the affairs of men, and we are praised or blamed merely as we swim with or against them. Right wins, wrong loses; and we are not to cry out against the grossness of the victor nor pause to pity the gallantry of the defeated. To me it seems that there are good states of being, to be sought for their own sakes, however much the world is shifting round us; and all its shifts are destructive except in so far as they serve to establish such good states of being. But Hamish, with the rather Germanic mind that overlaid his Celtic temperament, was ready to accept some inclusive philosophy of change . . . it meant a fight, and his Celtic temperament was spoiling for a fight. The war had exalted and transformed him.

Yet I sensed a contradiction in his attitude. He was not only a Marxist but a Scottish Nationalist, and in Scottish history his sympathy was not with the winning faction, the Lowland Whigs, but with the Highlanders, who 'rode into battle, but they were defeated'. Hamish's instincts were with the last stand and the lost cause; his mind, trained in the schools of Germany, sought to hallow any victory. For the moment, Marxism was helping him to solve his emotional problem. It must, he thought, win in the end; but it was not winning at that time in Western Europe, and in

135

standing by it he was standing by a threatened minority. He saw Marxian Socialism, also, as the means by which the Highlands of Scotland and the Celtic enclaves of Europe generally, from Scotland and Wales to Brittany and Spanish Galicia, could regain their old cultural autonomy.

Scotland, he admitted, was going through a cultural revival in any case, but that was not enough. The politically central power always imposes its own culture on the outlying provinces. Look, Hamish said, at the case of Provence, with its sophisticated culture, its wonderfully poetic language, so perfectly adapted, unlike the language of the North French, for singing; Provence goes under politically to the North French, and culturally it is not absorbed but simply knocked out. Its language, its literature, become provincial. So it was, he said, with the Highlands of Scotland; when the Lowland Whigs became supreme in Scotland, their policy towards the Highlanders was to destroy their clan system and 'root out their Irish language'. The '15 and the '45 were the last desperate rallies of a proud, ancient people in defence of old ways, and Hamish, a Marxist in the modern world, became when he considered Scottish history a Jacobite and a Tory. He was so eager about the old feuds, which he felt stirring again beneath the surface of our time, that it was hard not to catch his enthusiasm. An age of battles! What a splendid prospect . . . if one had a temperament like his.

I had not ('a thrawn little dominy', Hamish used to call me, as I tried to answer his arguments). My temperament was not combative. I felt that the war must be won and some foundation laid for a juster society. But history was so full of violence and suffering, suffering breeding violence, violence breeding suffering, that I stood back and wished the process to run down to a standstill. I remembered the process in myself, in my earliest days in the army. Hurt and humiliated, I had cried out, 'Somebody must suffer, somebody must suffer!' But nobody had suffered but myself; violence and suffering had shocked against each other, and at length the weary clash wore them to stillness. A burden of resentment would disperse itself now and then, harmlessly, in mild little shocks of verbal malice: nothing more. I was persuasive about this. Yet what, from Hamish's point of view, could it mean but, 'Sit back, be silent, do nothing'? An attempt to contract out of history! I felt that until enough people with practical sense, administrative grasp, and the power of command achieved such a detachment, history could be little more than the clash of mass passions. We lack in affairs of state even the most rudimentary domestic virtues, the virtues of the nursery.

Sometimes I tried to enter into Hamish's enthusiasms. When he was dictator of Scotland, I said, I would write his propaganda for him. 'Ah, man Geordie, but it had better be I who carry the pistols!' So he rallied me and, in the middle of our most obstinate arguments, suddenly broke into a lilting Gaelic song. Once, while he sang in a bar, some New Zealand soldiers stared at him in disgust. It was unusual in 1941 to see a lieutenant drinking with a private (though by 1945, as far as distinctions of rank went, Cairo had become a very informal city); and it was uncanny to hear the lieutenant entertaining the private with songs in an unknown tongue. 'Stow it, you bloody pommies!' they shouted. Hamish got up, revealing his tremendous height, and for a moment was most imposingly military. He was not going to stand on his rank, he said; he was not a bloody pommy, he was a Highland gentleman; he would drink with what friends he pleased, and sing the songs of his ancestors if the mood so took him; if any of the gentlemen cared to discuss the matter further with him, would they step outside? Nobody did want to step outside, but when Hamish came back to our table, I felt wretched. 'I don't like this place any more, Hamish,' I said. 'Let us go.' Grimly, Hamish shook his head; I could feel the New Zealanders staring at us; I sat miserably self-conscious over my glass; but Hamish ordered another two beers; and began again in a coaxing voice to sing to me. The song with its firm grief penetrated me. I sat back, relaxed, and my eyes took our enemies in at last, quite casually, impersonally, as one takes in people sitting opposite one in a tram.

To those who know and admire Hamish's later poems, it may be interesting to see two things of his I printed at that time, in the shoddy and uneven unofficial soldier's magazine that I helped to start, *Orientations*. I give myself credit for recognising at once the poet in him at a time when, to many of the people to whom I introduced him, he seemed merely a strange and noisy swaggerer. This is a translation, a fragment from Hölderlin,

> Near is,
> And hard to catch hold of, God.
> But where danger is, grows
> That which can save.
> In the darkness the eagles
> Have habitation, and fearless

The sons of Alps cross over the abyss
On narrow flimsy bridges. Therefore
Since around us are heaped
The peaks of time, and our beloved
Live near, yet tiringly
On the farthest of mountains,
Give to us holy water
O wings give us, that we may truly
Cross over and come back again . . .

And this is a poem written in hospital, which shows the sensitive
observer that hid behind the swaggerer's mask:

In the hand projecting from the blue pyjamas
The nerves dart like a pond of minnows,
Betraying a brief agitation in the brain,
Timid deer start in the parkland spinneys:
Through our shutters the fine sand blows like rain.
The waves of heat loll lazy aggression
Against our feverish island of illness,
The bumble buzz of an electric fan
Makes a weakly wind in a covey of coolness.
We lie out of sheets in defeatist languor.
The wardrobe mirror takes up my attention.
After lunch, feelings grow fat in the heat.
My nihilist brain nods in its own suspension,
On a tide of treacle drifts off to sleep . . .

6

Early in 1942 I was offered a job, more responsible than my work
on *Parade*, and involving promotion, on a bi-lingual newspaper in
Asmara, the capital of the conquered Italian colony of Eritrea. In
some ways, I was glad to go. The heat of Cairo was wearing me
down and Asmara, eight thousand feet up on the Eritrean high
plateau, was reported to be a cool, pleasant city. I did want a
more responsible job; and I felt that in Cairo I was outstaying my
welcome. Nobody minds helping a lame duck over a stile, but it is
another thing to help him over an endless series of hurdles. The
thing to do would be to get me some responsible and fairly
independent job in Cairo itself. But what job? I seemed to fall

between two stools. I was a scholar among journalists, a journalist among scholars; poets teaching in Cairo thought that anybody who turned out popular articles as rapidly as I did, on all sorts of subjects, must be a bogus poet, and newspapermen thought that nobody who wanted to be a poet at all could be a very safe sub-editor. There was no place in Cairo, in 1942, where I properly belonged except the group of my intimate friends in the Army, and these were my friends partly because they shared my sense of not properly belonging.

And yet these friends often rather disliked each other. It often occurred to me that getting on with me was the only thing that held my friends together, and that when I left what had been a group would break up once more into a set of individuals, blind to each other's qualities. Were these qualities perhaps a hallucination of my own? Many people, for instance, found Campion tiresome. He was a 'character', I would say—a weak defence, since we were all 'characters' in Cairo—to which I remember Reggie Smith once replied in that peremptory way of his: 'Well, describe him! What sort of character? Make me interested!' I showed Reggie a poem that Campion had written, a poem that made vague gestures that somehow failed to come off,

> I'll pluck tomorrow's Southern Cross,
> Ten tranquil rubies in my hand . . .
> And fell you half an albatross . . .
> One plaintive motion of my wand,

and Reggie snorted. And yet in conversation the plaintive motions of Campion's wand could produce magical effects. Reggie had not sat beside Campion outside a barracks cookhouse, in the baking sun, while Campion, lean, sick, and miserable, scratched the sores on his legs till they bled and talked about the Sephardic Jews of Constantinople who speak the Spanish of the Age of Gold.

The last time I saw McKechnie and Campion together was in the flat of a charming, elusive Irish journalist, Keith Scott Watson, who had a beautiful Spanish wife, Nieves. While Keith prepared tea, Nieves read Lorca to us, and I made her turn to the lines about a girl's thighs, escaping like fish in a pool in the moonlight. She patted her own thighs, shapely under her light frock. 'Half light, half dark, half warm, half cold!' she said. 'You understand?' And Campion talked to her about the dialects of Spain, and McKechnie asked her if she was a Catholic. She said

139

once, but no longer. 'Like so many of my friends,' he said. 'That declension. *Labor, labi, lapsus sum.*' McKechnie and I talked about her extraordinary Spanish looks all the way down Soliman Pacha; Campion, impatient, and with concerns of his own, hurried away.

My very last vivid memory of my first period in Cairo is of a lunch in a restaurant, in a decayed garden, on the edge of the river, where Campion and I and another good friend of mine, the journalist Haig Gudenian, celebrated the birth of *Orientations*. There one could sit in a thing like a beach hut and stare at a low wall, beyond it the green river, palms, moving feluccas, a few white square buildings in the background; no human figures bulked large in the scene, and it produced an illusion of peace. Over our omelette, our beer, our ice, and our coffee—how good things taste when one is poor and hungry and while companionship is still what matters most in life!—neither I nor Haig said much, but we savoured the sadness of a parting that was more than personal. This city, too hot, not beautiful, except with such beauty as is lent to any great city by the stars, by lights and by a river; obscene in its poverty, its bent women blackmailing you with their starved babies to buy lottery tickets; obscene in its luxury, a greed, an ostentation, a sensuality that showed no taste, no heart, but only the eagerness for food, objects, flesh; this lively and wicked city, with its broad and its narrow streets and its odd jostlings—the Arab boys in the El Azhar, sitting on their heels, swaying slightly, and swotting up an abridged version of *Rodney Stone!*—in its complication and irregularity, I found a rich metaphor for the creative disorder of my own life. So many things had met in me because my soul, like Cairo, was a place of commerce. If I did not possess Cairo, neither did I possess or understand myself. What is the self? The platform for a debate, the stage for a play; and in my case, a crowded street, full of jostling strangers.

'I feel so sad, Haig,' I said. Partly this was what I should have said but partly I meant it; with the horror one always has that one will make no more friends. We walked for the last time towards the Embassy and past it. I turned into the offices of *Parade*. I bought a stiff whisky to fortify myself to say good-bye to everyone, and then got my kit together; I would pile it soon on a lorry, starting on another journey.

It was a journey by train, paddleboat and lorry, that lasted for about ten days, and since they were days of almost complete solitude—the soldiers who travelled with me were sunk, as I was, in their thoughts and memories—some scenes remain imprinted on my mind with dreamlike vividness. I remember how, in Cape Corps lorries, we bumped out of the Sudanese plain towards the Eritrean highlands. The buff terrain became thicker with scrub, and then the soil gradually changed to a red crumbly clay. There were twisted, dry watercourses, giant stony cactuses, slim green trees like English birches. Virulently blue birds flashed across the path; here was a herd of speckled goats, the dark herdsman leaning on his spear; here we passed a camel, bleeding to death by the roadside. The lorry jolted heavily and made me feel sick. The man beside me, an oafish creature, constantly plucked at my arm, entranced by the lurid enamelled sheen of the darting birds. 'Look,' he would say, 'lovely, lovely! Look, parrots!' At length, for the last lap, we were bundled into a train. I sat down on a wooden corner seat and looked at the darkening landscape outside. By a high-hanging bridge, we passed over a deep and wide watercourse, nearly dry, but with a pool of green scum in its centre. Over there was a reddish mountain, faintly peppered with green, like a mountain on a Chinese scroll painting. Gradually, in my cramped, uncomfortable position, I dozed off . . . When I woke, it was a cool, clear morning and as the train ran into the station at Asmara women were hanging out clothes to dry on second-storey balconies. Asmara seemed like some provincial town in Europe, growing up a little untidily, but not yet having grown beyond leisure and space: villas set in their own gardens, patches of green wasteland, cafés with pavement tables, strolling figures hovering by second-hand bookstalls. I lumped my kit onto the platform, already, as I breathed the mild, clean air, beginning to feel a sense of relief. Life might be often dull here, but it would be restful. This was the size of city I could manage; Cairo already seemed garish, and confused, and very far away.

To Hugh MacDiarmid

Since mine was never the heroic gesture,
    Trained to slick city from my childhood's days,
Only a rambling garden's artful leisure
    Giving my mind its privacy and ease,

Since Poverty for me has never sharpened
    Her single tooth, and since Adversity
So far has failed to jab me with her hair-pin
    I marvel who my Scottish Muse can be.

I am Convention's child, the cub reporter,
    The sleek, the smooth, conservatively poised:
Abandoned long ago by Beauty's daughter;
    Tamed like a broncho, and commercialised!

Perhaps I have a heart that feels . . . I wonder!
    At least I can salute your courage high,
Your thought that burns language to a cinder,
    Your anger, and your angry poet's joy.

O warrior, with the world and wind against you,
    Old sea-bird, in your bleak and rocky coign,
Only my fears can follow where you fly to . . .
    Beneath these rocks, how many souls lie slain!

Your journey has not been the private journey
    Through a mad loveliness, of Hölderlin.
Against the windmills, sir, you choose to tourney.
    And yet, by marvellous chance, you hold your own.

O true bright sword! Perhaps, like Mithridates,
    Before the night has fallen, you may say:
Now I am satisfied: at least, my hate is:
    Now let me die: I saw the English flee.

Facing boys' faces, whom your world of thunder
    Is massing clouds for, whom the violet forks
Seek out from heaven . . . simulating candour
    I face both ways! A secret question carks.

Because my love was never for the common
    But only for the rare, the singular air,
Or the undifferenced and naked human,
    Your Keltic mythos shudders me with fear.

What a race has is always crude and common,
    And not the human or the personal:
I would take sword up only for the human,
    Not to revive the broken ghosts of Gael.

142

Nilotic Elegy

Sometimes I seemed to see gliding the green
Ghost of a landscape, sometimes other summers
Were marginal upon the summer scene,
Sometimes the river's waft was wet with rumours
Of other scents, the tingle of the sea,
Sometimes the passing walker was the echo
Of one who waits on other shores for me,
Sometimes the sliding mask of the felucca
Spoke of enchanted summer voyages
Through rhododendrons or past shining bathers
To all my lost imaginary Venuses:
Sometimes these thoughts would have their doubtful sharers,
Sniffing the odours of a greensick youth
That spilt its promise on the soils of fancy
And in the rose and tulip found its truth.
Sometimes I thought how broken and how chancy
The tides of every sexual river are
That make the sandy valleys black and fertile
To crop a maggot summer of despair.
But yet I weave the rue and yet the myrtle,
But yet I weave the laurel, and I find
Still stained with a green magic from the south,
Weeds of a boy's desire, my Theban flood.
O walls of Karnac, buttress in your blind!
From the high sources to the stammering mouth
I chose the sun and every chance of blood . . .

Egypt

Who knows the lights at last, who knows the cities
And the unloving hands upon the thighs
Would yet return to seek his home-town pretties
For the shy finger-tips and sidelong eyes.

Who knows the world, the flesh, the compromises
Would go back to the theory in the book:
Who knows the place the poster advertises
Back to the poster for another look.

But nets the fellah spreads beside the river
Where the green waters criss-cross in the sun
End certain migratory hopes for ever:
In that white light, all shadows are undone.

The desert slays. But safe from Allah's justice
Where the broad river of His Mercy lies,
Where ground for labour, or where scope for lust is,
The crooked and tall and cunning cities rise.

The green Nile irrigates a barren region,
All the coarse palms are ankle-deep in sand:
No love roots deep, though easy loves are legion:
The heart's as hot and hungry as the hand.

In airless evenings, at the café table,
The soldier sips his thick sweet coffee up:
The dry grounds, like the moral to my fable,
Are bitter at the bottom of the cup.

Opening Out

1

AS I sat late at night at my desk in the offices of *The Eritrean Daily News* in Asmara, there, in Reuter's sheets on my third tray (sheets taken down from a Morse transmission by an Italian radio operator who did not understand English) lay the world. There were the ruins of Stalingrad in pale print on grey paper, the starving children in Greece, the American baseball scores; there was news about trouble in India, angry debates in the House of Commons, the various items which, in a conquered territory, it was advisable not to print. There too were the official communiqués from various fronts, skeletons of what was really happening. 'Milne Bay', I would read; and I would go to the map of the world pinned on the wall, and peer at New Guinea, and come back to my desk and write, 'Milne Bay, the thin forked tip at the eastern extremity of the island.' Or the communiqué might mention Rzhev, Vyasma—and after pencilling a triangle on the map, I would type out the headline: NEW RUSSIAN OFFENSIVE ON MOSCOW FRONT. War journalism was a great teacher of geography. Only China, elusive and somehow always on the edge of other interests, failed to form a shape in my mind. As I copied out the communiqués from Chunking, I had a vague sense of dishonesty.

I had not been so useful or so comfortable since I joined the Army, and yet not perhaps so alone. But my slow, vegetative life was nourished by this solitude; it was better to sit at night in my office, waiting for the paper to be put to bed, and slaving away at translations of Guido Cavalcanti, than to spend my evenings discussing the weary weight of the unimaginable world, in a Cairo soldiers' club, with glumly intellectual Corporals. I had been too much afraid of loneliness, I thought; loneliness, when combined with security and leisure, suited my poetry. And now, too, I had a good conscience. Here there were jobs, the supervision of translators, the writing of leading articles, the ordinary grind of sub-editing, which had to be done, and some of which I could probably do better than anybody else. I was away at last, too, from the atmosphere of the barracks. Our sergeants' mess was an old *pensione* on a top storey, in the Viale Mussolini, and in the morning our housekeeper would waken me with her golden-toothed smile and her cup of weak sweet tea. It was fine to wake up and realise I could go to sleep again; to sip my tea and roll over; and then to come in late, when everybody else had gone, to a solitary breakfast, glancing slowly over the paper which I had helped to put to bed the night before, and of which I knew every word.

Breakfast over, I would move down the Viale Mussolini (we did not interfere with the street names, nor with the chalked slogans on the walls, 'Believe, Obey, Fight'), past the red and yellow brick cathedral with its clock tower, past the cafés where unshaven Italians were already drinking tiny cups of black coffee and green and yellow *bibite* in broad glasses. At a corner, I would sit in a bootblack's chair and get my shoes done very thoroughly. The bootblack would be grateful for the thirty cents (a hundred cents are an East African shilling) that I gave him, and I would feel the relief of the contrast with Cairo, where the bootblacks follow you down the street, threaten to spatter you with blacking if you do not stop, and, whatever you give them, clamour for more. How strange, after Cairo, that there were hardly any beggars. Only sometimes tiny, plump, brown children, sometimes with silver earrings, comically frizzed and shaven hair, pot bellies, would patter after me, chuckling, *'Meskeen, meskeen!'* I sometimes gave two or three of them five cents each, but then they seemed to spring up from the pavement, always smaller and more insistent, so that finally I would turn on them and say fiercely, *'Gheess!'* There might still be time for a hot bath before I went to the office; and at the public bathhouse, an Eritrean woman, in one of the ankle-long Regency dresses they affect, would patter up on her brown bare feet with towels; her shrivelled face would be a little like a monkey's—not in the features, but in the way the expression had set for good, in a blend of innocence and vivacity. Similarly, it was a strange sight to see a native boy and a monkey capering along the street together—taking each other off. And yet the Eritreans were a noble and dignified people. I remember a tall, thin old man, with a grey Tudor beard, and robes cast loosely round him like a Roman toga, riding on a donkey, his bare heels almost touching the ground—and yet with a straight back, and an air of chivalry about him, that recalled Don Quixote. Such figures enlivened the calm, provincial scene. And one had only to go a mile or two out of Asmara to lose the sense of that scene altogether. The bus might draw up at a roadside halt on the steep, winding road to Decamere; and there in a boulder and cactus landscape, there would be the carcass of a mule, and bald, ungraceful birds moving around it—vultures. And above the rocky plateau the scavenger hawks would be always circling, with their serrated wings, and their queer, low, plaintive cry, like the noise made by kittens who have not yet learned to miaow. The sense of that landscape all around gave to the most ordinary comforts of Asmara a strangely poetic quality.

And one's ordinary work had a strangely poetic quality, too. By ten o'clock, I would be sitting at my desk, but with no real sense of urgency. The Reuter's sheets did not begin to come over the radio till noon. If it were a Monday, Mr Padulli, one of our two translators, would have his weekly war summary—'La Settimana e la Guerra'—ready, and I would start at once on an English version. This job of translation made Monday interesting and different. Padulli (he was a Count, but being a Mazzinian Republican did not use the title, though he had the coronet on his notepaper) was a strange personality. He was very tall and hideous in a melancholy, sympathetic way—a long pallid face, protruding and slightly squinting eyes, and a spastic grin which suggested that he was concealing intense pain. Probably he was. He did not sleep much, suffering, like Job, from boils. He also had terrible headaches; he would say that because of the height of Asmara, and the rarefied air, everyone who stayed there long enough sooner or later got cerebral anaemia.

One of the first symptoms of that malady is the forgetting of common words. Padulli often paused for a word while talking to me, but then he knew English as I knew Italian—with a large passive vocabulary for reading, but a small active vocabulary for talking or writing. In conversation, he translated the Italian idiom directly. We had been worried about him once for days because he was suffering from an inflamed appendix; but he came in one morning with a grin which suggested agony but expressed relief—'After all, it seems, a surgical intervention is not necessary!' His Monday articles were always sound and well-informed. When he went home from the office, he spent his spare time listening to the radio and making notes. Ill, ugly, comic, and yet intelligent and noble, he typified for me what the anti-Fascist in Italy must be. Men who cut themselves off from the currents of life among their fellows acquire certain physical eccentricities. It is the penalty of isolation. The war had become for Padulli like one of his illnesses, something to be nursed tenderly, with an almost grotesque care. 'I cannot read anything,' he would say to me, 'no poetry, no *romanzo*, only war.' Only war: on weeks when there were no important battles or speeches, he looked a little lost . . .

Rampone, on the other hand, our second translator, was a brown, cheerful pock-marked little man, who was very literary. He tried to take the war seriously but, after all, it was very far away, and cheerfulness kept breaking in. He showed me his poems in rhymed free verse, and I tried to do them into English for him; here and there, I remember, there was a good image,

> a petticoat on a rope
> that the wind swells and fills
> with an anonymous shape,

and that anonymous shape, the abstract idea of the female body, was his main poetic topic. We used to have long talks about English literature and it was the romantic personalities, Byron, Shelley, Wilde, who appealed to his imagination. But he was also fond of long, realistic novels about English middle-class life, of Galsworthy and Bennett, for example, because he liked the reassuring, comfortable background of everyday detail. A life of romantic aspirations built on a foundation of routine was what he was after—there are sillier ideals—and so the atmosphere of Asmara, which cramped and thwarted Padulli, suited him. For the moment, it also suited me. Talking about poetry, or gossiping about personalities, we sometimes cast a guilty sidelong glance at Padulli. He was following our conversation, and putting in a word now and again, for he was an extremely courteous person; but he cracked his knuckles absent-mindedly, there was a wandering look in his eyes. His mind, like the Laird of Cockpen's, was taken up with the things of the State.

In these early days in Asmara, however, I was not so happily settled as Rampone. I loved my work; but in the sergeants' mess in the evenings, pleasant as its atmosphere was, I often felt at a loose end. People sat around drinking beer and playing poker or pontoon. I had a couple of whiskies, and began to feel talkative, hoping that somebody would start a discussion, or sit down at the piano. When neither of these things happened, I went off to bed with a book. I felt frustration. I ought to get a tooth stopped. I ought some evening to visit the brothel round the corner. But my procrastinating spirit kept putting off both pleasure and pain . . . The war had treated me more kindly than it treated most people, but because of that, I had a sense of existing on the margin of life. In the mornings, when I looked at my maps and pencilled in, in Russia, the latest German setbacks or, in New Guinea, the progress of the Australians, I would wonder if for all of us, all over the world, the sense of life had become a little marginal. The boy in Athens, lying in the gutter, coughing up his blood; the Serb guerrilla looking down telescopic sights at a distant enemy; the clerk at GHQ putting tabs in a new file; the generals and the politicians, at their important conferences, at long tables, in impersonal rooms—did any of them have the sudden, vivid feeling, 'Now I am at the centre'? Life was with us and then not with us; we did not know why. But a man with an acute sense of life would suddenly say, for instance: 'It is no longer any use writing poems', and would go like Rimbaud into scrubby Sudan, a rifle under his arm, a belt loaded with gold around his waist. That was the awkward little truth which, since one was busy and contented enough, one's mind kept evading: 'It is no longer any use.' Yet might not something that was no longer of obvious use to oneself still be of use to others?

Our complicated and imperfect world had to be kept going somehow. It could not be allowed just to run down. There was a phrase that the army used, one of its many sinister and compelling phrases—'the necessary bodies'; we were all necessary bodies now, and if we would rebel against that, we must find a desert more remote than the Sahara or a secret city farther away than Harar. It was not our own satisfaction, or even the satisfaction of self-sacrifice for some concrete tradition, that mattered, but rather the patience to go on working for some purpose only vaguely apprehended. It was the sense of the future, of what might somehow be brought about, if we clenched our hands, and calmed our nerves with a drink or a smoke, and somehow carried on. There was no longer a centre, but we on the margin might somehow create one.

A Native Girl in Decamere

She in her straight transparent muslin swayed
Like water in a glass. The brittle light
Upon the plum bloom of her body played;
And the mimosa tree was twice her height
That scattered yellow pollen at her feet.
All the clock faces told a different hour,

Only the hens were scratching in the street,
And in the sun she opened like a flower.
Like water in a glass, my thought was swirled
A moment by the garden and the door:
Then I climbed up to where the shite-hawks whirled
With kitten cries above the plateau floor,
And where the snaky, slaty road wound down
To sting, with lecherous fang, the sleepy town.

2

While I was thinking of the world my sons would live in, my father died; run over by a tram one evening, in Aberdeen, in the blackout. I found myself at nights dreaming that I was having long conversations with him and then, when I awoke, I realised that I could never have any conversations with him again, and that these dreams, with their atmosphere of peace, might mean that I wanted to die. And I started to ask myself about the nature of the peace that I had found in Asmara. Was it a peace like the peace of death, and was that what I wanted? I was more contented and more free from anxiety than I had ever been anywhere else. But it was a strange kind of contentment. One worked, drank and talked to a routine. One day seemed exactly like another. Time no longer seemed to matter. How can I convey that static atmosphere? I had better take a single Sunday in Asmara, for Sunday in Asmara was the day that was quite our own, saturated with the atmosphere of our personal lives.

We would all have been drinking heavily the night before, and the rhythm of Sunday morning would be one of slow recuperation. I would leave my room-mate, James, still sleeping it off, and with my other close friend in the Mess, John, who had a harder head, I would stroll round the town. After drinking coffee, we would go to the Viceregal Garden, where there was a small zoo. We would feed the monkeys with nuts. The fun was the complete selfishness of a patriarchal monkey who snatched nuts even from between the lips of members of his clan, and howled with rage when he missed a nut. 'He ought to be in the Mess,' James would say. James had a phrase for everything, a phrase stylised, as was the pattern of our exiled lives. Sitting in a sunny café, we would look over the women, so near and inaccessible in their white Sunday frocks, and James, meeting the impenetrable gaze of an oval Italian face, would say, 'I would charge her a very

150

small fee.' When John joined us, after Mass, and we drank the first beer of the day, James would smile and say, 'You know we are a set of broken reeds.' Such phrases, repeated again and again, had become for us something like the password of a little clan . . .

Sunday lunch in the Mess was by tradition heavy and indigestible—pork and crackling, rich creamy pudding. It was not a meal to be missed. There were always some shattered characters just up, after a whisky jag, but even they made a brave show of it. Fred Saunders, his usually pink face white, except for the rims round the eyes, felt in honour bound to manage at least a mouthful. 'Good English cooking,' he would say. 'None of your Italian falderals.' And he would push the plate away from him, hardly touched, and clump off to bed.

Back in my room after lunch, I would take off all my clothes and get under the blankets. I might smoke a cigarette and pick up a volume of Dante. The room was littered with books in English, French, Italian, and Spanish, which John and I had bought at various times, and of which we read a few pages, on Sunday afternoons, before going to sleep. But no, Dante was not to my mood. Instead, I would tackle one of John's books on Thomist philosophy. The categories and subsections swam before my eyes. Make substance solid and existence real. Like a man slipping into his only refuge, I curled the blankets over my head. Outside the window it was a lovely afternoon and the tall trees were swaying.

My dreams moved in regular grooves. I knew well the dream St Andrews, a town quite unlike the real one; the Glasgow, a grey labyrinth; the generic railway station, ominous of disaster; the vague white figures that eluded my questionings. I did not know what the nightmare was that sometimes made me wake sweating in the middle of the night. But always, when not too drunk, I locked my bedroom door.

John, snoring slightly on the other side of the room, always dreamt about women. Once he had dreamt that he found one of the typists from his office outside the Mess, quite naked. He went up to our bedroom, which was on the top floor, to fetch her a blanket. But on the way down he met the Mess President, who held him in conversation, and when he finally got downstairs, she was gone.

James, who was older, and whose life had been better managed than John's and mine, did not dream at all. On his dressing table there was a photograph of a girl from Yorkshire, in his desk letters from a girl in Scotland. But he stirred a little in his sleep at times, perhaps at some image of his wife, whom he loved, and who was suggesting in her letters that they ought to separate. He lay flat on his back; his face, its lines smoothed out by sleep, its alcoholic flush fading, was beautiful, gentle, noble. His long graceful body was like the statue of a Crusader on his tomb; but with the arms extended, the hands flat. On the table by his bed were detective stories, anthologies of verse, and selected works of Lenin. A great half-empty wine-flask stood in a corner of the room and a half-eaten tin of Red Sea caviare.

At four o'clock, we would all awaken and drink a cup of strong stewed tea. The pleasantest part of a Sunday was this quiet interregnum, when we used to talk seriously about going to the cinema, having a quiet night for once, and getting to bed sober. The light was beginning to fade from the brilliant equatorial sky. We sat in dressing-gowns on the couches in the lounge and talked about the appalling sanitation of the Mess, and the sinister new element—people were always coming and going—who spent their time drinking tea and eating buns and playing whist at the Church Army Club. Yet we envied their ability to be happily dull. For evening would find us at the Greek Club, a bottle of brandy in front of us, the usual women, with their usual male hangers-on, at the table. The three of us, by that time, were beginning to feel normal. James was going round the tables, clapping various people on the back. 'You know what you are,' he would say genially, 'you are a broken reed.' He had his usual conversation with the tiddly major who always talked, in the Greek Club on a Sunday evening, about starting an RASC club in Asmara. Certainly it was true that, busy with our daily office jobs, most of us had lost any acute sense of belonging to any particular regimental unit. 'What I say,' the major would say, articulating carefully, 'is, you could get the chaps together. Not enough social life, in this place . . . no, that's not it exactly. Too much social life. Not enough corporate sense. We could talk about old times, eh?' 'And we could have a drink,' said James thoughtfully. The major's face composed itself, as nearly as it could, into a mask of formal dignity. 'Drink's not point. Very good thing in its place, drink—must keep in place. Point is corporate sense . . .' John, meanwhile, would have found himself one of those motherly women who always attached themselves to his tough, worn masculinity. And I would be dancing. The girl yielded easily, put her cheek against mine. She was like this with everyone, I thought, as impersonal as a glove, but I shuddered against her. I stammered amorous phrases in Italian. 'Take it easy, George,'

152

she said, 'take it easy.' It was the one phrase every personable young woman in the territory had learned from the Americans in the Douglas Aircraft Factory at Gura.

The evening would wear on, the women would leave. Soon there would be only the three of us, a yawning barman, a table littered with cigarette stubs and half-empty glasses. John, in a gloomy mood, would try to remember a poem of Leopardi's. 'How does it go? I only remember the sense. And, and there is no reason why I should live at all and, and—*e fango il mondo*. And the world is mud.' Leopardi was ill, I would say, so was Pascal, none of these attitudes were universal. And we would wander back to the Mess. A wicker chair and an empty bottle bounded off the pavement as we turned a corner. 'Making a night of it apparently,' said James happily. The Mess would be splashed with beer and crowded with people, a group round the piano, some attempting to sing 'Blaydon Races' while the pianist persisted in playing 'Roll Me Over', and others pouring beer into the piano's interior to give it a more mellow tone. We would go behind the bar to join the group of quieter and steadier drinkers, who were getting rid of the last of the whisky. Fred Saunders, all pink again, would be discoursing on his favourite subject, the English character.

'What the Englishman wants,' he would say, 'is his house, his garden, his drop of beer at the local. You can say what you like about Socialism, but we've all been pushed around enough in the last four years, and I, for one, am not going to be pushed around again.'

However many drinks he had put down, James was always ready for an argument about politics.

'I dare say you were happy enough before the war, Fred,' he said, 'but what about the poor bloody unemployed? It's all very well to talk about free enterprise, but what is our own job here in Asmara? Controlling prices and prosecuting profiteers. If we didn't do that, the people would starve. The law of the market is just the law of the jungle.'

'I would rather starve and be free,' said John.

'John, you are being romantic,' said James. 'Fred, you are being sentimental.'

'All I say,' Fred Saunders went on, 'is that let me get home, let me get my army boots off, let me get into bed with my wife, and you can stuff your politics up your jumper.'

John said, 'I shall spend six months in Tuscany after the war.'

I said, 'I am afraid to go home. Nothing is as I left it. My family are in London, a place a strange and foreign to me as Cairo. I shall feel lost. "In streets I never thought I should revisit when I left my body on a distant shore." So much of life is like that. As if one were a ghost haunting a place, as if I had never left Aberdeen, as if my body were only real to me on a bleak morning, with a grey mist coming off the sea.'

'George,' said John, 'you are an extraordinary sentimentalist. I suppose it's being a literary man.'

'I dare say,' I said. 'I dare say I have a cold heart. I write poems but forget to answer letters. I become estranged from old friends. I talk too much when I'm drunk.'

There was a period of silent drinking and the company began to break up. 'And we seem to have settled nothing,' said James. 'The night wears on, the last of the drinkers has departed.' He was growing more remote, his eyes glazing, a smile of disdain on his lips like that with which Farinata degli Uberti, in Dante, regards the landscape of hell. He went into the next room and sat down at the piano and began to play 'Swanee River'. And the three of us started to sing about the old folks at home. John and I slipped our arms round James's shoulder, clinging to his stability. James smiled at us affectionately. 'We're all broken reeds, you know,' he said. He went on playing, improvising a jazz symphony from scraps of half-forgotten tunes. John went over to a window, flung it wide, and looked out on the wide clear night, pin-pointed with stars. A fresh breeze blew on his face. He belched. 'But it hasn't been a bad day,' he said insistently, 'not a bad day at all.' It had been a day, indeed, like so many other days, satisfying expectations born of routine. I emptied the remainder of my brandy on the floor. A libation. James went on playing. We moved at last upstairs, and James turned at the end of his corridor, the charm of his smile frozen almost to vacuity. 'Good-night,' he said, 'good-night, you broken reeds!'

3

So weeks and months went round at Asmara, restful in their repetitions, like a water-wheel. But at last Cairo claimed me again. John Waller now had a job in the MoI, he needed an assistant, and he pulled strings. I wrote to him that I was quite happy where I was. The point for him was not whether I was happy, but whether I was productive. In my first unsettled period in Cairo I had written poems that had moved him; in Asmara, I was writing nothing but translations of obscure Italian poets, and these he found very dull. I had to be dug out. It would do me good to get a whiff again of the garish metropolitan atmosphere. So late in 1944 I found myself back in Cairo. The change, on the whole, told badly on my nerves. I no longer belonged anywhere, as I had in Asmara. I slept in the Ministry of Information, and I soon gave up having my meals at a Sergeants' Mess; I was still a most unsoldierly figure, and people stared at me inquisitively, wondering how I had got my rank. I had my meals out at restaurants and ran through my pay too quickly; for two or three days before payday I often went hungry. Moreover, churning out much mechanical prose—I used to write two or even three special articles a day—I felt my touch for poetry, and indeed for life, coarsening. I could no longer be happy in solitude. I needed company, and, to make myself amusing, I was ready to play the part of eccentric and buffoon. Yet, if I was unhappy, bored with myself, I nevertheless made friends during my last year in Cairo more readily than at any other time in my life. For many of these friends I was at first a symbol of their own inner maladjustments, and also for a sort of precarious inner freedom. Looking back on my life in Cairo in 1944 and 1945, I think of it as a gritty, uncomfortable, and a wearing period; yet it was relieved, from time to time, by companionship and genuine fun.

My pleasantest memories of that last lap in Cairo are the Sunday mornings which John Waller, John Cromer, Jean Moscatelli, Raoul Parme—half a dozen poets, of diverse nationalities—used to spend in Keith Bullen's house in Gezira. Keith was headmaster of Gezira Preparatory School and the school and his house were one building. He produced, irregularly, a little poetry magazine called *Salamander* and our group called itself the Salamanders. Keith received us in a great white room, full of sunshine, and on low tables there were large, flat bowls full of the snipped heads of dark roses. Keith, dark, and red, often liverish on a Sunday morning, sprawled in an armchair in his dressing-gown, was himself like a great blown rose. He was enormously stout; his pebbly blue eyes seemed strange mineral intrusions in his rosy flesh. Something about his appearance and his attitude to life was very soothing to me. When he stood on the stone steps of his house, in a white panama and a floppy white jacket that fluttered in the breeze, he looked like a big captive balloon that the stick moored to the ground.

Sunday morning in Keith's room, talking about poetry, or the fourth dimension—Ouspenski's book was on the shelves in the corner, beside the first editions of Swinburne—or the odds on the races, or the literary and social feuds in which we found ourselves involved, was a soothing time in a fretful week. One drank brandy, there, too, but it was better brandy; one talked, but not to pay with clever talk for the drinks one could not buy. The chairs were deep and comfortable, the room at once cool and sunny. Keith moved clumpily about, showing us a new book, a rare old edition, or some poem that had been sent to him for *Salamander*. He was without malice, and he moved among his poems, good and bad, among his opinions, shrewd and fantastic, like a generous child among toys. He was a good and happy man, and these are rare. I was often too exhausted on a Sunday morning to take much part in the conversation. Keith, and John Waller, and Raoul Parme would talk vivaciously; I would listen intently, and pick off the floor a small dark red rose-bud and drop it petal by petal into a brass ashtray full of stubbed-out stumps.

Yet even in Keith's company it was impossible always to escape from the peculiar emotional prickliness of the general Cairo atmosphere or from the farcical squabbles that prickliness tended to provoke. There was once a Salamander party . . . but I had better quote the dry, deadpan description of that shocking evening which John Waller sent off, a few days later, to Erik de Mauny, then serving in Italy. The very lack of comment in John's letter is, in its way, expressive. The kind of social fiasco he is describing was something to which we had all become perfectly attuned.

'John Cromer leaves for England this week. The Salamanders had a farewell dinner for him at that peculiar place known as Parme's bistro at the Cairo end of the Bulac bridge. There came to it John Cromer, Keith Bullen, Raoul Parme, Jean Moscatelli, George Hepburn, Alan Arnold, Nicholas de Watteville, G. S. Fraser, and myself. Really, it cannot be described as altogether a success, since it ended up with everybody quarrelling with each other furiously. And really, the bistro—at which Parme had insisted the dinner should be held—was a quite odious little place and they just put screens round us in the middle of the public bar, where we were so tightly placed that if anybody wanted to go to the lavatory the whole company had to get up. The food consisted of lots of hors d'oeuvres and snick-snacks. Drink was not obtained very easily—I only managed to get one bottle of beer and one brandy at table, but fortunately everybody had consumed a considerable amount of Scotch whisky at Keith's house before setting out. In fact everyone was more than a little tipsy before the meal started.

'I endeavoured to make the whole party go with a swing by performing a few conjuring and juggling tricks, but Parme, who was taking the whole thing so seriously that he was almost in tears most of the time and choking with emotion the rest, considered that this was frivolous. Keith and John Cromer made very sentimental speeches. Parme could scarcely talk for emotion and most of what he said was to the effect: "I have supported French literature for forty years—ask my friend Moscatelli." Nicholas put a plate of omelette on Parme's chair while he was speaking and when he had finished he sat down on it, but didn't notice anything was wrong till half an hour later, whereupon someone remarked: "Well, that will be the only hot dish we've had to-night."

'All, however, was well so far. The crisis arose when Parme came back from the bar (where he had taken Keith to get some more drinks) and said that everybody owed seventy-five piastres for the meal, a ridiculous figure for what we'd actually had. Moreover, he asked for the money so unpleasantly that Nicholas was rude to him. G.S.F. and George Hepburn hadn't got seventy-five piastres anyway. Alan offered to pay for G.S.F. but then Nicholas found he hadn't got the money either. Parme then accused everybody of trying to bilk the bill. Nicholas was rude to him again. I was then rude to Nicholas, Cromer and Alan started up a quarrel about effeminate young men in Cairo, and Jean Moscatelli just looked on wonderingly.

'I then went up to the bar to find Keith pretty mellow. He bought me a drink and I bought him one. Then Keith had one hell of a row with the barman whom he accused of being rude to him. He stormed all over the bar declaring that the barman was a disgrace to his father (also present) who owned the bistro, and that he ought to be in the Greek army. The Egyptian police then appeared (it was half past eleven) and wanted to know why there was so much drink being sold after licensing hours. Nobody took the slightest notice of them. Everybody went on quarrelling. Moscatelli, who couldn't understand a word of what was being said, but felt it might have something to do with his being Italian and having spent the war in a concentration camp in Egypt, kept going up to Nicholas, who spoke all the languages being used, asking: "Excuse, please! But are they quarrelling about me?" Nicholas then said: "I suppose you know, Mr Bullen, that there has been a lot of disagreement here." Keith looked at him amiably from the bar and replied: "Has there? Tell me about it."

'Anyway, so it all went on till about half an hour after

midnight, when I found myself back in my flat, having had a hearty quarrel on the way with G.S.F., about which neither of us could remember anything the next morning. Keith had to stay in bed the whole of the following day, Cromer has not been seen since though expected at Keith's on Sunday, and the rest of us have had hangovers. On Sunday, Keith (who had been standing at the bar most of the time the rest of us were quarrelling at the table, and so had no idea at all of what had been going on) remarked: "I thought it was a very successful and enjoyable evening, didn't you?" But even he was certain we had been absolutely swindled by the bistro and he is going to take it up next week with a view to recovering some of the money.'

Keith hoped to retire from his headmastership, to settle in London, perhaps to open a bookshop there, specialising in poetry, like Harold Monro's, and to provide for young poets some hospitable centre like his open house on Sunday mornings in Cairo. We would all have rallied round him, for there was something in his nature that inspired affection and respect. People felt at ease with him and yet, at the same time, they showed themselves at their best. His plans were all made and, a few months after I had left Cairo and settled in London, he gave a magnificent farewell party. Shortly afterwards he had a stroke, fell dangerously ill, and died. I felt his loss deeply. He had treated me, as he treated every young poet who came to his house, with fatherly kindness.

An Elegy for Keith Bullen

(Headmaster of Gezira Preparatory School, Cairo, and a friend to English poetry and poets)

A great room and a bowl full of roses,
Red roses, a man as round as a ripe rose,
Lying in a bowl of sun. And who supposes
Such a sad weight could support such a gay pose.

Flying his sad weight like a round baby's
Petulant balloon! He has blue pebbles for eyes,
Petulant, bewildered, innocent eyes like a baby's;
Like a great baby or a clipped rose he lies

In a white bowl of light in my memory;
And expands his tenuous sweetness like a balloon;
I shall die of feeling his dear absurdity
So near me now, if I cannot cry soon.

Keith was particularly Sunday morning,
Red roses, old brandy, was unharrying Time,
Was that white light, our youth; or was the fawning
Zephyr that bobs the gay balloon of rhyme,

He bobbed incredibly in our modern air;
With his loose jacket, his white panama hat,
As he leaned on his walking stick on the stone stair
He seemed a balloon, moored down to the ground by that.

As he leaned at the bar and ordered us pink gin
Or arranged a flutter on the three-fifteen
He seemed a child, incapable of sin:
We never knew him prudent, cold, or mean.

Or tied to the way the world works at all
(Not even tied enough for poetry);
All that he was we only may recall,
An innocent that guilt would wish to be,

A kind, a careless, and a generous,
An unselfseeking in his love of art,
A jolly in his great explosive fuss;
O plethora of roses, O great heart!

4

Cairo, in fact, in that last year of the war, was unsettling me.
'I never enter,' I wrote to Henry Treece, 'any great centre of
our war organisation—a headquarters, with its enormous
corridors, a barracks enclosing the Spanish cruelty of its square,
or even the huge mess where, as in an enormous third-class
waiting-room, so many strangers eat together—without a
shuddering sense of personal impotence; I expect at any moment
a thousand fingers to point, whistles to blow, and I expect then to
be brought, like a Kafka character, before some tribunal in a
small, shabby room that will condemn me to unexampled

penalties for the crime of being myself. This is a sort of persecution mania; but, to judge from the stiff, nervous faces around me, widely diffused. Moreover one *is* guilty in being oneself. The act of surrender to a huge machine, however frightful its consequences, would be an act of love.

'On the other hand, with what a sense of restfulness, travelling through the flat and scrubby Sudan, or in the highlands of Eritrea, I have come upon some military post so small, so isolated, that the few soldiers have been forced to know each other like a family; so that, entering such a Mess, from the baking heat outside, and finding nothing but bare whitewashed walls, scrubbed wooden chairs, benches, pin-up girls, a smell of cooking, I have nevertheless had the sensation, so reassuring, so refreshing to the traveller, of *entering a room* . . . When we say a "room", to-day, the word has as much emotional content as the word "home": how often have I sat in misery within four great walls that are not a room; or turned my eyes on an abstract construction that is not a scene; or watched, hunched over their tables, working to rigidly neurotic rules . . . typing with the exact margin of two and a half inches . . . the clerks performing their activity that is not an act. How I have been terrified of order!'

I meant the mechanical order of an organisation, like an army or a state according to its ideal notion, in which the dumb growth of tradition has been destroyed, in which everything is organised, by stated formulas, from the top down. But I was afraid too of the freedom of mere evasion; of the drifting isolation which I was beginning to know too well.

'The passions are not evil,' I wrote later in this same letter. 'But they are autonomous; they seek their own fulfilment, not ours. Does not freedom, I mean responsible freedom, which is the only sort worth talking about, depend upon the creation of an interior order (perhaps, for personality, what form or total intention is for a poem)? If we had this sense of interior order would the outward mechanical order terrify us so much? Would we feel so impotent in the face of it? Might we not transform it?'

In Cairo, I explained to Treece, I lived the life of false freedom, drift, of sick evasion. 'How much better,' I wrote, 'if we could be more soberly and patiently ourselves; the life in the small town, with the few serious friends, the many who smile in the street, the daily task with its satisfying drab detail, the grip on something, the chance for infinitely patient observation, over years, of tiny changes against a static background—changes to be recapitulated in memory, as one watches in the cinema the

160

unfolding of a flower. But here, the need for small satisfactions, the habit rather than the urge, the countless erotic half-loaves that add up to no lovely bread: this is a city where everything is permitted, where nothing excites surprise, and where nothing, therefore, has much moral or emotional importance. It is this which makes me sad and heavy, which gives me a nostalgia for virtue, for the small towns . . .'

So I moved towards a conclusion which was only a restatement of hesitation. 'A truly vital organism always hesitates. It chooses from, perhaps it *creates*, alternatives.'

Treece replied in a cheerful vein, determined to blow away my cobwebs.

'My faith in my fellow-men has increased to a degree,' he wrote, 'which before I joined up would have seemed fantastically impossible. All round me I see a rough kindness and co-operation, every one of us united to win a war, to get a square deal for each other and ourselves. And in every case, this kindness and co-operation is not, cannot be, imposed from above. It comes from the individual heart. I have known it, have felt it for five years, and no amount of theorising, however cleverly put, will seduce me from the results of that experience.

'As for *love*: yes, it's what we're all searching for, whether we know it or not. If we don't get it, we become gangsters, take to dope, power-politics, or psycho-analysis . . .

'I am quite impractical as a politician. I will only say that, if one decides to love a person that person, if he is normal, must ultimately cease resistance, allow himself to be loved, and finally love in return. To love, in this sense, requires a greater degree of self-abnegation than does almost any other activity. Perhaps the further we get away from the Self, the more nearly we approach happiness. And aren't you just a little overpowered by the weight of your own Self, George? Don't you rather drag it around, like a ball and chain on your leg? I mean that in the kindest way; I should have said possibly, aren't you too constantly aware that you are George Fraser and not Dick Smith, and don't you too often put the stethoscope of your sensitivity to George Fraser's heart or take the measure of his pulse as he reacts to the cruel world?'

Finally, Treece tackled my point about hesitation. He did not agree with me.

'For hesitation,' he wrote, 'like its near relative, pro-crastination, is a thief of energy. To know the way and to pursue that way, however inviting may be the irrelevant

161

sidetracks, is to use the energy God gave one to its highest advantage. The man who lacks a goal is already half-lost. Conversely, the man who has forged for himself some purpose, some goal, provided it be a Christian purpose and goal, is proof against all corruption. For is not corruption only another way of compensating for one's lack of faith in oneself and one's fellows; is it not only a substitute for happiness and completeness?

'Lack of faith, corruption, an uneasy conscience, fear of the machine, fear of one's fellows, fear of love . . . All these I see as a contemporary disease. You confess, whether you like it or not, that you suffer from some of these troubles, and I am smugly glad that at the moment I don't.'

So, I thought, as I read Treece's letter, I was projecting my own procrastinations, my sense of futility, my inability to forge some purpose or goal—I thought Treece's use of that equivocal verb 'forge' unfortunate—on the world at large. Perhaps, on the other hand, when Treece spoke of 'a contemporary disease' it might have been more accurate to speak of 'the contemporary disease'. No doubt I did rather drag my Self around, like a ball and chain on my leg; but reading my letter over again, I did not feel that I had been speaking for my own self only. I wondered if Treece considered me a writer, as he considered Henry Miller, who was out—in a phrase used of Miller and some others by a very different person, Dr Leavis—to 'do the dirt on life': as a writer always plaintive, defeated, discouraging. I did not see myself in that light. But I did not seem a person who could arrive at light, except by way of a long dark tunnel.

5

I must not make too much of my gloom. Cairo was full of rewarding characters and places. There was the grocer's shop, for instance, discovered by John Waller and the young New Zealand writer, Erik de Mauny, who always cheered us up with his vivacious good humour when he turned up in Cairo on leave or attachment from Italy or North Africa. For Erik, the war, though tragic, had elements also of a spree or a lark. He and John were always looking for original places to spend an evening, and they liked the little grocer's shop, on a sidestreet off Soliman Pacha, because of the creaking, rickety chairs, the smell of oil, the crates on which we balanced our glasses; the bottled beer was always just off the ice, and one could help oneself to olives and crisps out of great bowls. An Arab would come round to the shop during the evening with a brazier like a chestnut brazier, but piled high with little roasted birds, birds that fed on figs and had a sweet, delicate flesh. We would eat these greedily with our fingers, crunching them, bones and all.

It was in the grocer's shop that we first met the poet John Gawsworth. Erik de Mauny had brought with him from Mahdi a very untidy RAF sergeant with a long, thin, saturnine face, drooping eyelids, and a twisted nose. A cigarette hung slackly from one corner of his pliable mouth. Occasionally one eyebrow would cock upwards, sardonically, and simultaneously the corner of the mouth would move and the cigarette would point upwards towards the raised eyebrow. The RAF tunic was stained and short of buttons; but there was a little coloured button in the lapel, that of a Chevalier of the Court of the Bey of Tunis. There was a certain rakish and piratical air about this sergeant; an air, also, of grave and secret ceremony. He poured himself out a glass of beer with a slightly shaky hand. He asked for a small glass of water. He put the water down on a crate, passed his glass of beer over it in a small circle, and drank solemnly, muttering to himself, 'Mon roi!' De Mauny and Waller were frankly baffled by this performance. I was not. 'Ah,' I said, 'you are a Jacobite. The King over the water.' The sergeant cocked his sardonic eyebrow, his cigarette twitched upwards. 'But, hist!' he said. 'We are observed.' He laid a finger along the side of his boxer's nose.

John Gawsworth was, as we were soon to discover, not only the last of the Jacobites, but, according to his mood, a Sinn Feiner, an Indian Nationalist, or a French Republican. Gawsworth, whose real name was Terence Iain Fytton Armstrong, came of the same family as the Border riever, Johnny Armstrong, who was hanged by James IV of Scotland, and his family was connected also with the Lady Mary Fytton who was once believed to be the Dark Lady of Shakespeare's sonnets. He numbered distinguished Frenchmen and Irishmen also among his ancestors and, though he had spent most of his life in London, it was his foible to affect a harsh disdain for the English. 'Ah, you English,' he would say to us loudly in bars. 'What a set, what a set!' In his Scottish mood, he would say glumly, 'Had we our rights, my eldest brother would be Earl of Gawsworth in the Jacobite hierarchy.' In his Irish moods, he would talk about 'my president, Douglas Hyde'. In his French moods, he was ready to take the Bastille over again. All these loyalties of his were fierce and sensitive, and later, when he went to India, he became a great friend of Nehru's and ready to block argument with another gambit: 'You may not be aware, Sir, that you are talking to a Hindu.'

As John Gawsworth collected loyalties, so also he collected honorific distinctions. He was not only a Chevalier of the Court of the Bey of Tunis, he was a Freeman of the City of London, the youngest Fellow of the Royal Society of Literature, the Society's youngest Benson Gold Medallist, and since coming to the Near East he had become a travelling delegate of the Federation of French Writers of North Africa. He was heir to the Kingdom of Redonda (he is now King Juan I of that kingdom), a small, rocky, barren island in the West Indies, of which his great friend, the romantic novelist M.P. Shiel, had been in his childhood crowned King. John, in fact, had a great fondness for institutions of all sorts; it was owing to his enthusiasm that our informal Sunday gatherings at Keith Bullen's became a definite club, the Salamanders. It was owing to Gawsworth that the grocer's shop became an institution. John Waller, Erik and I would let things slide; John Gawsworth was a great man for keeping things up.

Gawsworth was to become one of our best friends, but there were difficulties to be got over first. He was only four or five years older than myself, but poetically he belonged to a quite different generation. His friends were survivors from the 1890s like Shiel and Machen, or neglected elder poets, like Anna Wickham; and, as he was the fierce champion of elderly slighted merit, so he tended to be extremely suspicious of sudden youthful fame. When Michael Roberts brought out his famous anthology, *New Signatures*, which for the first time introduced Auden, Spender, and Day Lewis to a large public, Gawsworth had immediately counterblasted with an anthology called *Known Signatures*. He himself was younger than Auden, younger, I think, than most of the leading poets of the '30s; but he had started writing in his 'teens, under the influence of older poets like Masefield and Abercrombie; he had never absorbed Eliot, and he was so much at home in the 1890s, so full of gossip about the private lives of Lionel Johnson and Ernest Dowson, that it was hard sometimes to remember that he was not the contemporary of Shiel and Machen, his surviving heroes.

When he read my poems, and to his surprise understood and liked them, in his relief he praised them too much. He wrote poems at a bar with a glass beside him, tossing the sheets over to me for my suggestions. He talked, while he wrote, but not about his poetry. 'Here I am,' he would say humorously, 'a pore

164

scruffy sergeant, a pore gorblimey, and me wife, God bless 'er, is an orficer of field rank in the ATS' (When John was in a good mood, he tended to talk in this way, in stage Cockney.) 'Stow it away, George, stow it away. I got millions of 'em. Millions of poems at home. Write 'em on little scraps of piper and stow 'em in an old tin trunk.' Another sip of brandy and more concentrated scribbling. 'What rhymes with "diaphanous", George?' I would pause and think. ' "Cacophonous",' I would say, 'nearly.' 'Nearly ain't good enough for the old traditional school. Cacophonous, eh? And what rhymes with "dastard", you old unutterable, you!'

John Gawsworth was good but dangerous company. Rows always seemed to start up round him in bars, and it was also hard for us always to remember his extremely various, and easily wounded, loyalties. There was an evening when he, de Mauny, Waller, and I took a taxi to Mahdi. John Gawsworth fell asleep for a quarter of an hour, and then woke up, looking startled, bad tempered, and not quite sure where he was. He started off on one of his usual diatribes about the English. 'Come, come,' I said petulantly, 'a very civilised people.' John Gawsworth suddenly gritted his teeth, shuddered, and said, 'Gentlemen, you forget you are talking to an Irish Republican. I am afraid I cannot bear such company one moment longer.' The taxi was moving rapidly, but before we could stop him, John Gawsworth opened the door nearest him and tumbled out on the road. We pulled up and shouted after him, but he was limping bitterly away. It was a poor quarter of Cairo. 'The silly old beggar,' said Erik, 'he'll get a knife in him.' Gawsworth limped to the nearest Arab café, where he asked for a doss-down for the night. He pushed the scanty furniture of his room against the door, so that if anybody felt like cutting his throat he would at least have fair warning. He slept soundly, and in the morning, on his way out, met a Provost-Captain who was looking for soldiers out of bounds. Gawsworth went straight up to him, saluted, and was told the way to Mahdi. He had borrowed twenty-five piastres for his taxi before the Provost-Captain had time to think of putting him on a charge.

He was admirably resourceful and his extravagance was contagious. We found ourselves playing up to him. Was he living in a world of fantasy? Well, what sort of a world were we, of Groppi's Light Infantry, living in? Really, there were no flies on John. Out of the corner of his mouth, without shifting the drooping cigarette, he occasionally muttered an obscure comment on some acquaintance of ours—' 'E's a purty little bunch o' roses, ain't he, chums?'—and one detected, behind the

flourish and panache, the shrewd bohemian who had kept afloat
so long on London's deep waters, and whom the Nile would not
drown either. Gawsworth was always short of money, as many of
us were, but the MoI was a resource to him. He would come
into our office in the afternoon, looking weak and shaken, and
sitting down at a desk would scribble out a feature article with
incredible rapidity. Writing so rapidly, he naturally often wrote
at the top of his voice. From India, I received a copy of an article
he had written about me, with the striking title: 'In the Sky of
Poetry, A New Star Rises.' I could imagine John tossing the pages
over, and saying, ' 'Ow's 'at, chum? I bet, now, you think no
small potatoes o' yersel'!' I was embarrassed, but touched.
Gawsworth always seemed hovering on the verge of some
romantic disaster. When he finally limped off to India, we waited
for bad news of him. But all the news was good. An Indian
publisher brought out volume after volume of his poems and
anthologies. He met all the leading poets and political figures of
Bengal, and came back with yet another loyalty. His character
had been formed long before the war; so he came back to London,
in the end, less changed than any of us. It was to his office in the
premises of the Poetry Society—he edited *The Poetry Review* and I
do not know how many other magazines—that I turned when I
wanted to revive the pleasanter side of Cairo life. He would be
sitting there at a desk piled high with proofs and manuscripts,
working through them, with that famous cigarette still drooping,
and an open bottle of beer beside him. He greeted me with that
upshooting eyebrow. And when the pubs opened, we would stand
by the bar for hours, talking about the good old days, which
became of course, in retrospect, better and better.

6

So the war for me ran mildly to an end, in a kind of flat twilight,
relieved by moments of comedy. But younger friends, new to
Cairo, were still able to feel a sort of fresh anguish. To them I
seemed almost horribly at ease in my shabby bohemian
atmosphere. Iain Fletcher, a young poet with short-sighted angry
eyes, a comic snub nose, and a mouth that twisted eloquently in
disgust and sorrow, wrote a long prose piece about an evening
that he spent with me and Kenneth Topley—a blunt young RAF
officer, an intellectual hearty—in a café which was a haunt of
rather decadent and off-colour characters. Iain's purple patch

conveys little to me, and I am not quite sure how far he was merely 'projecting': 'About us, as we talked with frantic abstraction, there was specific vacancy, specific insufficiency of purpose . . . With George, it was different. The most tenuous, as the most learned of us, in a sense, the most "innocent" of us, he nevertheless moved with a myopic assurance through this underworld. If the senses contracted through reading about cults of violence and then continuing as a quiet citizen, that would explain his languor in the face of what was done in the open street and what was also done tigerishly in the evil air through which this particular place moved. It did in fact move. With each coming together of "characters" at a table, in a corner, at the foot of an abrupt stair, a certain eddy was to be perceived through all the bodies whose looks were never directed at anything in especial, but who were busy in some indefinable way, on the margin of the eye and ear, whose conversation was always cleverly inaudible except for an arresting fragment which might expose or delimit the "characters" in the picture.'

It was, Iain added, to gratify the 'sense of evil', that Kenneth and he drank coffee with me night after night in this particular café; but I simply went there because it stayed open later than the others, and because I wanted to go on talking. My sense of evil was not something that needed an airing, and I was long past the stage when I could get what Iain called a suburban *frisson* from the social manners of the sexually eccentric (these, in fact, are what he is talking about, in that portentous paragraph I have quoted). But on that particular evening, we had an experience that, for Iain and Kenneth at least, assumed a definite symbolic importance. We were talking politics; and we were interrupted by the booming, as from a deep sea cave, of a drunken captain. I had been expounding the sociological theories of Karl Mannheim. What the captain said was, 'What you are saying, young man, sounds to me like pure Herbert Spencer.' The Captain provoked in Iain a certain suburban shudder. He drew up his chair to our table; and he would occasionally look away, with a benevolent eye, towards a handsome youth sitting near the door, observing each time, sentimentally, 'It is the harlots who go to heaven.' Iain was rude ('An instinctive loss of breeding,' he had once said to me, 'is my only charm') and he found the Captain genuinely shocking. But the latter, blandly ignoring his snubs, went on talking, switching the conversation from politics to theology. This was Iain's favourite subject. The Captain was good at it. They were soon talking about Hell. 'God is not absent from Hell,' said the Captain. 'Or his absence is a kind of presence. God is present there in the shape of his Justice.' 'God's absence,' said Iain, rolling the phrase with relish over his tongue, 'is a kind of sinister presence.' The Captain said that it was a permissible private belief (it was, he indicated, one that he inclined to himself) that Hell, though eternally existent, was eternally empty. Yet, he added thoughtfully, salvation was only to be found in the free cooperation of the will with God's grace. God wanted us to be saved but was not going to force us to be saved without our own cooperation. 'God is not lust,' said the Captain thoughtfully, and his eye wandered again to the youth by the door . . . Iain was held between horror and fascination. And it added a last touch to the Captain's character when (the conversation switching to politics once more) we learned that before the war he had been a follower of Sir Oswald Mosley and was still rather Fascist in his general opinions. 'I would call myself,' he said, 'a Radical of the Right.' Finally, he left us, springing up to greet a friend who had just come in. 'Hello, my dear! How's tricks?' and the two vanished. Iain sat silent for a long time: that the same person should be at one and the same time a congenial mind, a comic drunk, and a moral horror. I thought the Captain just a type. Iain turned on me. 'You have a frightening calm,' he said, 'because you think it all evens out in the long run. But in the long run, we are all dead, and damned perhaps.'

'What did the Captain stand for, then?' I asked. I was a little bored.

'You wouldn't see it, because you have no real sense of evil. No, what the Captain did for me—and I think, really, for Kenneth, too—was to burst open any fabulous idea of innocence we might have had. We shall never believe now that anyone is untouched, can remain untouched, can remain on the margin of guilt. How that guilt is to be expiated is another matter. But we are all guilty. No will is pure. There is no great gulf fixed between me and the Captain, or between me and anybody else. I feel a kind of peace after that encounter. But it feels quite unlike the peace of God.'

I was past or I had not reached the stage for such revelations and such certainties. My strength lay in an ability to suspend my judgment. Leaving Iain sitting over his coffee with his tragically twisted mouth, I went my ways with precise indecision. The end of the war came with more parties and with little dramas in the streets. Australians and New Zealanders, on VE night, wrecked a few of the more exorbitant Levantine bars. Egyptians, as our carousing and sometimes obstreperous troops strolled the streets

168

of Cairo that evening, expressed their injured sense of national self-sufficiency by emptying their slops on us from top-storey windows. In Emad el Din, a crowd of soldiers had got hold of a long pole and were trying to batter down the front door of a block of flats, from which such slops had been slung at them. I strolled about the streets with a young Captain, Tony Schooling, who was prancing on his toes from excitement at the tense scene. 'I'd move off, Captain,' said an MP sergeant, respectfully but impatiently. 'You'll only encourage them if you stand and watch. This is not exactly a spectacle, sir.' 'Come away, Tony,' I said, 'come away. Let's go somewhere quiet, if there is anywhere quiet, for a drink.'

We went in the end to Keith Bullen's, where a wonderful victory party was going on. All the feuds of Cairo were for one night forgotten. An old enemy of mine (a writer of great talent, who generally resembled a codfish but to-night, flushed with wine, a red mullet) wrung my hands. 'Tomorrow the knives and the poison,' he said, 'tomorrow the knives and the poison. But to-night the truce, the temporary forgiveness, the full glass.' I took the glass he offered me. I gulped at my drink and clapped Tony on the shoulder. 'Better than brawls in the street, Tony. And it's strange to think it's all nearly over. And on the whole one feels, doesn't one, real relief?'

A Winter Letter

(To my sister in London, from Asmara)

Like an unnourished rose I see you now, and yours the
Pallor of that city of soot and pigeons
Where the leaf is pale, that seems to curl its tendrils
Always around the painted green of iron,
I imagine you pale among the pigeon droppings,
And with your eyelids shadowed like the violets
They sell in bunches from their pavement baskets,
And I imagine you not with your old buxomness
But slim like the young ladies in the advertisements,
With your hair preened in a mode of cockney smartness
And your hands in the pockets of a heavy coat . . .
Do you think wistfully as I do, my darling,
These mornings when your heart is not in that city,
Reluctant stroller to the Board of Trade,
Of our glittering and resourceful north, with its

Terminus smell in the morning of cured herrings
And its crackling autumn suburbs of burned leaves?
Though I write in winter, and now except for the hollies
The trees in our old garden are all bare:
Now as they walk these streets of flashing mica,
They puff white steam from their nostrils, men and horses,
And their iron heels strike out sparks from the frosty road!
Now the white mist seeps round the red brick baths by the sea-
     front
And the children are girning at play with blue fingers
For a sea-coal fire and the starch of a Scotch high-tea,
Now with nipped red cheeks, the girls walk the streets rapidly,
And the shop-window's holly and tinsel can hardly delay.
I think of the swirl of the taffeta schoolgirls at Christmas,
Remembering Bunny whose skin was like cream upon milk,
Remembering Joy with her honey-dark skin and dark glances,
Remembering Rosemary's chatter and eloquent eyes,
Ahimé! and sigh because war with its swoop and its terror
That pounces on Europe and lifts up a life like a leaf,
Though its snell wind whirl you into a niche where you're cosy,
Yet its years eat up youth and the hope of fulfilment of youth.

And last night I dreamt I returned and therefore I write,
Last night my train had drawn up at a black London station,
And there you were waiting to welcome me, strange but the same,
And I shook your gloved hands, kissed your light-powdered
     cheek, and was waiting
To see your new flat, and your books, and your hats, and your
     friends,
When I suddenly woke with a lost lonesome head on my pillow,
And black Africa turning beneath me towards her own dawn,
And my heart was so sore that this dream should be snapped at
     the prologue
That I send you my soreness, dear heart, for the sake of this
     dream.

A Beginning of Peace

1

I CAME back, wearing no ribbons (I was entitled to a few, for having pounded my typewriter in the same area where other soldiers had fought battles, but I had never thought it proper to apply for them) and holding the inappropriate rank of WOII. My conduct, according to my discharge sheet, had been exemplary; the note on my character, by the Major in charge of the section of the MoI in Cairo, said that I had great talent and was a glutton for work, but was untidy and eccentric, and that the employer who gave me a job would have to conquer an initial prejudice against my vague manner and my wild hair. Vanity and ambition are two other facets of my character, so I never used this note. Lieutenant Fowler, in Eritrea, had been wrong when he said that after the war I would probably settle down quite happily to a sub-editor's job on a provincial paper at seven pounds a week. My character is dutiful but not docile. In the army, I allowed more practical people to make the most sensible use they could of me. I did not intend to do that as a civilian. After using my brain on my country's behalf for about six years, I wanted, for a year or two at least, to use it on my own. I was determined to see if I could earn my living by creative writing. Like the young man in Balzac, I wanted to be loved and to be famous.

I remember few details of that voyage home. We came by the Mediterranean from Alexandria and then across France to Dieppe. I was in charge of a draft, kept busy checking papers, changing money, and calling rolls. The troopship was as crowded as it had been on the longer and drearier voyage out round the Cape of Good Hope. I was cheerful and talkative, and on our last night at Dieppe, I remember, drank rather too much whisky in the Sergeants' Mess; coming across the Channel, the next morning, I stood at the bows, feeling ragged, holding on to the rails of the bucketing little steamer, and letting the wind punish me. It soon blew away my hangover. I noticed that the Channel is a deep and virulent green where the Mediterranean, like the sea in poems, is a translucent blue. I had forgotten this northern

171

scene. As we approached Newhaven, the cliffs seemed not white, but of a yellow, sad colour, like tartar-stained teeth; a mist lay over them, and the island of Britain seemed wrapped in a purple cloud. At the docks, there was a steady grey drizzle. I had never, in all these years, learned to carry my kitbag properly and I went down the gangway swaying and staggering. In the railway waiting-room reserved for us, I drank lukewarm, oversweet tea from a large coarse mug. It was Sunday and a little boy was selling papers. He mocked my accent and my choice. 'Ooh, yess,' he mimicked, 'ooh, yess, *The Observah*, of course!'

In the carriage of the train that was to take us to our dispersal centre at Aldershot, I lit a cigarette and looked out of the window. The red brick of the houses, the bomb rubble, the grey weather, even the damp indigestible green of the fields, all seemed strange. Looking round the carriage, I saw that the soldiers' faces had acquired, like my own, a withdrawn look. For years we had been making a great effort to get on with each other. It would soon no longer be necessary. At Aldershot, when I had signed in the draft, I walked out with a couple of sergeants into the streets, harsh with December fog. A grim, glum town, full of poky little shops and Methodist chapels. We asked a soldier the way to the nearest pub, and he shook his head. He was a Pole, or a Norwegian, and spoke hardly any English. We found a pub at last, dark, brown and stuffy, so different from the bistros of Cairo, with their marble-topped round tables and their shutters run up to a sunny, dusty street. We ordered half-pints of mild beer.

We wandered back into the dispersal centre with a feeling of anti-climax. We were told to gather our remaining kit, to have it checked over. I was short of several pieces of webbing equipment and told the sergeant, but he merely winked at me and checked over in a loud voice all the pieces I had not got. I had been worried about that all through the voyage; a slight weight had been lifted. Finally, we passed along a row of small tables, collecting pay, money orders, discharge books, I forget what else. A stout officer seized my discharge book, asking suspiciously what the piece of typed paper stuck in it was. The young officer who was handing out the books said it was a tribute to my character; and then shook hands with me, as he must have shaken hands with hundreds that day, and thanked me for all I had done. I passed out of the long room, and realised that I was a free man again—with nothing to struggle against now, except life and my own character. I expected to feel a certain exhilaration; I felt only a kind of blank relief.

The next morning we were packed into lorries and taken to Woking to pick up our civilian clothes. I chose a grey pinstripe suit, a solid pair of brown shoes, a mackintosh, and, for comedy, a green pork-pie hat. A few hours later I got off a number nineteen bus at Beaufort Street in Chelsea where my mother and sister were now living, and humped my kitbag and my little cardboard box with my civilian clothes in it along a street of ugly, old-fashioned flats, with trams clanging towards a bridge over the grey Thames. Opposite my mother's flat a bomb had shaved a church in half. I was to grow fond of Chelsea, but at the moment it seemed to me only to have the character of drabness. I got my things up to the first floor and rang the bell. My mother came to the door and stared at me for a moment with a white face. We stared at each other for a moment, as if not quite believing what we saw; then she was in tears and in my arms.

2

My mother had brought most of her furniture down from Aberdeen with her, and in her large front room with white creamy walls and a bay window, looking out to the noisy street, I had, for the first time since I had landed, the sense of being at home. There was the piano, and on top of it the familiar photograph of my father. He must have been about thirty when that photograph was taken, and I was about thirty now; as I stared at him, standing, as a soldier should, with a slight air of swagger, I looked down also a little guiltily at my own baggy battledress and the crown and laurels on my sleeve. And there was one of the things that my grandfather had picked up on his early voyages; a round Japanese painting in a square lacquer frame, of fishes coiling through a freshwater pool, over the edge of which hung a blossoming branch. An old friend of my father's in Aberdeenshire, a connoisseur of painting and the keeper of a country inn, used to brood over this piece. 'Life, life,' he would say, 'vivid, pulsating life!' The saying had stuck in our minds and had become a family name for the picture. 'Have a look,' we would say to our friends, 'at life, life, vivid, pulsating life!' Looking at it now, I remembered my grandfather, the smell of his cigars, of his sickroom, and the strange affinity between childhood and old age.

As mother talked to me, I glanced again at the piano, and that seemed to bring me closer to her than whatever she was saying. In moods of anxiety, in Aberdeen, she had been in the habit of sitting at the piano, improvising for hours; her hands were broad and strong and capable, and seemed to pounce on the notes—my own hands, small and thin and elegant-looking, are my father's, and good for nothing practical. I remembered the evenings of singing; how my mother, as she played by ear, concentrating fiercely, would close her eyes; my sister would also close her eyes when she sang, but because she was nervous, and for the same reason would dig her nails into the palms of her hands. I remembered how my father and I would listen patiently to the trilling pieces, and then ask for the simple, melancholy songs we liked. Gravely, we would enjoy a sort of pure sadness.

The room meant these things to me, but I had not come back to them. Grandfather and father were dead, mother did not play or sing so often. My mother looked tired and worried. My father's death, and her uprooting from her old surroundings, and the bombing raids on London, had told on her nerves. My sister, too, was different. She was married to a young engineer from Hamburg, Fritz Kestner, whom she had known since her university days in Aberdeen. She was expecting a baby. During the war years she had continued to hold down a responsible job. Where I had left behind me a lovely, fierce girl, I found myself facing a serious and composed young woman. The lines of Jean's face spoke of a character more fixed than my own, and as I talked to her I realised that the atmosphere that had once existed between us no longer existed in the same way; she would not listen now so patiently to my ramblings; with her strong brows and her clipped, incisive speech she seemed more than ever like my father.

I would be living, I realised, in a house full of women, for Paddy—a friend of Jean's, also at the Board of Trade—was sharing the expenses of the flat. I met Paddy later that first evening in London, when she came home from work: a tall, dark, thin girl, with eager, slightly gawky movements—though graceful even in her gawkiness—big dark eyes, and a gentle face. I hardly took her in, that first evening, though within a year I was to marry her.

The London I came to know well was a private London, like everybody else's, the shape that one carves out for oneself in a huge amorphous map. Its centre was the offices of *Poetry London* in Manchester Square. A day or two after settling in at Beaufort Street, I went to see the head of that concern, Tambimuttu, who had published a volume of my poems during the war and who had sent me kind and encouraging letters. Nicholas Moore was also in these offices, reading through and rejecting an incredible number of poetic manuscripts, but usually sending them back with helpful and practical comments. Nicholas's desk, on which a few files were neatly arranged, contrasted with the desk of Tambi, which was heaped in the most chaotic fashion with books, letters and manuscripts, a pile into which Tambi would dive a hand at random when he wanted to show me something, usually landing by a kind of uncanny luck on just what he wanted. But certain things did get lost, sometimes poems which the authors had sent in months or years before and about which Tambi would get plaintive, enquiring letters. 'Dear Mr Tambimuttu: I sent you from Cyrenaica, in 1942, a long poem called 'Soldier's Pay'. You said you thought it had promise and you might conceivably use extracts from it. It is now January, 1946, and . . .' Tambi's conscience would be stirred and there would be a wild hunt through the piles of manuscripts on his desk and through cluttered drawers. And perhaps (for if his memory was of a rather disorderly kind, he never really forgot anything) he would dig out 'Soldier's Pay', with the dust of time on it; and Nicholas would send it back for him with a very polite letter.

When I went into the office, Nicholas would be hammering away methodically at his typewriter. Tambi would be crouched over the gas fire at the end of the large room, silent and moody; or walking up and down with his hands behind his back like Felix the Cat in those early film cartoons. Their social habits were also different. Nicholas set out for lunch at precisely half-past twelve, and if one ate with him one had a solid meal at a Czech restaurant of chicken and dumplings and then more dumplings, sweet, with jam and poppy seed; or if one came in to the office in the afternoon, one would go out with him to some small expensive teashop, and eat several little sweet cakes, before he dashed away, looking, with his neat clothes, his spectacles, and his rolled umbrella, like someone in the City, to catch the train to Cambridge. And conversation with Nicholas would consist of precise analytical discussions of current poetry, in which he displayed his dry, sad, humorous mind. He spoke of poetry often in terms of cricket, of which he was a devotee; and seemed to think of most of his contemporaries as a set of awkward, dogged stonewallers.

With Tambi, on the other hand, one would go out to lunch about one; and we would be drinking beer in 'The Hog in Pound' in Oxford Street almost till three, snatching then a late, hasty

175

meal; back to the office about four (Nicholas would already be on his way back to Cambridge) and then out again to the pubs about half-past six, returning to Tambi's flat near Regent's Park about midnight, when he might feel like cooking a meal. Tambi's conversation, unlike Nicholas's, would be intermittent and often apparently inconsequential. At lunch-time, till he had drunk his first pint or two, he would often merely sit in gloomy silence, muttering occasionally, 'My stomach is bad this morning.' With his long black hair, his beautifully moulded, rather bird-of-prey-like brown face, his angry flashing eyes, and his dangerously eloquent smile, he was, even in his oldest, untidiest clothes, a person of physical distinction; one felt the background of Tamil grandees, the atmosphere of a childhood spent in a mixture of rustic simplicity and feudal state. A childlike directness was Tambi's great quality, and for the sake of that one was quite willing to put up with his occasional outbursts of rage. In the evening, there would come a period when he felt like reciting poems. His voice had a booming resonance, that seemed to make something different of the verse he quoted; something admirable in itself, but often rather aside from the poet's intention. *'Come,'* he would intone, *'come, my December lady, to my side, amid the tick and tock of the mixed seasons . . .'* 'Who wrote that, Tambi?' 'That was Nicholas. At sixteen. He has written nothing since that I really like so much.' Or he would assume the manner of burlesqued pomposity. 'Come, come, George. We need form. We need concentrated force. We cannot be doing with this glib, garrulous writing.'

I had come home at the end of the great wartime 'boom' in poetry. During the war, Tambimuttu had been producing his magazine *Poetry London* with comparative regularity, every few months, but he had finally accumulated so many manuscripts by new poets that he decided to produce a bumper number, in book form, that would give almost everyone a showing. The sheer size of this volume, which sold at eighteen shillings, was staggering and discouraging, and after producing it Tambi felt incapable of getting back to his old method of comparatively rigorous selection. He carried round with him habitually (losing it sometimes in taxis, but always recovering it again) a fat file of typescripts and manuscripts. He looked gloomily through them as we sat at a long table in some pub. He was waiting for his sense of the occasion to tell him the right moment to start his magazine going again. This was early in 1946 and it was not till 1948 that *Poetry London* started appearing again fairly regularly.

176

Tambi's procrastination was shrewd, though not on his own account, since his inability to plod like so many editors and publishers in a safe routine, in the end led to his firm and his magazine—which he had started at the beginning of the war, with hope in his heart, and ten pounds in his pocket—falling into other hands, and he left the London literary scene. The war had provoked a great many people into writing sincere occasional verse. Peace removed that provocation. Even I, who was not an 'occasional poet', felt in 1946 no immediate urge to write. The spur of exile and loneliness had gone, but when it came to expressing any more positive theme my voice faltered. These first years of the peace were a fallow period for many poets. We were growing into a new atmosphere, and it was Tambi's job now not so much to publish us as to help us grow. As a Ceylonese, he was indifferent to the religious, political, or social differences that cause petty feuds between English writers. His friends were a good representative cross-section of the younger generation, as well as some of their interesting elders. He felt at ease with everybody, and one felt at ease in his company; not that his manner was marked by what Mr Asquith called 'a flaccid geniality', for he never flattered anybody, or concealed boredom or much stronger negative emotions. But he was always himself, and it was easy to be oneself with him. My awkwardness, provincial oddities of manner, occasional bursts of absurd self-assertiveness, were things he took for granted, or about which he would rally me only in the kindest way. Through him, in this new scene, I gradually began to feel sure of myself.

He introduced me to useful people, hoping that I would get a job as a lecturer in a university or, like so many poets of our time, on the BBC. I had a series of meetings, at the suggestion of William Empson, with Dr Crow of London University. Dr Crow was anxious to find out what period of English literature I had a special interest in. I was glib and evasive, and Empson finally said to me in irritation, 'Crow thinks you are just a know-all.' I was for a moment abashed. 'He's quite right,' I said at last. 'I haven't really kept up my reading as I should. There isn't any period I know thoroughly. There are several that I have a feeling for, and think I could get up, if I had to.' 'Well,' said Empson, 'you should have told him so.' Similarly, when I had an interview at the BBC with Mr Gilliam—again through Empson's kindness—I was stumped when I was asked what my special interest was. I thought of subjects as things to 'get up': the fault of my journalistic training. And when I interviewed the rather stern

177

editor of a famous literary weekly, to see if I could get some reviewing from him, the same difficulty cropped up. I had now decided that it was important to have some special subject (it would have been arrogant to say what would have been the truth, that what interested me was the free play, over a wide range of topics, of my own mind, and that I liked to approach every subject with a freedom from preconceptions). I said that I was very interested in philosophy. 'But if you don't know Greek and if you don't know German,' said this editor, 'I would leave philosophy alone. This is not the age of the amateur.' An amateur was what I was; there were few subjects on which I could not make a few pertinent remarks; however, there was no subject that I felt I thoroughly possessed. This was a slender foundation on which to build a career in polite letters.

I did land one or two odd jobs. I started writing, and never completed, a radio script about Captain Cook for Rayner Heppenstall (it pleased me to hear that before the war Heppenstall once started writing, and never managed to complete, a radio script about Columbus). I got a contract for a short book about Scotland, which I wrote rapidly, filling in the gaps at the Chelsea public library. Through a casual meeting with an old Cairo friend, I got a contract to translate a fascinating, difficult little book by the French poet, Patrice de la Tour du Pin. And in the summer of 1946, by a great stroke of luck, I got a literary award of two hundred pounds a year for three years. This, with the other odd money I was earning, made it unnecessary in the meantime for me to seek a regular job. The Harvill Press, for which I had translated Patrice de la Tour du Pin (my version was generally praised, but Tambi disliked it, hinting that it smelt of pietism and Pater), got used to having me around, and made me a junior director; and in 1947, my luck holding, I got the chance to go on a cultural mission to South America, and signed a contract with Harvill Press to write a short book on the trip. My income was helped out by reviewing which, infrequent at first, latterly became so regular as to be something like a burden. There was an ironical side to all this. I had managed to remain independent, to devote all my time to writing; but I was so busy with books, articles, translations and reviews, that I had less time than I would have found if I had been doing some routine job, to devote to poetry. I wrote fewer and fewer original poems; but tried to keep my hand in with verse translation.

The habits of industry which I had acquired writing daily

leaders in Eritrea and daily feature articles in Cairo, helped me to get my literary journalism done on time; and the passion for convivial sociability, which I had also acquired in the Middle East, helped to put such work in my way. But I would not advise any other ambitious young Scotsman who wants to establish himself in London, to imitate my lack of method. I had not really pulled any strings; I had been around and things had come my way. But it would be perfectly possible, I imagine, to spend years drinking round the bars of Chelsea, Soho, and Bloomsbury, and to return to Scotland at the end with nothing but an empty purse and a range of casual acquaintances.

Tom Scott, for instance, whom I ran down again, selling books in Barker's, in High Street, Kensington, represented the other side of the medal. He was living, in 1946, in a single room, with books piled on the bed and a small gas ring to cook his meagre meals on. Since his discharge from the army, he had held a succession of odd jobs—working in the post office at rush periods, doing crowd work in film studios, or serving over Christmas in big shops. He was still writing poetry and later, with his unshakable faith in the people, he became one of a group of young poets who read their work regularly in Hyde Park. But these waters, to which I was taking like a duck at that time, had bedraggled his plumes. He loathed London bohemian life; the same drift, evening after evening, on the great beer route between 'The Wheatsheaf' and 'The Highlander'; his Scottish puritanism and shyness reacted against what he regarded as an atmosphere of promiscuous exhibitionism. He still retained his intransigent idealism. He kept his enormous diary, full of his dreams. There was a set of aphorisms at the beginning of one of these volumes which he called 'First Principles'; there seemed to be about a hundred of these, and I thought that was too many first principles altogether. But Tom resembled Tambi, whom in many ways he rather disapproved of, in that he was a creature of intuition. Everything that he genuinely thought or perceived *was* a first principle, not a weak logical derivative from something else; he liked, disliked, approved, disapproved, praised, condemned, not according to some set of 'attitudes' but according to the blind, obscure reaction of his whole being. This was true of Tambi, also, except that Tambi was more liable to go back on his intuitions. So the two of them, chary of each other as they generally were, got on rather well. Both of them had the same protective attitude towards me; regarding my ploddingly rational processes of thought rather in the light of an interesting curiosity. 'Everything you say is so *pertinent,* George,' Tambi observed to me once, with more than a touch of mockery; and Tom observed, 'For you, George, everything that happens is an illustration of an idea.' I spent some pleasant evenings with them together. Tom still sang to himself as he wandered along the streets with us, and song, for him, was still the life passion for which the writing of verse was a most inadequate substitute.

I was curious to see how Tom would react to somebody who seemed, temperamentally, at quite the opposite pole to himself. I took him along one evening to drink mulled beer with William and Hetta Empson in Hampstead. Empson would heat a poker in the fire and plunge it, red hot, into a pint glass of mild ale. There was a sizzling noise, and a moment of suspense, while we all waited for the glass to crack, which it never did; a rich froth gathered on the beer and it acquired a delicious creamy flavour. Tom's remarks on the evening were acute. 'G.S.F. took me along,' he wrote, 'to meet William Empson the other night. I was surprised to find a short gypsy-dark man in bohemian clothes, with a Norse goddess of a wife. I suppose he is the most intensely intellectual person I have met, with just a touch of that puckish, childish sentimentality about him. His degree of introversion was another surprise; I had imagined he would be rather arrogant and socially poised; instead, he has humility, is pedantic, keenly observant of people, intellectually precise, athletic-looking, and erudite. He is a born scholar, of complete integrity, and "really what he is". I was quite unable to take part in the conversation between him and G.S.F. I liked him best for his impersonal sincerity. He is not like the average denizen of these parts who delights in "helping" others; he has too much respect for truth and candour to say things which are supposed to benefit the imagined psychology of a "person". His sincerity was such a relief—or would have been in better circumstances—from the damnable modern craze of "personalism" in which everybody peddles his amateur psychology in phrases and references that look like artificial walls. (I gathered he thought that I was in grave danger of being devoured by that monster!) I liked him but felt out of place in his company. His wife has a wealth of physical rest in her.'

It may have been true in Tom's special sense that Empson did not delight in 'helping' others, but in the sense of doing generous and practical things for one, nobody could have been more helpful. I had met him first, through Tambi, as I met everybody, at a party of Roy Campbell's. He had liked some of my wartime poems, especially 'Letter to Anne Ridler'; and I, for my part, since I first came across it at St Andrews, had been impressed, even when its subtleties confused me, by his critical prose and later by the melancholy and passionate wit (more by this than by the deft obscurities, which tended to stump me) of his poems; the poem that begins 'This last pain for the damned the Fathers found' is one of the half dozen best short poems of our time. In my undergraduate days, Empson had been like a tone of voice, a ripple of speech, that fascinates, even if one cannot quite make out what it is getting at; and it was possible to make that out in the end, if one took enough honest trouble. It is all very well to talk as Mr John Sparrow does, in his hostile little book about modern poetry, about Empson's 'perverse ingenuity'. *Seven Types of Ambiguity* and *Some Versions of Pastoral* are, for the ordinary reader of poetry, like a gymnasium; he will be forced to use muscles he never used before, he will ache and sweat, but in future he will tackle any difficult poem that comes along with suppleness and assurance. He will be up to all the poet's dodges. Mr Sparrow's polar opposite to 'perverse ingenuity', his cult of common sense, is on the other hand like a Turkish bath. Mr Sparrow's ideal reader is not to make any effort at all; he lies prone and flaccid, a passive lump, and the poet, as if he were a masseur, must do all the work. Any critical method that promotes *active* and *alert* reading is to be encouraged, even if it should occasionally result in exhibitions of excessive ingenuity.

I had noticed in Empson's writing several pleasant little tricks, of the sort that keep a reader wakeful: a way of saying 'of course', when drawing some conclusion that seemed likely to jar and startle; a habit of alluding to rather out-of-the-way quotations as 'these famous lines'. In conversation, Empson had similar ways of jogging one: a trick of saying, 'To be sure, to be sure', for instance, before taking hold of some vague and inept remark of one's own and handing it back twisted by irony or perception into some new and intriguing shape. Tom's description of him does not bring out this spriteliness, especially when he could be persuaded to read his own poems. I remember him doing that at a British Council party given for the Chilean poet, Gabriela Mistral. Dylan Thomas had been reading earlier, in that voice like the thundering of a gong above a sea of treacle: the vowels bursting from the small round mouth like viscid bubbles. Then Mr Eliot read in his dry yet rich voice, with its extraordinary exact variations of pacing, almost like those of a motor changing gear. Finally, Empson read with his head on one side, cocking it up a little with an alert and pleased look when he came, every three lines or so, to some pungent equivocation; and with his legs astride, and swaying to rest his weight, now on this foot, now on that, to mark the broad movement of the rhythm. His gaiety, his physical enjoyment of his own poetry were infectious; the dryness of which some critics complain in his verses became a positive quality; one was no longer aware of his obscurities as hampering the communication of the total intention of the poem.

The boyish zest for life, that went with an extraordinary intellectual equipment, was the most taking aspect of Empson's personality. He was a person it was impossible to be with and not like. Yet I sometimes felt a little awkward about him, for he arranged so many opportunities for me which I muffed; and I wondered whether as a person I was coming up to the opinion he had formed of me from my poems. I had a sense of personal inadequacy, for instance, when a Chinese friend of his said to me very politely, 'We have a high opinion of your verse in Peiping.' But I need not have been so worried, for the dents that one makes on the London literary scene, whether by vanity or modesty, by being glib or by being inarticulate, by taking what is said to one literally, or as chaff, are not so deep as all that. It is a world one easily slips into and out of. Empson, when he went to China, wrote suggesting that I should try to get a teaching job there too. 'When you come back,' he wrote, 'you will find the same people talking about the same things, even after a lapse of five years . . . unless, indeed, you find it was wise to get away in time.'

There was a sense in which it might have been wise to take that advice. For certainly London seemed to have a strange effect on one's sense of time. Thus one of my best friends in Cairo came back with a whole set of literary schemes; for a trilogy of novels, for a series of verse plays, for new magazines, for anthologies of his friends' writings. First, however, he had to settle down and establish contacts. It is, as I write, almost 1950, and I know that if I meet him, it will be at a pub, talking over the same schemes that he talked over in 1946, and keeping his contacts warm. In fact, it is not necessary to write very much to establish a reputation as a London literary character; for the reading of one's friends' works, like the writing of one's own, makes sad inroads on the time that could otherwise be spent on the great beer route. The friend I speak of was unlucky enough to have a little money, and I was lucky enough to be forced to write for the little money I needed. But it was typical, this instance, of a disparity I was soon to notice, in so many young friends whose vitality and eagerness had attracted me in the army, between their aims and their achievements.

Thus, one friend (who had already, before the war, taken a degree in psychology at Cambridge) was taking classes at the London School of Economics. He, too, had a little money. His life seemed nicely balanced between books, parties, and periods when he shut himself up in his bedroom to listen for hours to records of hot jazz. But somehow, when the time came for him to sit his finals, he did not feel quite up to it; or quite up to looking around for the job for which he was already well equipped even without a second degree. He had discovered the pleasure of routine, of marking time; he could make one week very like the week before, and forget that he was growing older. But he was living on his capital, which would run out by the time he reached his fortieth year; and then he would have to look for a job without ever having held one. Meanwhile, his personality expanded, he relaxed, it did not seem to his friends that he could ever change in any way or grow older. And, in fact, one was constantly meeting in London very well preserved characters who had apparently been going round the same bars, meeting the same people, saying the same things, for twenty or thirty years.

This new awareness of the pleasures of habit was a sign that none of us was as young as he had been. A charming woman once described the group of us who had known each other in Cairo—a large, loose group, with several competing centres—as 'the old chums' league'. This was too true to be funny. In the Middle East we had lived rackety lives because we were harried by a sense of instability. We had looked forward to stability in London, to building for the future, but when we met in the evenings it was of the past that we found ourselves talking. The habits we had formed were stronger than our hopes and ambitions. It is dangerous to let one's emotions feed on the past, for it is finite and exhaustible. Friendships based on shared memories become formal and unreal, yet it is only friendships of this sort that wear well. We had our different ways of life now, ranging from idleness to plodding, from dalliance to marriage; we had different political fancies and diverging tastes. The way to keep friendship going was to create more sharable memories, to repeat, so far as one could, the old 'good times'. And these old good times would, of course, be the thing to talk about, the gap-bridger—though they would shift a little forward, of course, as the years shifted. Our attitude towards the concept of the good time was, in fact, almost religious. There must have been a first good time, some time; the

183

genuine original of all good times; but it seemed to veer backwards and forwards—when we clearly envisaged any period in the past, there was never a time when we had not been anxious and worried, and looking forward to some sort of change—and it would be tactless to pin it down to date and place. It was an idea, and an evening or a day spent drinking and gossiping was an attempt to make it real. Meanwhile, we had not written the books and poems our friends expected of us, and we were getting a little too old for the reviewers to go on talking genially about promise.

Thus, sometimes, when I go to a party given by old friends, or revisit, after a lapse of time, one of the bars where they congregate, I have a feeling as if I were slipping back smoothly, frighteningly, into a discarded skin. There, at the corner of the bar, is that same short-story writer, in that same camel-hair coat, with the long cigarette-holder, flicking away, in 1950, the ash that began to smoulder in 1946. It is like the feeling one has in the cinema, 'This is where I came in'; or like the feeling when one starts reading a detective story and realises, after fifty pages, that one must have read it years ago, since one knows the plot and the solution; or like dreaming, and realising that the dream is familiar—and shaking oneself awake, shaking oneself into the sense that time does pass, with a little shudder. It is only at such moments, of compulsive trance and compulsive awakening, that the sense of time, in London, becomes acute; which explains the strange, uncanny vivacity of many of the figures one meets, the grey hair slicked back, the crowsfoot wrinkles round the boyish twinkling eyes, the fishermen's jerseys and corduroys, the whole apparatus of youthful charm affixed, so indelibly, to promising middle-age! One wants to creep up behind such figures, to whisper in their ears, 'It is later than you think!' And in the bars, of course, every night, there *is* a ritual reminder: 'Time, gentlemen, time!' And once we are out in the cold street again, our clocks begin to tick.

3

London, then, keeps one young, but at a price. One can become a nomad, drifting and gregarious. One can cease to believe that one will ever have a position, responsibilities, a home, children, or grow old. There is merely time to be filled in till one dies—to be filled in as pleasantly as possible. For many poets this may be a proper mode of life. I shrank from it, remembering the feeling I had known in Aberdeen, of belonging to an organic community; even though that feeling had come to the surface as a sense of dissatisfaction and constraint. Though Aberdeen was an organic community, it was not one that had contained an appropriate place for me. London had a place for me. But though my group of friends in London did not either dissatisfy or constrain me, it was not a community in the same sense. It was held together by memories and likings; it performed no function. Individually, some of us might have a great deal of drive; but collectively we expressed drift.

I was saved from the worst pangs and oppressions of this social anxiety by individual love. I had been living, all through the war, in a male society, and I had been living for work and friendship. Knocking around pubs and parties with Tambi, I discovered to my surprise, that I enjoyed the company of women and that they seemed to enjoy mine. I realised, looking back, that at these dances in Aberdeen I had never thought of girls as persons at all—they had appealed to a thwarted appetite and a raw fancy, they had been a cloud of images to weave into poems. Because they had not been real to me, I had not been real to them.

Drinking with Tambi one evening, I met a tall, untidy girl called Amanda. She was in her late teens. Her straw-pale hair was tied with a green ribbon, and she wore a man's green coat into the pockets of which she thrust her hands. She seemed to hate consecutive conversation, and spent penny after penny playing against Tambi and myself for beers on the bagatelle machines. Later, when I used to stroll along the streets with her in daylight, she would prevent conversation by pointing out to me, and trying to make me identify, the various makes of motor-car. She was not obviously beautiful or graceful; her eyes were downcast, her face unhealthily pallid and powdered too heavily, and her body had the lovely strength of youth but was held clumsily, with legs astraddle and shoulders hunched forward. Her eyes, when she raised her head, were of a light blue colour, and miserable. She smoked, as I did, incessantly. Her voice was thin and flat, with a certain mincing refinement of phrase (she had been to an expensive boarding-school, but had run away from it to live with a man much older than herself, who at the time when I first met her was just about to desert her). She exaggerated this mincing tone deliberately, with an effect of mockery. She was desperate that first evening for money, and I made over to her a cheque which I had just received for some literary work. For some months afterwards, she became an obsessive element in my life; I

185

felt for her a torturing tenderness, in which the mind might isolate conflicting strands of lust and pity, but which was compulsive in its effect. I might call the feeling love, for I did not wholly yield to the lust, though I found myself kissing her again and again, and I did yield to the pity.

Having missed the last bus home one night from the Tottenham Court Road area, where we had been drinking, I went back with Amanda to her cottage in the outer suburbs. She lit a fire and cooked me an indigestible meal of fried potatoes, spaghetti, and black puddings, for she had the gross, hearty appetites of a raw and sullied young body, combined with the whimsical, hurt refinement of a childlike mind. The cottage was picturesque and singularly slovenly; I lay down on a mattress by the fire, watching Amanda's shadow as she undressed and went to bed, leaving the door open, in an inner room. I wanted very much to go to her bed, but I stayed obstinately by the fire, and at length slept uneasily. In the morning, she came over to the fire in her shift and lay down beside me to warm herself. I ran my hands gently over her body and kissed her. Then I hurried away to get my own clothes on, and we went out to have breakfast together. 'I haven't been kissed,' she said excitedly, 'I haven't been kissed by anybody but Harold, for months.' When we met after that, and when there was any privacy, and sometimes when there was not—saying good-bye to each other, for instance, in a tube station—we would kiss passionately. And Amanda rang me up in the mornings for long, pointless conversations, ending always with the remark, 'Say something sweet to me, George, say something sweet'; and I looked uneasily around the room to see if my mother or my sister or Paddy—whom I was also now kissing, and who knew all about Amanda, and was showing an extraordinary patience about her—was in earshot.

Amanda also knew about Paddy, for I have never been able to conceal my feelings about persons. 'She is very nice,' Amanda would say, 'but then there is only one Amanda, and there are so many Paddies.' This was an unkind and unfair remark, like many of Amanda's remarks about her own sex. As well as lust and pity, there was another element in my feelings for her; an element of exasperation, and at times almost of terror. She had a fierce possessiveness of nature, which made me understand why her lover had deserted her. 'I have no respect for Harold,' she would say, 'he is a failure in every way, but I need him, I need the feeling that I have got him safely locked away.' This fierce possessiveness was not wholly concentrated on Harold, though for ten days she and I travelled about the southern parts of England, trying to run him to earth (he had disappeared, leaving no message and no address) in all his old haunts. If we did not find him, she said, she would die. And we did not find him, and she alarmed me when we got back by producing a pistol and some cartridges, which I failed to wrest away from her—she was a strong girl, far stronger than I am. Yet she could be equally possessive with me. She insisted, during that queer ten days of hunting for Harold, on travelling as often as possible without a ticket; she made me walk ten miles through the night along country roads towards a village where there might be news of him; so that, exhausted in the small hours, I had nightmares, and was knocking on her door, waking her up, to see if she was safe; and then, on the train journey back to London, she kept badgering me to ask a young sailor to give her his white silk scarf, to which she had taken one of her sudden craving fancies.

If she finally gave Harold up, I thought, she might make do with me, absorb me completely into the melancholy disorder of her life. I could bring no order into it; it was something raw and hurt in her that at once appealed to, and found an answer in, something raw and hurt in me. I was no good to her, I could not even pretend that I was being chivalrous, for she had only to kiss me, and let me play with her green ribbon, and make me run my hands through her hair, for all my exasperated resentment, and all my flat common sense, to melt away; I wanted then merely to say silly, consoling things, to stop her crying as one stops a child crying. And she was like a child who has been abused. Raising her head towards me, I would press my lips to hers, and think that this was not how one should kiss a child. I too was abusing her. It was not true, I knew, that I was the only person, except Harold, whom in so many months she had kissed; it was not only Harold who had made free with her. It was perhaps the most absurd scruple that prevented me from doing so.

I occasionally did talk sense to her: she must forget Harold, go back to her family, or, if she stayed in London, start training for some job (the jobs that Amanda got were part-time and tended to be in the black market); then I would see she was becoming stiff and sulky, and would change the subject to get her into a good mood. Amanda was complicating my life; the time and money I was squandering on her alarmed my mother and sister; the scenes of quarrel and reconciliation, of cold formality ending in kisses, of discussions that led nowhere, and plans that came to nothing, sent me home in the evenings irritable and exhausted; to find

Paddy full of sweetness and patience, but with dark smudges under her brown eyes that suggested sleepless nights or hidden tears.

It was not, in the end, an episode to be tragic about. Amanda would reappear, and disappear, in the most erratic fashion; and when, after one such disappearance, I told her that I was now engaged to Paddy, she took it remarkably well. I was much more marginal in her life than she had been in mine. We had, over a month or two, some more companionable cups of tea and cigarettes, even a farewell kiss or two; I noticed that she was becoming tidier, cleaner, and smarter, more of the quiet country girl, which was one of her parts, and less of the town tomboy, which was another; and, after a final disappearance and a lapse this time of quite several months, I was glad to hear that, Harold happily forgotten, Amanda was now married to a suitable, pleasant young man, and settled in the country. She rang me up one day; I went to lunch, and the husband (one of Amanda's traits was a childlike pride in her possessions) was benignly displayed to me. I did not see Amanda after that lunch for almost two years. I ran into her in a pub in Soho; she seemed now radiantly beautiful. She had a baby, and I saw in her the look that I had divined from the first. It had turned out happily. I too was married and happy and could look back on her with a tenderness that was no longer tortured; she had given me a rapid, drastic and very necessary education in the relations between the sexes. She had perhaps given me the courage to love Paddy and make Paddy love me.

4.

There is no end to restlessness. I was happy now, I should have settled down to work. But over drinks one lunchtime in 'The Hog in Pound', a friend of Tambi's, a young Chilean of English ancestry called Jorge Elliot, said casually, 'Tell me, would you like to go to South America?' Jorge was the secretary of Sir Eugen Millington-Drake, the founder of the Hudson Institute, and formerly Minister in Montevideo. On retiring from the Foreign Service, Sir Eugen had decided to devote his time to the furtherance of friendship between Great Britain and the River Plate Republics. He was sending a dozen young men out that year to Uruguay and Argentina, and Jorge—we had made friends rapidly through a common admiration for the Chilean poet,

Pablo Neruda—thought that a poet would be a suitable addition to the party.

That was in June of 1947. In August of that year I found myself at sea again, and since my life has been so much like a drifting voyage, touching at so many ports, it is at sea that I had better end my story. We travelled across France and at Bordeaux embarked on a steamship, the *Groix,* that was to touch at Dakar, Rio de Janeiro, Santos, and Montevideo, where we were finally to disembark. The voyage was pleasant. Jorge and I spent hours by the rails, watching the clouds at the approach of sunset. There was a tiny green flash when the sun finally went down. Just above the water, the cloudscape was a yellow desert, but higher up in the sky there was a band of vivid green, reflected in the far edge of the ocean. Higher up still were other clouds of all shapes, red and golden, flatly extended or bulky, thinning out at the edges into transparencies. The sea itself was worth observing, with its patches of cobalt in the wave hollows near the boat and its little vanishing red vermicular shapes. At night, one of our number had written home, the sky was full of witches and there were peacocks in the sea. But while we watched, it grew cold, and Jorge and I retired to the saloon, to work away at a translation of a poem of Neruda's about the magic of the sea and the ghostly presences that infect old steamships. Neruda's steamship phantom was composed of the misery of stowaways, the squalor of the steerage, the decay of plush furniture, and the smells of machine oil and cooking. He could not get beyond the edges of the boat:

Only the waters reject his influence,
his colour and his smell of forgotten ghost,
and fresh and deep they roll open their dance
like lives of fire, like blood or scent,
new and strong, they rise up, at one, and made at one again.

Unwastingly, untouched by habit or time,
green by quantity, efficacious and cold,
they touch the ship's black belly and its stuff
they wash, its broken crusts, its wrinkles of iron,
gnawing, these living waters, at the husk of the ship
swaggering their long flags of foam
and their salt teeth flying in drops . . .

Jorge pointed out how close the feeling of this was to a famous poem of Lawrence's,

> The sea will never die, neither will it ever grow old
> nor cease to be blue, nor in the dawn
> cease to lift up its hills . . .

Time went by. We drew near Rio. Our voyage, like all long voyages, was beginning to grow tedious. Our main amusement had come to be the endless discussion of the characters of our fellow voyagers. (It has been my own main amusement throughout the long voyage this book recounts.) By now we knew them as well as we were ever likely to know them, and we went on talking about them with a sense of diminishing returns. There was a man called Vladimir who won during two or three days a reputation as the ship's comedian. He was thin, sad, he looked at once faintly absurd and very ill. He wandered round the ship, mocking life, mocking his fellow passengers. He invented the greeting, 'Woo, woo, woo!' This, in our tropical tedium, seemed to mean something: 'How absurd life is, and what pompous fools we are to take it seriously. Look at us filling in the days with our long, pointless conversations. We might as well make noises, like the animals, or faces, like the children.'

For a day or two we all said, 'Woo, woo, woo!' when we met each other. Vladimir (who used to enrich his performances with mimicry and grotesque little shuffling dances) regarded this with faint contempt. 'You are making a fool of yourself,' his bright, jaded smile seemed to say, 'if you think you can make a fool of yourself like me!' People began to grow embarrassed. They wondered if Vladimir had quite the central significance they had imagined, if it was not more reasonable, after all, for voyagers to be dull and heavy, for a voyage to be a vacuum, a gap. Vladimir induced a self-consciousness with which nothing could be done, at sea, once it had been induced. As people began to question his position as a comedian, he himself began to value it. Yet he was afraid of inventing a sequel, a new extravagance. 'Woo, woo, woo!' had been a success, and he kept on saying, 'Woo, woo, woo!' People responded to this in a faint, embarrassed fashion, as one responds to a child who, instead of being a little man, is being consciously and winsomely childish. (In all this, echoes, echoes.) Poor Vladimir began to fade away, like the grin of the Cheshire cat . . .

Jorge was getting bored with talk about Lawrence and Neruda,

190

with our translation, with literary conversation, even with the clouds. Often snubbed, but full of an undampable enthusiasm, he was out after the girls. We had no beauties on board. There was a nice, pleasantly plain little Norman girl, Jeanne, who came every day to Jorge's Spanish lessons, and sat in sandals wiggling her toes. 'Jeanne is a very nice girl,' said Jorge one morning thoughtfully, 'but I am afraid she may be frigid.' 'Don't you think, Jorge,' I replied, 'that that may be a subjective judgement?' There was also, but rather out of our reach, a splendid creature whom one of our number had christened 'the Brazilian Ambassadress'. She was large, lovely, dangerous, and simple, like one of the great cats. Jorge, with a poem of Eliot's in mind, had christened her 'Grishkin'; the same poem had given him the adjective 'pneumatic', which he was now applying, with monotonous regularity, to every attractive young person who swam into his ken. 'What do you mean by "pneumatic"?' irritated young women would ask. 'How do you mean that I am pneumatic? Do you mean that I am hard and corrugated, like a rubber tyre?' Jorge would smile subtly and say, 'Oh, no, no, not that. Really, you know, it is rather a compliment. A great English poet uses the word.'

I and some other members of our group (who took a more awed and distant view of Grishkin than Jorge) called her, more respectfully, 'Tiger, Tiger'. At the concert when we crossed the line she looked magnificent in white velvet, and sang 'One Fine Day' with a large, simple sincerity that went straight to the heart. Jorge, however, was not really attracted. Very large women put him off. At times, he talked nostalgically of the girls of the 'traditional families' in Chile who were, he said, the most beautiful creatures in the world.

At Rio, we were to lose some of Grishkin's brittle and expensive entourage. She liked lively young men about her. There was nevertheless one very rich young man, who hung passively on the edge of her group, who was anything but that. He was an American. We had seen him first on the day we came aboard, sitting alone in the bar, in a too beautiful white suit, with a bucket of iced champagne in front of him; on his lap, a small French poodle; black glasses made his pallid, thin face quite inscrutable. We had thought at first that he might be an interesting, intellectual type of decadent. But as soon as, within earshot of us, he opened his mouth, it became obvious that he was not. The little remarks that one overheard were quiet and serious and concerned with his daily round of small self-indulgences: 'Oh, I say, isn't it a shame? They won't give me another brandy fizz!' He disliked us; sometimes refusing to let us borrow a spare chair from the table where he was sitting, alone but for the company of his poodle. It was to Jorge, on the day before he got off at Rio, that he voiced his complaints. 'They are so very strange. They are not at all like Americans,' he said, alluding to our British group. 'Why can't they behave like ordinary people? And why can't that man with glasses'—meaning myself—'go and get a haircut?' We had been considering *him* as peculiarly abnormal! And perhaps we were right. On the evening before we reached Rio, something went wrong with his expensive camera and, in a fit of petulance, he flung it into the sea. Sitting with a sad smile on the edge of lively companies, he was not happy even in his own world; but his own world did not begin to be ours.

Others of our fellow passengers seemed more healthy and serene. There was a full-bodied Jewish tenor (we never heard him uncork his voice) whom we called 'old Mr Disraeli'. He wore his hair in a long bob, but otherwise, plump and open, he bore little resemblance to the great romantic statesman. Because he carried a pair of binoculars, with which ever and anon he would scan the far horizon, later we changed his name to 'stout Cortez'. He had a perpetual cheerfulness and struck us as vaguely comic: a figure in a static attitude.

But while we are at sea (or while we are drifting, as now, with so little say about our destination) are we not all vaguely comic? On a long voyage, it is as if the pressures that induce change and growth were removed. The blue sky might be the round top of a great glass air-pump; some atmosphere that we generally breathe is slowly but continuously being removed. In the new emptiness, one bobs up and down with extraordinary lightness; feeling that if the voyage were to go on for ever one would ultimately swell up, like the frog in the fable, and burst. There is more repetition than there is in ordinary life, less novelty to adapt oneself to; one becomes less of a personality and more, in the theatrical sense, of a personage. Everything that is typical and habitual is given enormous relief and becomes a main course of entertainment for one's companions. Yet these 'characters' of shipboard life (or of one's days in the army, one's rounds of the literary pubs, one's whole range of contacts in this drifting time) are also, in a sinister way, a little like waxwork figures. They stand in their fixed poses, which day after day become a little more irritating, meaningless, unreal.

On a sea voyage there is no conflict of interests, the whole business of life is eating, drinking, sleeping, talking, and flirting; there are no real acts, or what acts there are have no real consequences. And the background sets for this stage on which nothing happens, the sea and the sky, if they are always different, are also always the same. These are the remarks that people make about the sea, and according to which one has been made first, it is correct to make the other.

'The sea is always the same,' said Jorge, whom boredom was making irritable. It was a little after sunset and early the next morning we would enter the great bay at Rio.

'The sea is always different,' I replied.

'Tell me, George: I do not want to waste my time entirely on this voyage, and lately I have been thinking of writing a little fantasy. It is about a ship that voyages on and on for ever, and gets nowhere. About the world, in fact. The passengers in the end realise that it is going to get nowhere and adapt themselves to an eternal routine. But, on the other hand, though the voyage does not come to an end, my fantasy must. How? What happens to the passengers?'

'The sea gradually expands, Jorge. The ship gradually expands. The passengers gradually expand. Everything grows less and less dense. The ship grows lighter than air and floats off the sea. The sea itself, losing density, follows it up. The passengers begin to float off the deck but the ship, still expanding and still moving upwards, pursues them. This terrific expansion continues . . .'

'George, how wonderful! Go on!'

'Like an electric light bulb. Or like a balloon. Everything shatters into splintered fragments. Everything bursts and sags.'

'And what happens then?'

'Nothing can happen. It is a quite general catastrophe. Everything has burst, sea, sky, ship, passengers, everything. Everything has burst and there is nowhere for anything to settle down.'

We moved along to the bar for our customary Cinzano.

'But do you realise, George, that this may in the end happen? The universe *is* expanding . . .'

'I realise I want a drink.'

5

Lying in my bunk that night, I wondered about these things. Was that all that one had to say about life? Either, as Jorge said, our

193

life was just a drifting, on the edge of death, with no purpose, so that one had to fill in the time as amusingly as one could? Or (as I said earlier, in one of the many arguments with which we diversified the voyage) the wise in our day were the shallow, those who ignored or had never discovered the deep uneasiness of living, and who gave themselves up to humane, practical purposes? Here was no abiding city, but a makeshift dwelling, and day after day we had to patch the walls, keep out the deathly draughts, always deluding ourselves that the patching was final— was that it? What purpose made any sense of my life? Habit and affection made a kind of sense of it, lingerings, parentheses. I had let my life slip by, thinking what I would say about it; it was rich in scenes, faces, remembered words, empty of achievement: a series of uprootings, of farewells. I switched on the light over my bunk and read a draft of a poem I had written, one of many on such themes, on Aberdeen, or really on my idea of a city that might endure and on all the things that threatened it. The city in my poem stood for all our attempts to create stable and permanent patterns,

> I sought to build the mind, as they the walls
> Of complex and of memorable rock
> That my words might not wear
> But take an added glitter from the weather:
> But all rock fails,

and the sea, and the images connected in my mind with the sea, the gulls swooping down for scraps of bread, the hands in the fishmarket, shiny with scales, ripping out the guts of fish, the line of the waves wearing away the coast, stood for the wider natural context that thwarted human effort, but gave it, too, its dignity:

> Gold between rivers
> And sterile, like my gold, there stretched the shore:
> I lay and watched from that the lashing waves;
> Fancied them gutting the soft shore like hands,
> Imagined history as watery beaks
> Pouncing for human fragments.

It was not a good poem—the concepts, mind, city, history, sea, were too vague, the images, like that of the 'watery beaks', too wilfully fanciful—but it was a rough first attempt to say something I felt. It would need to be destroyed, forgotten, and done again.

I remembered, underlying my memories of Aberdeen, my vision as a child when I said my prayers, grandfather's dining-room at Brooklands, with its rich browns changed to a swimming transparent white. I remembered how, curled on the window seat, I would look out on the lawn, and admire a holly tree, its leaves smooth and glossy like the wood of the dining-room table and sideboard, but of a more living colour, and the lawn sloping steeply towards the garden wall, so that, looking out of the window, I could imagine the sensation of rolling over and over down it, and how in my vision I was never able to see out of this window, and used to wonder if the holly tree, too, had become a sort of dead cream-colour in heaven or a shiny papery white; or whether heaven, for its outdoors, had even livelier greens. And I remembered my grandmother explaining, 'George, you can't expect God to make you a good boy if you don't take the trouble to be a good boy yourself.' My prayers were infrequent now. I had not been a good boy. I had the sudden sense that comes in loneliness of having spoilt much promise; of the gap between what I was and what, if I had cast down my vanity, built up my courage, and lived by my love, I would have been. I had the sense of many insights, glimpsed and not grasped, going by in a flutter of papers. I felt my words go by me, last year's words that do not meet to-day's occasions, and I felt their weak, eloquent flutter, like the flutter, when I talk, of my hands.

I put on my dressing-gown, and went into the corridor, up the companion way towards the rail, into the thin rain and the pearly dusk. I lit a cigarette and peered towards the approaching bay. This was at the dead time, four o'clock in the morning. Vital forces were at their lowest ebb. It was a dim and rainy morning when we entered the great bay at Rio, a great sad circle and, above a gap between skyscrapers, as if flying, a huge statue of Christ on a conical mountain blessed a grey day. Yet the weather could not prevent me from having an impression of gaiety. Planes from the airfield that thrust out, a small oblong peninsula, into the water, kept crossing and recrossing the bay, flying very low. There were green-painted warships of the Brazilian navy at anchor, beside a naval installation of the same steely green. Like a backcloth in a theatre, green hills behind flat white façades of skyscrapers, green hills covered with low, old-fashioned houses, their roofs tiled red, the farther scene piled up in high and shallow recessions. The bay at Rio is enormous, elaborately spiked with queer conical hills out to the farthest stretch of its semi-circular arms. Yet the grey peaks straight ahead of us, just peeping above the clouds, embraced and minimised the sprawling city. Lines of trees grew here and there at the very water's edge, so that one felt one was approaching not a busy dockland but a seaside esplanade. And the sun, as I watched, was beginning to dry up the morning mists, to dissolve the fine rain, and to beat down on the flat façades of pink, buff, yellow and white stucco. The chill left my bones, I puffed my cigarette with more vigour, my heart full of mild acceptance.